Discovering
Old Bar Harbor
and
Acadia National Park

COVER: Bar Harbor, Maine, *1870s, W. W. Brown (Collection of the Farnsworth Art Museum, Rockland, Maine).*

This painting shows the Bar Harbor summer colony at about 1875. At the time, Bar Harbor had more than a dozen hotels, the largest of which was the Rodick House, the large yellow building with the red roof and twin towers. The spire of the Union Church is just visible behind the Rodick. Although Brown obviously was influenced by Hudson River School painters Thomas Cole and Frederic Church, he captured the dramatic–and accurate–look and feel of a typical summer afternoon's rumbling thunderstorms and squall lines.

Discovering
Old Bar Harbor
and
Acadia National Park

An Unconventional History and Guide

By Ruth Ann Hill

DOWN EAST BOOKS • CAMDEN, MAINE
1996

❧ To John ❧

Cover painting: "Bar Harbor, Maine," W .W. Brown, oil on canvas, c. 1870.
Collection of the Farnsworth Art Museum, Rockland, Maine.
Book design by Ruth Ann Hill
Color separation by Roxmont Graphics
Printed and bound at Capital City Press, Montpelier, Vt.

9 8 7 6 5 4 3 2 1

Down East Books / Camden, Maine

LIBRARY OF CONGRESS CATALOGING-IN-PUBLICATION DATA

Hill, Ruth Ann, 1958–
Discovering old Bar Harbor : an unconventional history and guide / Ruth Ann Hill.
p. cm.
Includes bibliographical references (p. 141) and index.
ISBN 0-89272-355-6 (pbk.)
1. Bar Harbor Region (Me.)--Guidebooks. 2. Bar Harbor Region (Me.)--History, Local. I. Title
F29.B3H55 1996
917.41 ' 45--dc20 96-24747
CIP

For those who came before.

This 1886 guidebook cover enticed the visitor to Bar Harbor and Mount Desert Island with views of favorite recreations of the time: a trip on the Green [Cadillac] Mountain cog railroad; a buckboard ride through the Gorge to see the scenery; and a visit to the Indians in Bar Harbor to rent a canoe for a romantic paddle on Frenchman Bay. (Courtesy of Maine Historic Preservation Commission.)

"Just before coming into Bar Harbor there is an excellent opportunity of observing the cluster of islands to which it owes existence. These are the Porcupine group, and beyond, across a broad bay, the Gouldsborough hills appeared in a Christmas garb of silvery whiteness. The Porcupine Islands, four in number, lie within easy reach of the shore, Bar Island, the nearest, being connected with the main-land at low ebb. On Bald Porcupine General Fremont has pitched his head-quarters. It was the sea that was fretful when I looked at the islands, though they bristled with erected pines and cedars.

The village at Bar Harbor is the sudden outgrowth of the necessities of a population that comes with the roses, and vanishes with first frosts of autumn. It has neither form nor comeliness, though it is admirably situated for excursions to points on the eastern and southern shores of the island as far as Great Head and Otter Creek. A new hotel was building, notwithstanding that last season had not proved as remunerative as usual. I saw that pure water was brought down to the harbor by a wooden aqueduct that crossed the valley on trestles, after the manner practiced in the California mining regions, and there called a flume. There is a beach, with good bathing on both sides of the landing, though the low temperature of the water in summer is hardly calculated for invalids."

From Nooks and Corners of the New England Coast, *Samuel Adams Drake, 1875;*
courtesy of Carl Little, College of the Atlantic.

ACKNOWLEDGMENTS

I owe abundant thanks to Deborah Dyer, curator of the Bar Harbor Historical Society, for her good-humored willingness to share her knowledge and help with research. Many of the photographs in this book are under her care. Deepest thanks also go to Earle Shettleworth, director of the Maine Historic Preservation Commission, for his help and generosity in the matter of reproducing images in the commission's collection. I am grateful to curators Edith Murphy and Pamela Belanger of the William A. Farnsworth Library and Art Museum for their willingness to explore new techniques, and their invaluable assistance with the reproduction of the painting that graces the cover. I would also like to offer a special thank you to Gertrude Lawrence McCue for graciously allowing me to reprint portions of the journals of her mother, Marian Lawrence Peabody.

Heartfelt thanks for assistance with research go to the following: curator Brooke Childrey, Paul Super and Linda Gregory at Acadia National Park; Bar Harbor town clerk Jean Barker; Earl Brechlin, editor of the *Bar Harbor Times*; librarian Charles Campo at the *Bangor Daily News*; curator Rebecca Cole-Will and project director Betts Swanton of the Abbe Museum; Marla Coffin; head librarian Marcia Dworak at the Thorndike Library, College of the Atlantic; David Gordon; Fred Hadley; chief librarian Nancy Howland and Alison Hamor at the Jesup Library; Joan and Reggie Hudson; Phyllis Joyce; Carl Little, director of public relations for College of the Atlantic; Bar Harbor town planner Jonathan Lockman; Tim O'Brien; the late Gladys O'Neil, whose work and research lives on in the Bar Harbor Historical Society collections; Captain Steven Pagels, Down East Windjammer Cruises; Alison Salsbury; Richard Sassaman; Ralph Stanley; Patricia Tierney; and Heidi Welch. I also would like to thank the many people who answered my questions, suggested leads, and offered their support for the project.

The following institutions generously permitted me to reprint images or writings from their collections: Abbe Museum; *Bangor Daily News*; *Bar Harbor Times*; College of Environmental Design, University of California, Berkeley; William A. Farnsworth Library and Art Museum; Harvard University Art Museums; The Jackson Laboratory; Maine Historic Preservation Commission; Milwaukee Art Museum; Mount Desert Island Biological Laboratory; National Park Service, Acadia National Park; The Art Museum, Princeton University; and Rockefeller Archives.

The staff at Down East Books is the finest. I would like to thank publisher Tom Fernald for his trust and patience; managing editor Karin Womer for her understanding, perspective, and thoughtful insights; copy editor Alice Devine for her fine application of the sharp pencil; and scan meister Phil Schirmer for his elegant work bringing the old photographs and illustrations in this volume back to life.

Wonderful family and friends made it possible for me to spend many months dwelling in the past. My husband John contributed many fresh ideas and suggestions in addition to feeding me and generally taking care of everything while I was buried in old papers or glued to the computer. My parents, Betty and Ray, and mother-in-law, Toni, gave their enthusiastic support. I could not have done it without them. Jean, as always, offered the best advice. Amy, Rob and Jake supplied timely suppers and water balloons.

Although many people contributed to this book, any mistakes within are mine. I welcome comments, stories and corrections.

Contents

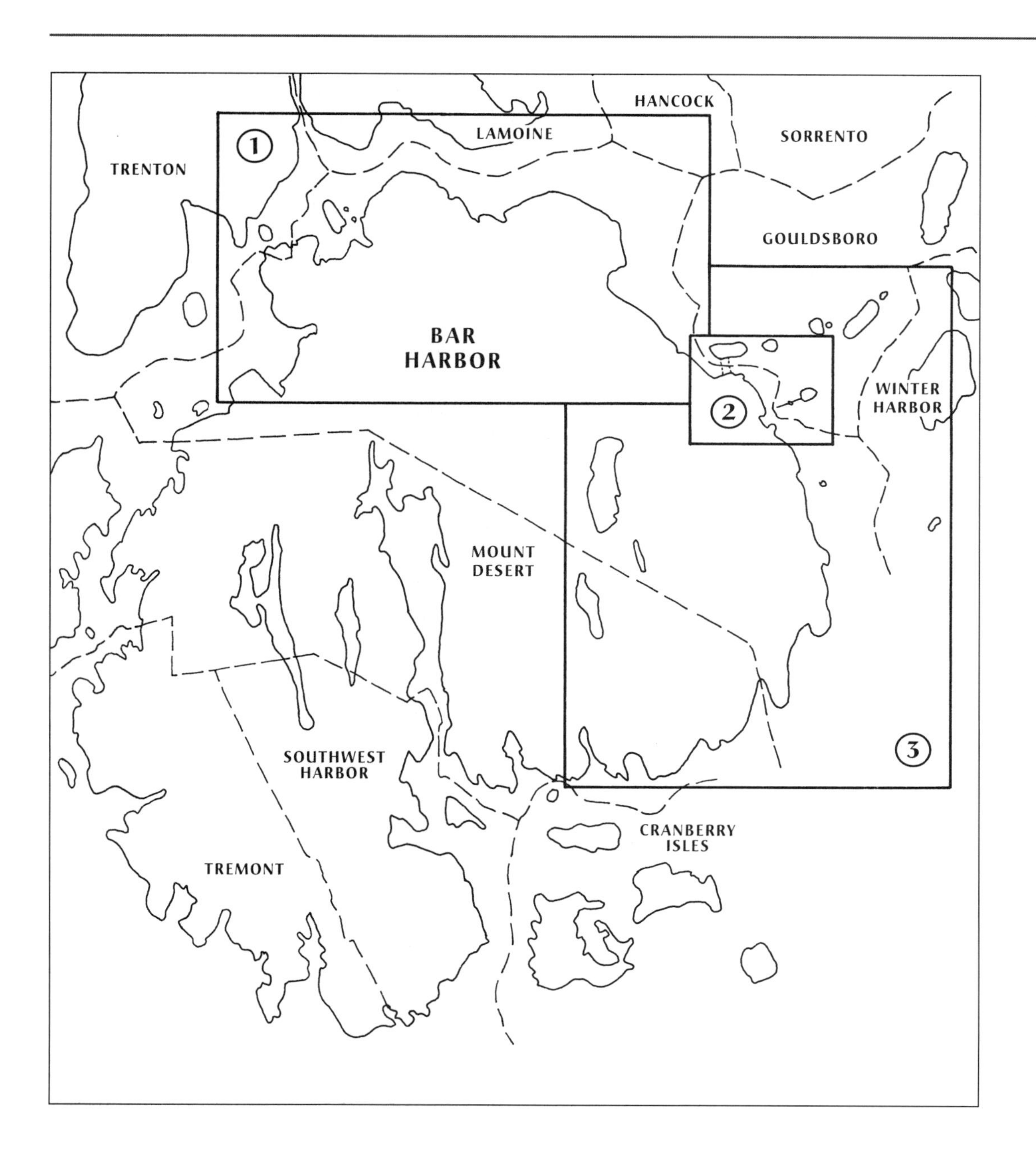
HANCOCK
LAMOINE
SORRENTO
TRENTON
1
GOULDSBORO
BAR HARBOR
2
WINTER HARBOR
MOUNT DESERT
SOUTHWEST HARBOR
3
CRANBERRY ISLES
TREMONT

A Few Introductory Words

This book is divided into routes that explore three regions in the town of Bar Harbor and Acadia National Park. Each route includes sections that focus on specific places. The material within sections is arranged chronologically.

Although organized routes are presented, it certainly is not necessary to follow them.

Encouragement to the Curious

The stories and images that follow open a window to the past. There is much more outside this window to discover. Much of the fascination and joy of journeying back in time lies in following the path wherever it may lead. Some clues can be found in the landscape, others in drawers and on shelves in historical collections and libraries.

Almost all of the photographs and illustrations in this book come from collections that are available to the public, especially those of the Bar Harbor Historical Society and Maine Historic Preservation Commission. The stories are selected from the many contemporary writings that are also available in historical collections or local libraries. The Jesup Library has microfilm copies of Bar Harbor newspapers dating back to 1881, genealogical records and other historical materials. The most precious resources are people who can share their memories of times gone by.

References are given for each selection; a list of suggested readings appears on page 141.

Some Thoughts Concerning Place Names

Visitors to Mount Desert Island were fond of naming–or renaming–things. In particular, the early rusticators indulged in the romance of exploring the wilds of their newly discovered island. They enjoyed bestowing names on each place they visited. In later years the national park, led by George Dorr, renamed nearly all of the island's major peaks.

Reading the old stories is confusing until the old names become familiar. To help make things clearer, the current name is given after the first use of an old name in each section.

...Including Three in Particular

Mount Desert: The name comes from the French, *Isle des Monts Désert* (Island of the Desert, or Barren, Mountains), bestowed by explorer Samuel de Champlain in 1604. The English won North America in 1763, and the pronunciation of Mount Desert evolved in the same way as that of Calais and Isle au Haut. There are vehement proponents of both accent options for "Desert." We will stay out of that one.

Bar Harbor: From 1796 until 1918, Bar Harbor (East Eden in the early days) was a village in the township of Eden. There also was a village of Eden in the township of Eden. Since 1918, Eden has been a small village or place within the township of Bar Harbor. Neither name has any noticeable "R" sounds in it.

Eden: The currently popular theory holds that the name Eden was a last-minute second choice taken after the town's representatives arrived in Boston to find that another town had taken the name Adams, their first choice.

A Brief Discourse on the Subject of Trees

A person looking for the past in Bar Harbor spends a good deal of time mentally removing trees from the landscape. From the mid-1800s until quite recently, Bar Harbor had many fewer trees than it does today. There are hints of this in the old reports and stories, especially where they describe views.

The first settlers cleared some land for gardens and pastures, and began logging. Their descendants cleared more land and kept logging. In her 1866 guide book, Clara Barnes Martin described the island: "Except in one or two almost inaccessible valleys, the forest primeval is all gone; but huge trunks and scathed trunks show what the axe and fires have done. The three western mountains [Penobscot, Sargent and Pemetic?] and the Twins [Bubbles] are covered with second-growth, but the other summits are bleak and bare. In the valleys and on the open land, there is a larger proportion of the more graceful forest trees, than is common on the coast...." The shoreline plateau from Hulls Cove to Cromwell Harbor was cleared by the time Martin arrived.

By the 1880s, most people had given up logging for more profitable work filling the needs of summer visitors. The summer colonists built cottages, surrounded by elegant lawns and elaborate gardens with ornamental trees, along the shore and on the outskirts of town. They kept the land around town largely open. Photographs taken during the summer colony years clearly show buildings from the waterfront to the top of the hills.

The forests grew back on the mountains and uninhabited lands—until late October 1947, when a great fire burned from just south of Northeast Creek and Hulls Cove to Great Head and Sand Beach.

Most of the burned lands are once again covered by trees. Trees also have reclaimed estates and farm lands that have been abandoned during the last few decades.

An Admonishment to Collectors

Please refrain from removing or altering artifacts of any kind.

Useful Hints for the Traveler

On foot: Although some trails still follow the old routes, many more have been re-routed, at least in part, or abandoned. *Please use a current trail map.* It is fun to discover that a trail still follows the old route and walk along in the company of a storyteller from a century ago; it is much less fun to get lost following old directions that are no longer accurate.

By bicycle: Bicycling can be a great way to explore the rural parts of Bar Harbor. On back country roads, be aware that cars may be infrequent but they travel at the speed limit or better. Riding nonchalantly down the middle of the road is not a good idea. Unfortunately, there are no paved shoulders to make biking safer.

Biking in Acadia National Park is close to ideal. Bicycles must yield to walkers and horses on the carriage roads. On nice summer days the popular carriage roads can be very busy, especially those near Eagle Lake.

By horse: With the exception of the roads around Eagle Lake and Witch Hole Pond, the park's carriage roads are open for their original purpose: horses and carriages. Wildwood Stables, near the Jordan Pond House, offers carriage rides and has accommodations for visiting horses and their riders.

By automobile: Primary town and park roads are busy during the day, especially in July and August. Those planning to poke around and explore will have a much better time if they choose quieter periods. Early morning and suppertime (sometimes) are much less frenetic.

By small boat: Island visitors in the late 1800s were devoted paddlers and rowers. Rowboats and canoes were available for rent in the harbor and at Eagle Lake and Jordan Pond. Exploring by small boat is still a fine way to go.

Frenchman Bay looks like a bay and acts like the ocean. The summer afternoon sea breeze is usually a fifteen-knot wind that raises a foot-high chop. The quietest times in summer are morning and around sunset. The bay below the breakwater can get very rough, and there are no protected coves south of Compass Harbor.

The tidal range averages twelve feet, and tidal currents between islands can be strong. When landing, make sure that the boat will not float away on the rising tide.

Fog comes up the bay from the ocean. It arrives faster on a southeasterly wind and an incoming tide. Thunderstorms generally come down the bay on hot afternoons. They do not always survive until they reach Bar Harbor, but those that do can be surprisingly strong. Squall lines with shifting winds gusting over forty knots are also a regular feature of the summer bay. These may or may not accompany thunderstorms, typically arrive from the northern quarter, and last less than an hour. It is wise to head for home or a protected shore upon spotting any of the above.

Lake paddlers are spared the tide and usually the fog, but should be aware that the larger lakes can get quite rough on breezy days.

A note for the hot and dusty: Swimming in Eagle Lake, Bubble Pond and Jordan Pond is forbidden, since these serve as town water supplies. Swimming in the ocean is not forbidden, but is done infrequently because a cold flow from the north keeps summer water temperatures down in the refreshing fifties.

Maps

Historic maps from the 1800s begin on page 12. Current maps can be found on the page following the introduction to each region. These maps are for general reference only; a more detailed map, preferably one with contours indicated, is a worthwhile acquisition.

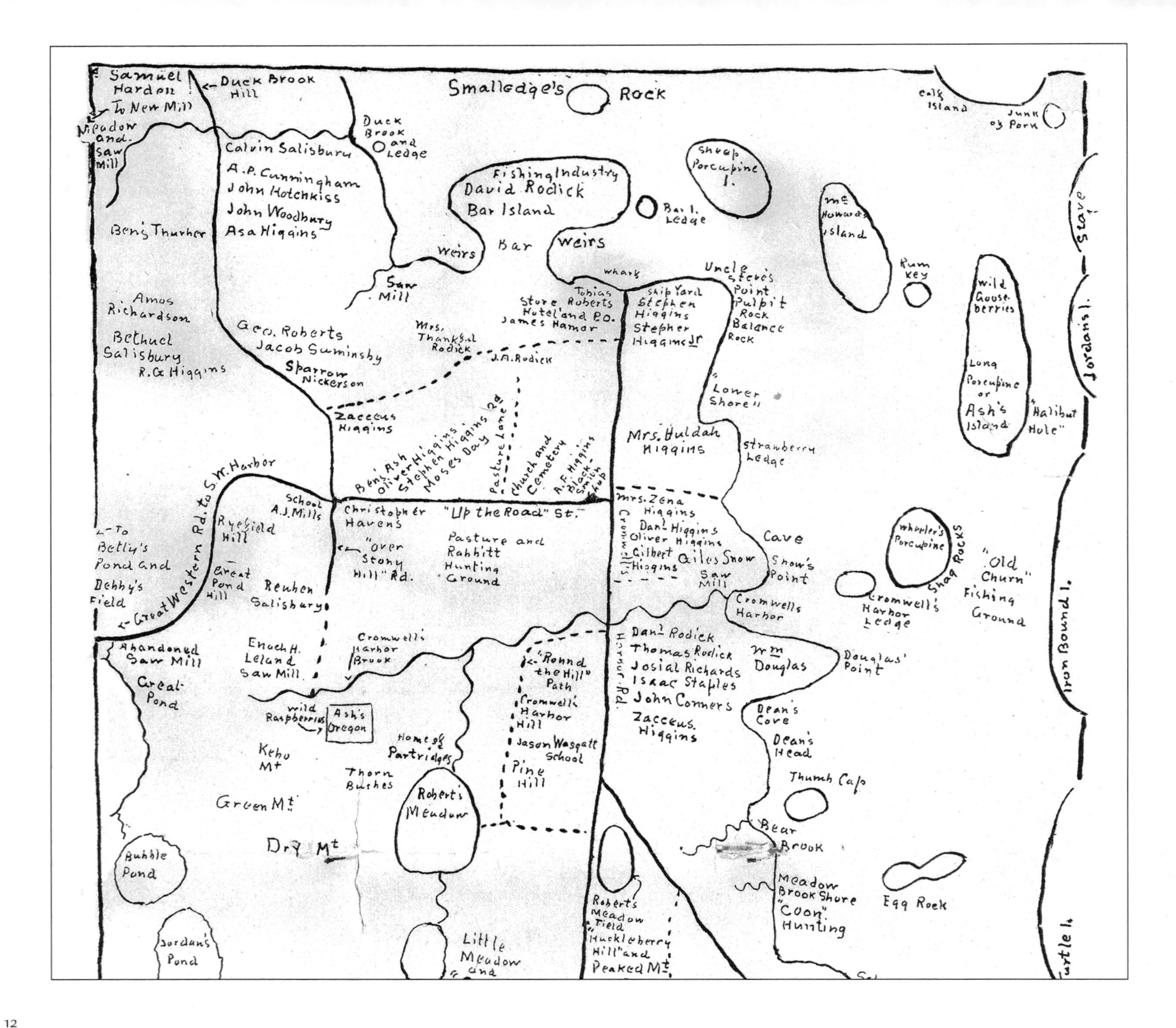
Samuel Harden
To New Mill
Meadow and Saw Mill
Duck Brook Hill
Smalledge's Rock
Calf Island
Junk of Pork
Duck Brook and Ledge
Calvin Salisbury
A.P. Cunningham
John Hotchkiss
John Woodbury
Asa Higgins
Benj Thurber
Fishing Industry
David Rodick
Bar Island
Bar I. Ledge
Sheep Porcupine I.
Mc Howard's Island
Stave I.
Weirs
Bar
Weirs
Saw Mill
Wharf
Uncle Steve's Point
Pulpit Rock
Balance Rock
Rum Key
Wild Gooseberries
Jordan's I.
Amos Richardson
Bethuel Salisbury
R.C. Higgins
Geo. Roberts
Jacob Suminsby
Sparrow Nickerson
Mrs. Thankful Rodick
J.A. Rodick
Tobias Roberts
Store Hotel and P.O.
James Hamor
Ship Yard
Stephen Higgins
Stephen Higgins Jr
"Lower Shore"
Long Porcupine or Ash's Island
"Halibut Hole"
Zaccheus Higgins
Benj Ash
Oliver Higgins
Stephen Higgins 2nd
Moses Day
Pasture Lane
Church and Cemetery
A.F. Higgins Black Smith Shop
Mrs. Huldah Higgins
Strawberry Ledge
Great Western Rd. to S.W. Harbor
School A.J. Mills
Christopher Havens
"Up the Road" St.
Mrs. Zena Higgins
Dan'l Higgins
Oliver Higgins
Gilbert Higgins
Giles Snow
Saw Mill
Cave
Snow's Point
Wheeler's Porcupine
Shag Rocks
"Old Churn" Fishing Ground
To Betty's Pond and Debby's Field
Ryefield Hill
Great Pond Hill
"over Stony Hill" Rd.
Pasture and Rabbitt Hunting Ground
Reuben Salisbury
Cromwells Harbor
Cromwell's Harbor Ledge
Iron Bound I.
Abandoned Saw Mill
Enoch H. Leland Saw Mill
Cromwell's Harbor Brook
"Round the Hill" Path
Dan'l Rodick
Thomas Rodick
Josial Richards
Isaac Staples
John Conners
Zaccheus Higgins
Harbor Rd.
Wm Douglas
Douglas' Point
Great Pond
Wild Raspberries
Ash's Oregon
Cromwell's Harbor Hill
Jason Wasgatt School
Dean's Cove
Dean's Head
Kebo Mt
Home of Partridges
Pine Hill
Thumb Cap
Thorn Bushes
Robert's Meadow
Green Mt
Dry Mt
Bear Brook
Bubble Pond
Meadow Brook Shore
"Coon" Hunting
Egg Rock
Jordan's Pond
Little Meadow and
Robert's Meadow Field
"Huckleberry Hill" and Peaked Mt
Turtle I.

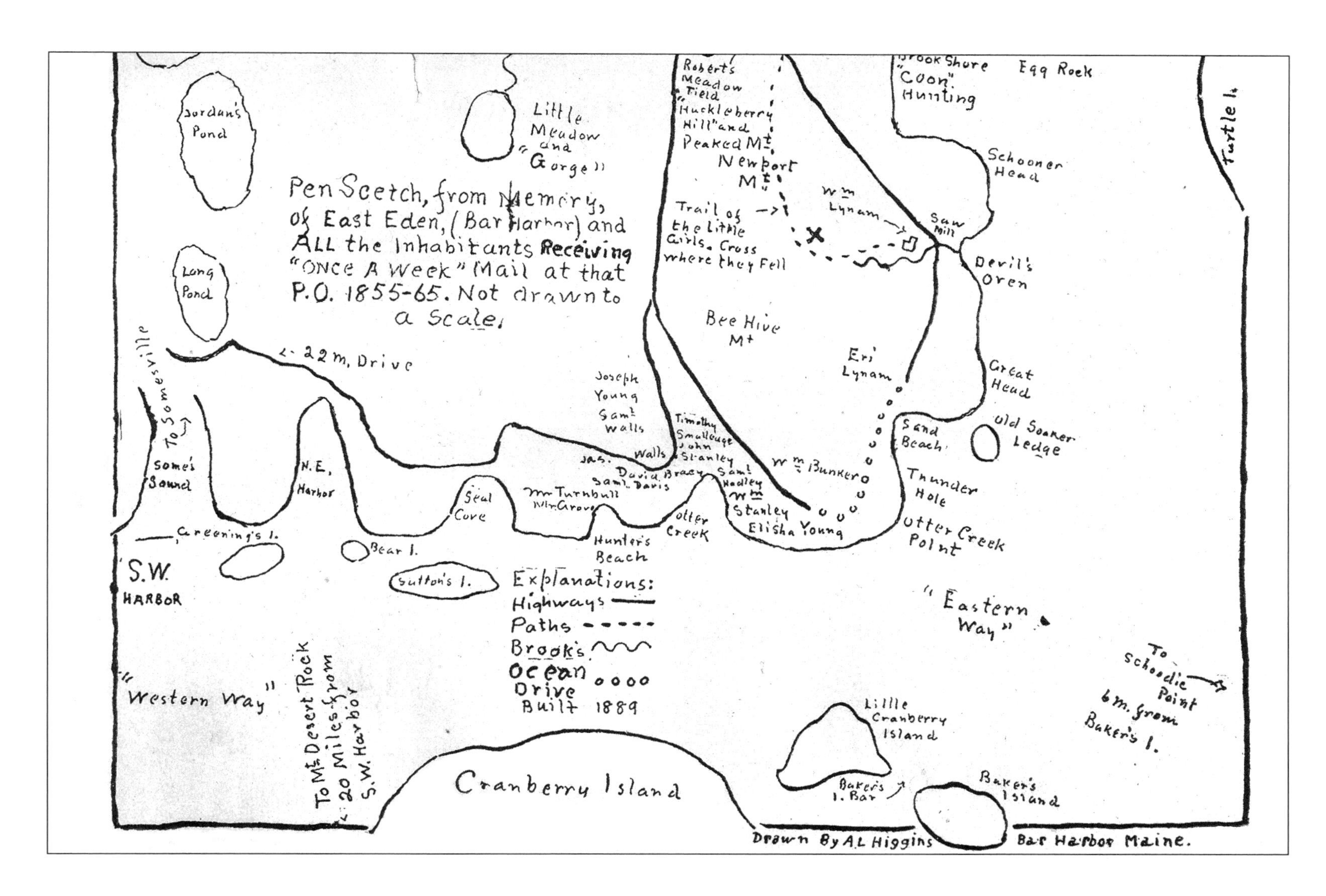

This sketch map, showing points of interest in the mid-1800s, centers on the village of East Eden (Bar Harbor); the western territory and Frenchman Bay are much compressed.

Key to Places and Names

- Road from Duck Brook to school intersection: Eden Street (Route 3)
- "Up the Road" Street: Mount Desert Street
- "Over Stony Hill Road": Kebo Street
- Great Western Road to S. W. Harbor: Eagle Lake Road (Route 233)
- Great Pond: Eagle Lake
- Green Mt.: Cadillac Mountain
- Dry Mt.: Dorr Mountain
- Newport Mt.: Cadillac Mountain
- Smalledge's Ledge: Bald Rock
- M. S. Howard's Island: Burnt Porcupine Island
- Wheeler's Porcupine: Bald Porcupine Island (Allegedly named after a captain who ran into it while paying more attention to his lady friend than his sailing.)
- Cromwell Harbor Ledge: now part of the breakwater.
- Thumb Cap: Thrumcap
- Robert's Meadow: Great Meadow
- Devil's Oven: Anemone Cave
- 22 M. Drive: The Twenty-two Mile Drive, an established buckboard route that went from Bar Harbor to Somesville past Eagle Lake, then returned by way of Northeast Harbor, Otter Creek and the Gorge. It could be done in a half day, but required a full day "to do full justice to all the points of interest."

Courtesy of Bar Harbor Historical Society.

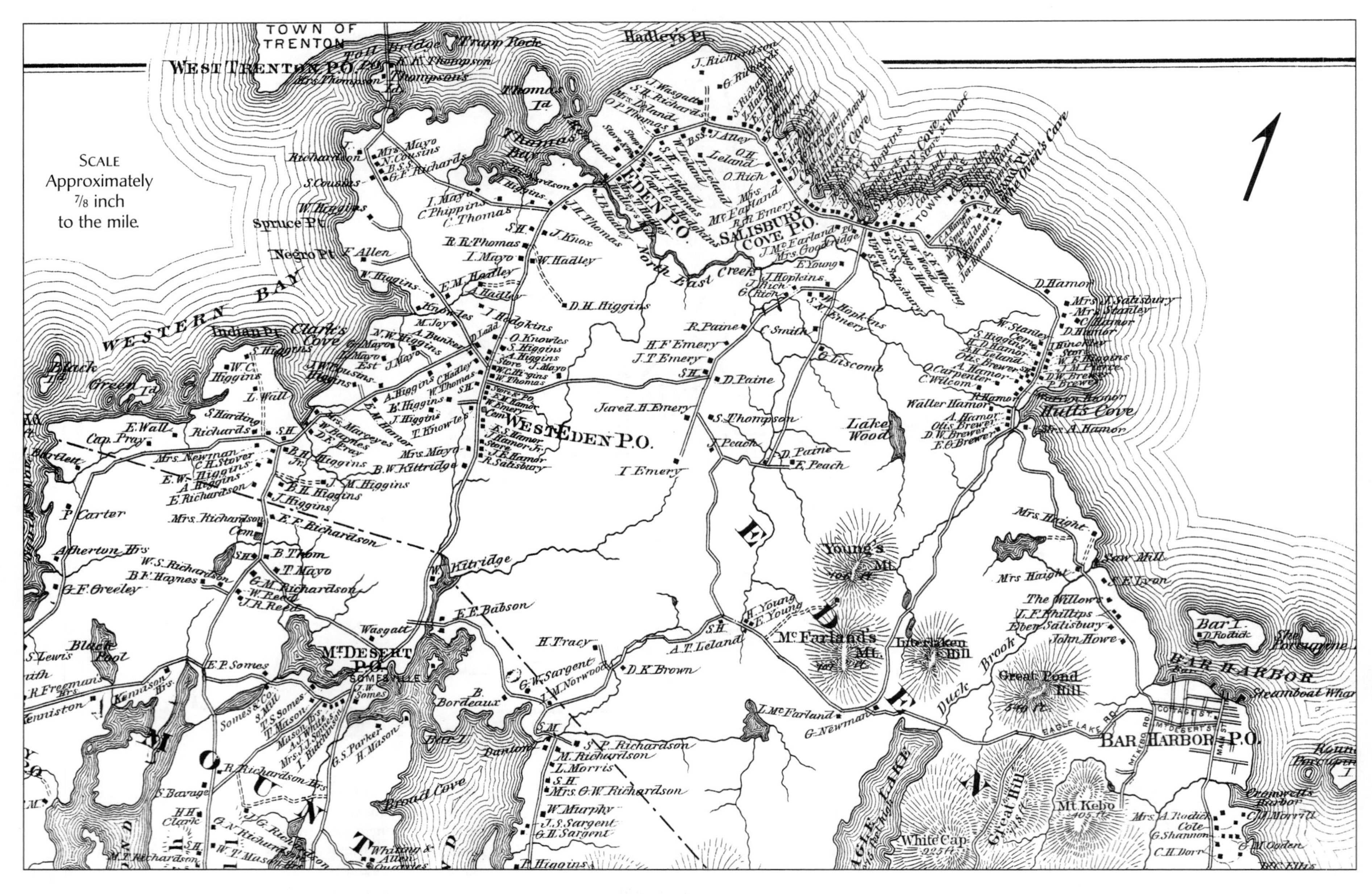

The maps on these two pages, and the Bar Harbor village map on page 16, are taken from Colby's 1881 atlas of Hancock County. The maps appear to be generally accurate, although the mapmaker apparently moved some buildings a bit so that he could fit everything into crowded places. (Courtesy of the town of Bar Harbor, Planning Office.)

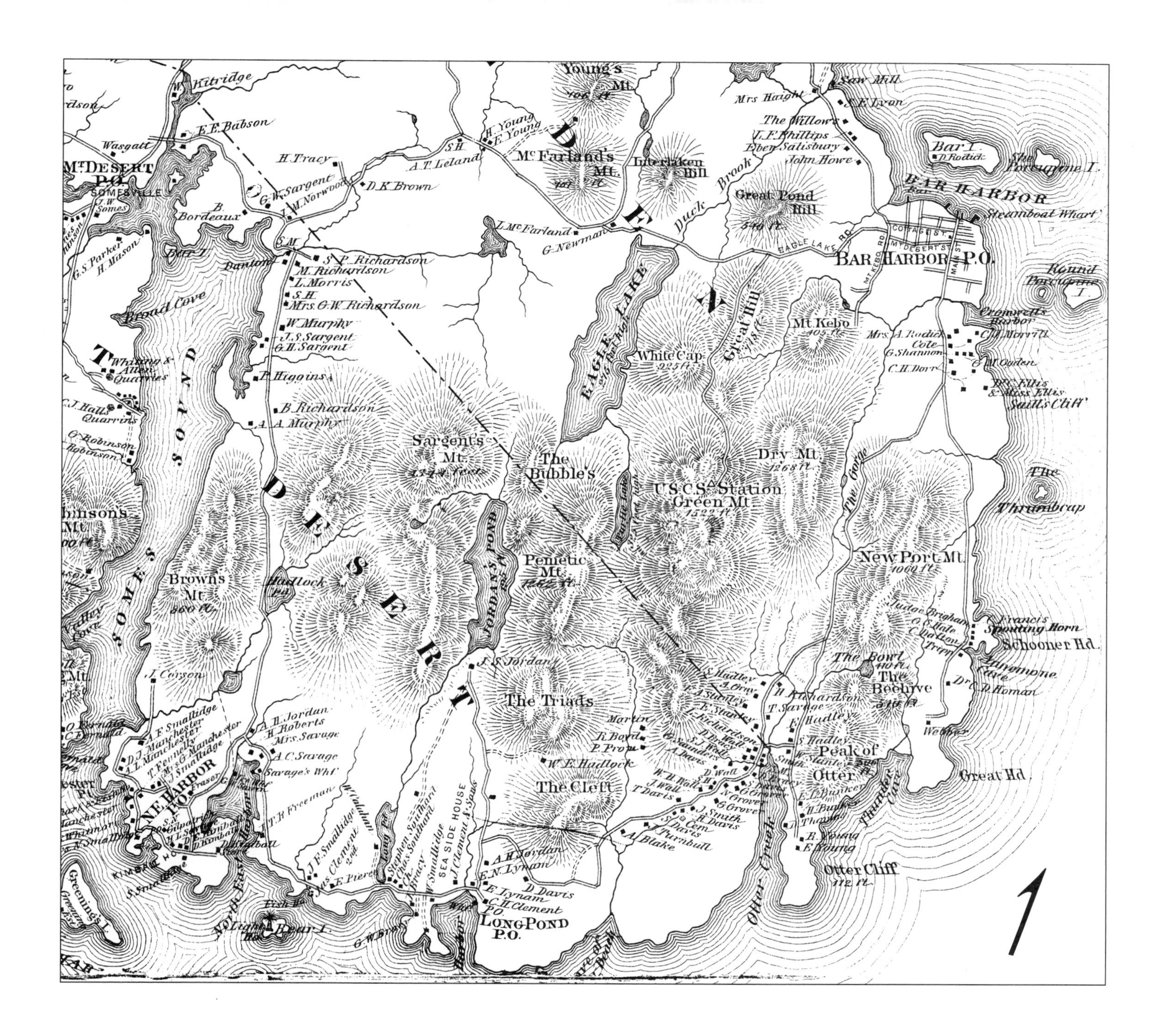
Bar Harbor
Bar Harbor P.O.
Eagle Lake
Sargents Mt.
The Bubbles
U.S.C.S. Station Green Mt.
Dry Mt.
Mt. Kebo
White Cap
Great Pond Hill
New Port Mt.
Pemetic Mt.
Browns Mt.
The Triads
The Cleft
The Beehive
Peak of Otter
Otter Cliff
Great Hd.
Schooner Hd.
Spouting Horn
Long Pond P.O.
N.E. Harbor P.O.
Mt. Desert P.O.
Somes Sound
Jordans Pond
Otter Creek
Steamboat Wharf
Bar I.
The Porcupine I.
Round Porcupine I.
The Thrumbcap
1

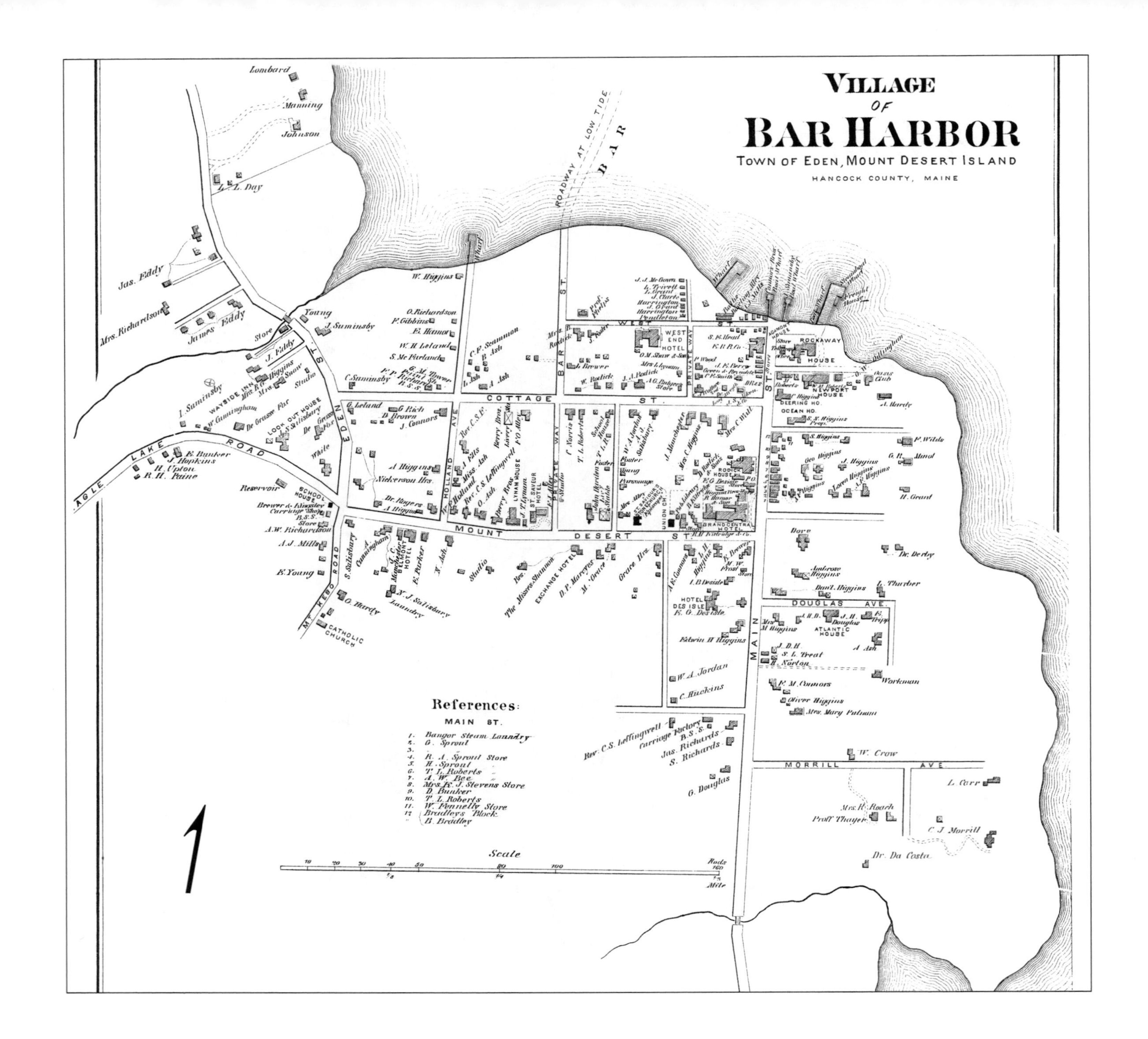
VILLAGE OF BAR HARBOR
TOWN OF EDEN, MOUNT DESERT ISLAND
HANCOCK COUNTY, MAINE
ROADWAY AT LOW TIDE
BAR
COTTAGE ST.
MOUNT DESERT ST.
MAIN ST.
WEST ST.
BAR ST.
EDEN ST.
HOLLAND AVE.
DOUGLAS AVE.
MORRILL AVE.
EAGLE LAKE ROAD
MT. KEBO ROAD
WEST END HOTEL
ROCKAWAY HOUSE
NEWPORT HOUSE
DEERING HO.
OCEAN HO.
RODICK HOUSE
GRAND CENTRAL HOTEL
LYNAM HOUSE
ST. SAVEUR HOTEL
EXCHANGE HOTEL
HOTEL DES ISLE
ATLANTIC HOUSE
BELMONT HOTEL
WAYSIDE INN
LOOK OUT HOUSE
SCHOOL HOUSE
CATHOLIC CHURCH
UNION CH.
Wharf
Reservoir
Studio
Laundry
References:
MAIN ST.
1. Bangor Steam Laundry
2. G. Sprout
3.
4. R. A. Sprout Store
5. H. Sprout
6. T. L. Roberts
7. A. W. Bee
8. Mrs. K. J. Stevens Store
9. D. Bunker
10. T. L. Roberts
11. W. Fennelly Store
12. Bradleys Block. B. Bradley
Scale
Rods
Mile

Eden

Eden is "Old Bar Harbor." The first settlers to venture down the Maine coast to the eastern side of Mount Desert Island chose its more appealing, more useful northern shore, leaving the unprotected coastline and mountains to the south uninhabited. By the time the town of Eden formed in 1796, there were probably at least two hundred people in residence, based on the recorded number of polls, or propertied men eligible to vote, which was eighty-nine. Most families lived in the area from Hulls Cove to Indian Point, on the better land near the shore.

There never was a big rush of people moving to Eden. To farmers, eastern Maine did not seem like paradise. It was a hard land then, it is a hard land now, for anyone trying to grow crops. In particular, the region between Penobscot and Schoodic was thought to be "a wasteland."

In 1790, Rufus Putnam reported, "...as to the eastern country it is a very fine place for lumber, and in that respect is of great service to Massachusetts: but any considerable number of people more in that district then to carry on this business will be a disservice distroying the timber which ought to be preserved—that country in general is not fit for cultivation and when this idea is connected with the climate, a man ought to consider himself curst even while in this world who is doomed to inhabit their as a cultivator of lands only; however I cannot suppose that the Ohio country will much affect the settlement of the eastern lands because those people who have not a double curse entailed to them will go to New York or Vermont, rather then to the eastward."

The settlers of Eden presumably spent little time worrying about what others thought. They made their living from the forests and the sea, and prospered in a small way. Eden was not a bustling place, and it did not appear that there would ever be a reason for it to become so.

One summer in the 1840s a New York artist came to the island to do a little landscape painting. Over the next couple of decades, a few more intrepid souls took the trip down east to see the glorious natural wonderland for themselves. After the Civil War, more people began coming to the hamlet of East Eden (now Bar Harbor), people who cared nothing about making a living from the land, but who came in summer to look at the scenery and enjoy something different called leisure.

Getting Around

The Eden route is primarily a driving excursion. The road connecting the villages has followed the northern shore of Eden since the late 1700s. Traffic on the road increased somewhat after the first bridge over the Narrows opened in 1839, but things really picked up when "flivver tourists" arrived in the 1920s.

With care, it is possible to explore the back roads by bicycle. Small boats can be launched at the Hadley Point boat ramp and Northeast Creek. This shore is often a fog hole, where warm land breezes hold back the fog that can persist all day in the lower bay.

Photograph courtesy of Maine Historic Preservation Commission.

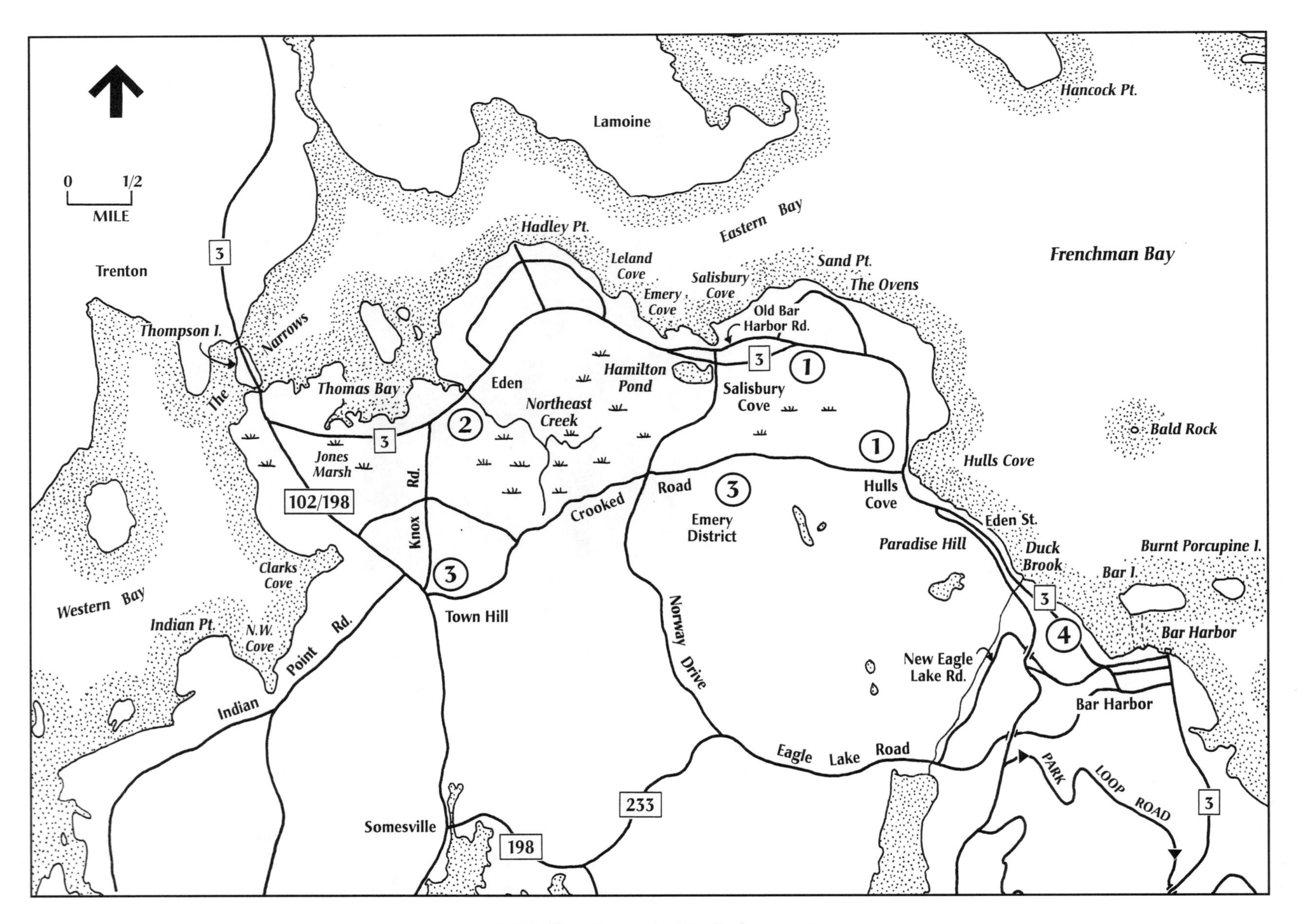

1. Hulls Cove to Salisbury Cove
2. Northeast Creek and Eden Village
3. Town Hill (West Eden) and the Emery District
4. Eden Street Shore

Hulls Cove to Salisbury Cove

In 1844 Thomas Cole, the leading artist of the Hudson River School of painters, traveled from New York to Mount Desert Island to sketch the scenery, three decades after Mme. Therese and Barthelemy de Gregoire were laid to rest in the cemetery just up the hill from where he stood to do this drawing of Hulls Cove. Cole took notes on his sketches for later reference in the studio. From left to right, the notes read "oaks," "Bar Island," "red roof" and "woods." Cole apparently referred to the sketch for other works, but never painted this particular view.

The schooner moored in the cove could have been built nearby, in Hulls Cove, or in one of the other small protected coves. Close inspection reveals a scattering of houses in the cleared land that is now the village of Bar Harbor (above and to the right of the schooner's bowsprit). The arched pole is probably the well. (Courtesy of The Art Museum Princeton University, gift of Frank Jewett Mather, Jr.; photograph, Clem Fiori.)

At some point, most visitors to Bar Harbor wonder where the "old New England" part of the village is.

Mount Desert Island, along with the rest of Maine east of the Penobscot, was not part of New England except during a couple of short intervals, one just before the Revolutionary War. It was part of New France, or at least the French thought it was. The two nations fought about this, and much more, from the mid-1600s until the mid-1700s. Very few people lingered in Bar Harbor. The first settlers did not arrive until the 1760s.

The settlers needed protected harbors for their boats; sheltered, sunny house sites; wild marsh hay for animal fodder; good land for farming; fresh drinking water; streams that could support mills; and forests worth logging. Hulls Cove and Salisbury Cove were the main villages in the northeastern part of Mount Desert, which became the town of Eden in 1796.

Trees now grow over much of the abandoned farmland and only a few boats use the coves. Some of the old villages have disappeared. The 1947 fire burned through Hulls Cove, taking many of the oldest homes. The center of community activity has shifted to Bar Harbor. But the essence of past days in Eden lives on in the villages, beyond the busy highway and its hurrying travelers.

Beginnings

On September 2, 1604, explorer and pilot Samuel de Champlain and his crew (including native guides) left St. Croix in a sixteen-ton boat on a mission to investigate the eastern coast of Maine for Sieur de Monts, who had a grant to Acadia (L' Acadie), a political "place" that included much of northeastern North America. They passed by Mount Desert Island on September 5: "I went near an island about four or five leagues long. The distance from this island to the mainland on the north is not a hundred paces. It is very high with notches here and there, so that it appears, when one is at sea, like seven or eight mountains rising close together. The tops of most of them are without trees, because they are nothing but rock. The only trees are pines, firs, and birches. I called it the Island of the Desert Mountains (Isle des Monts Désert)...."

Nine year later, a group of French Jesuit missionaries found themselves in Frenchman Bay praying for deliverance from the fog. They broke out into the sun just below the Porcupine Islands. The Indians they met on the shore invited them to their settlement at Fernald's Point on Somes Sound. The English fourteen-gun warship *Treasurer*, commanded by Captain Samuel Argall, found the Jesuits several weeks after they landed and invited them to leave.

Throughout the 1600s eastern Maine remained an unsettled territory inhabited by traders, fishermen and soldiers—along with the few Indians who were still alive after the plagues of 1616 to 1619.

In 1688, the self-titled Antoine La Mothe de Cadillac, Seigneur de Douaquet et des Monts Déserts (né Antoine Laumet) and his wife arrived to inspect Mount Desert Island, their gift from Louis XIV. They apparently spent part of the summer on the island's eastern shore, but left for new responsibilities and opportunities—and safer territory. The following May, France and England were at war.

From 1689 until 1760, eastern Maine was no place for settlers. Warriors and adventurers of all loyalties—Indian, French, English or a combination—passed by and may have stayed awhile, but the region remained a dangerous contested frontier throughout the period.

France was defeated in North America by 1760, although the treaty was signed three years later. The Indians retreated inland.

Sir Francis Bernard, the last colonial governor of Massachusetts, acquired the grant to Mount Desert Island in 1762. One of his officers described the island's finer points in a journal kept on the governor's fact-finding trip to his territory: "Its natural Productions are Oak, Beech, Maple, and all sots of Spruce and Pines to a large diameter, *viz*: thirty-four inches diameter. Ash, Poplar, birch of all sorts, white Cedar of a large size, Sasafrass, and many other sorts of wood, we know no name for a great variety of Shrubbs, among which is the Filbert. Fruits, such as Rasberrys, Cranberrys of two Sorts, Gooseberrys and Currants. It has all sots of soil, such as dry, wet, rich, poor and barren; with great Quantities of Marsh, a number of Ponds, with runs fit for mills. Quantities of Marble, and its generally thought from the appearance of many parts of the Land there are Iron and Copper Ore. Its Inhabitants of the Brute Creation are Moose, Deer, Bear, fox, Wolf, Otter, Beaver, martins, Wild Cat, and many other Animals of the fur kind, all kinds of wild fowl, Hares, Partridges brown and black.... Codfish is ever taken in any Quantitys with very convenient Beaches for drying and curing them. Shellfish of all sorts except the oyster, none of which we saw, fine Prawns and Shrimps...."

Settlers were not long in coming to the new lands. Abraham Somes and James Richardson established homesteads on Somes Sound in 1761, and brought their families down the next year. More followed; at least a half-dozen families found agreeable places on the northeastern side of the island. The islanders incorporated as the town of Mount Desert in 1776.

On February 24, 1781, the Revolutionary War came to Frenchman Bay. The British warship *Allegiance* sailed up the bay that evening and anchored off Duck Brook. They questioned Captain Ezra Young at his house next to the brook. They left him at home and sailed across the bay in search of Daniel Sullivan, a valuable hostage. They captured Sullivan, burned his house, spared his family and left the next day.

Another wave of settlers came to the island in the peaceful but hard times after the Revolution. The islanders farmed a little, fished, lumbered, built boats and traded their products for essentials, which included some food. Families grew steadily as relatives and spouses joined the first pioneers and children were born.

The first town meeting in the new town of Eden was held on March 26, 1796, in Samuel Hull's house in Hulls Cove.

The new citizens of Eden surely shared the feelings of their neighbors in Blue Hill, who said of politics and related matters, "...we are so as it ware out of the wourld that we dont hardley know wether we do rite or rong but we mean to do as well as we can."

First Church at Hull's Cove

1795–1890

E. M. Hamor

Mr. Editor:—In your very interesting account of the service of the laying the corner stone of "The Church of Our Father" at Hull's Cove, you say: "The first house of worship at Hull's Cove is the memorial gift of two ladies of New York, who have for many years passed the summer months on this island...."

Now to say that this church is the first house of worship at Hull's Cove is a great mistake, and if there is anything like this written in the documents deposited in this box in the corner stone referred to, it is doing great injustice to the first settlers of Hull's Cove.

The fact is that there was a house of worship at Hull's Cove from about 1795 till 1865. I well remember when I was a small boy walking with my father and mother, from Town Hill to Hull's Cove, Sunday after Sunday to attend meeting in that house. This house was a large high posted building. The wall pews were square, elevated about ten inches above the centre pews, and had seats on three sides of them. The pulpit was very high with a door to it, if I remember rightly.

There was a great deal of molding work about the inside of this house and it seemed to my boyish mind that it was a very grand and sacred place. Probably from the year 1810 to 1860 this was the best finished meeting house on the island.

E. M. Hamor

From the Bar Harbor Record, *September 11, 1890.*

(From Bar Harbor Days; *courtesy of Maine Historic Preservation Commission.)*

Mary Hamor was born in Harpswell, March 6, 1761, and came to Hulls Cove with her parents about 1768. She married Edward Hodgkins, of Trenton, who was ten years her senior, and was in her nineties when she died in the 1850s.

Taking Care of Grandmother

Mid-1800s

Dr. L.W. Hodgkins

My Grandmother, Mary Hamor Hodgkins, espoused to Edward Hodgkins, my Grandfather, I remember perfectly well, as a very handsome and a very proud old lady. That inevitable white cap with its set up crown and crimpled border must never be "dirty"; and her clay pipe must be "burned out" so often as may be to keep it as near its original whiteness as possible, and I got my first lessons in smoking from lighting that same old pipe for her when I was of the mature age of perhaps three or four years, for before I have any distinct remembrance of her she had the great misfortune to fall and break her hip, as the phrase is, and ever after was a cripple confined to her chair or crutches, hence my impressment and apprentisship as "pipe lighter." What was my reward? Well my Grammy saved me many a well-deserved trouncing and serepticiously fed me all the "Goodies" she could capture from my mother's small stores. "Peace be to her ashes." It was long, long ago but it comes to me now but as yesterday....

From an October, 1900 letter written by Dr. L.W. Hodgkins, of Ellsworth, to Eben Hamor; cited in Hamor's report on the families of Eden. Courtesy of Jesup Library.

Shipbuilding in Eden

On February 21, 1889, the *Bar Harbor Record* noted that "E. T. Hamor is getting out the frame for a sixty-five ton schooner which will be built during the Spring either at Hull's Cove or Duck Brook." Master builder John Salisbury and his crews kept at it, for the schooner was measured for her official tonnage on July 26, 1889.

The schooner *E .T. Hamor* left the ways at the end of Eden's shipbuilding era. She was part of a vital period in Bar Harbor's history that has almost been lost.

Ralph Stanley, who has dug deeply into Bar Harbor's shipbuilding past, has found that "there were a lot of schooners built in Eden"—more than he has had time to count, and he is sure that he has not found them all. He notes that not many people realize that Eden was a community of rather well-known shipbuilders. Throughout most of the 19th century, men came to Eden from the local area and beyond for their new boats.

Custom house records from 1809 to 1886 show that the builders of Eden launched at least seventy-three vessels from 1809 to 1886. Eighteen of these were brigs, a rig favored in the West Indies trade. The rest were schooners, all two-masted, used primarily for coastal transportation. Many of the vessels Stanley has discovered are not in the records, including the largest vessel known to have been built in Eden, the *Annie M. Gray*, a 443-ton, 116-foot bark built in 1864 for the coastal trade.

Eden's shipbuilders did not build grand clippers or giant ocean traders. They needed smaller vessels that they could use profitably, often to transport their own goods, especially lumber, staves and other products of the local mills. One of the larger, but still typical, brigs was the beefy 235-ton brig *Volta* (length, 90.8 feet; beam, 24.3; depth, 12.1) built in 1832. More typical was the 115-ton schooner *Ligonia* (73.5, 22.8, 8) built during the shipbuilding boom of the early 1850s. Many were much smaller.

A shipyard was not necessary. A few acres of protected waterfront with a gentle slope to shore, along with a ginpole, sawpit, steambox, pitch oven and perhaps a wharf sufficed. Schooners were built at Hulls Cove, Salisbury Cove, Hadley Point, Emery Cove, Leland Cove, Northeast Creek, Thompson's Island, Northwest Cove and Indian Point. One enterprising soul launched a small sloop in the Jones Marsh Salt Pond.

The *E. T. Hamor* went from stump to sailing in much less than a year, a pace that seems daunting today but that was entirely typical for the time. According to Stanley, this is they did it:

Each vessel had a master builder. He carved the model that determined the boat's shape and also managed the project. He often took a share in the vessel as at least partial payment. He supervised the various crews that came to work on the boat—and this is the secret to the speed of construction. A boat was not built by a group of men who worked on her from start to finish, but by a series of highly skilled, specialized crews that appeared at the proper time, then moved on to the next vessel. The keel crew was followed by the frames crew, who in turn were followed by a fairing crew, planking crew and caulking crew. Other crews rigged and finished fitting out. The boat was often fully rigged and nearly ready to sail on her first profitable journey on the day she was launched.

Some working schooners trudged along, but many captains delighted in getting the most out of their vessels. In his book, *Wake of the Coasters*, John Leavitt recalled sailing with Captain Ed Harper in the "homely" *Bloomer*, a bluff-bowed "cod's head and mackerel tail" schooner built originally as a sloop in 1855 at Indian Point. According to Leavitt, Captain Harper "never let the old girl loaf along easily. With full sail on, the *Bloomer* tore up the bay for hundreds of yards around and rolled white water up under her bow until it looked as through she were burrowing her way through a hillock of white wool." Leavitt's friend Freeman Closson remarked, "Yup, she could sail all right, but, oh God, how she hated to!"

For nearly a century, the *Bloomer* carried granite, lumber, sand, brick and lime.

Leavitt also reported the last days of the *E. T. Hamor*. She worked along the coast hauling assorted cargoes, from Mount Desert Ferry, then Portland. While hauled out at Blue Hill for a rebuild, she fell over and was scrapped. Her owner used her rig on the *Katherine Seavey*, which sailed until she was lost in the 1940s.

Some Useful Definitions

True *brigs* feature square sails on both masts for trade wind sailing, along with a small gaff-headed fore-and-aft spanker sail on the mainmast for better maneuvering close to shore. A *brigantine* is a variation, with square sails on the foremast, and a fore-and-aft mainsail. The term brig loosely referred to either type.

A *bark* is a three-masted vessel, square-rigged on the forward two masts, and fore-and-aft rigged on the third.

A *schooner* is rigged fore-and-aft, with a foremast that is slightly shorter than, or equal to, the main mast. The basic rig includes foresail and mainsail (traditionally gaff-headed), along with a boomed jib. Other sails can be added to this basic suit: more jibs, a jibtopsail, a balloon jib, gafftopsails and a staysail.

The schooner E. T. Hamor *after unloading at Fernald's store in Somesville, near the turn of the century. Her crew has been using her foregaff to lift cargo out of the hold.*

Coasting schooners regularly ventured into narrow, shallow inlets that required skillful navigation and full use of the tide. They served as the trucks of their time, carrying "anything they could get," including foodstuffs, wood, animals, coal, hay, stone, sand, manufactured products, and occasionally a few passengers. They typically sailed with a crew of two or three men and were usually run on a shoestring. Sails were patched until they finally blew out and leaks plugged or tolerated until the pumps could not keep up. Each vessel was as individual as her master: trim and finely kept or hogged, slovenly, and a wonder to see afloat. (Courtesy of Ralph Stanley.)

The small schooner Bloomer *(length, 64.3 feet; beam, 21.8 feet; depth, 6.3 feet) and the three-master* Isabel E. Wiley *loading granite at Hall Quarry sometime after 1906.*

The Bloomer *was stoutly built, mostly of hackmatack, and reportedly still had most of her original frames and planking when she finally went to the beach nearly a century after her launching. According to Ralph Stanley, her crew took her whaling at least once in the 1880s. They captured a half-dozen whales (of unknown species) out by Mount Desert Rock. (Courtesy of Ralph Stanley.)*

Reports of Eden

1859 AND 1881

A. J. COOLIDGE AND J. B. MANSFIELD
G. J. VARNEY AND B. B. RUSSELL

1859.—EDEN, Hancock County is situated on the northern part of Mount Desert island, and embraces an area of 22,000 acres, about 1,000 of which are covered by water. Its early history belongs to the town of Mount Desert, of which it formed a part until its incorporation. The surface and soil are similar to those of Mount Desert. The leading pursuits of the inhabitants are navigation and agriculture. Eden has one village, four religious societies (Baptist, Free-will Baptist, Methodist and Congregational), three of which have meeting-houses; fourteen school districts, with twenty-one schools; and four post-offices—Eden, West Eden, Bar Harbor and Salisbury Cove. It has also two saw mills, two shingle mills, and five ship-builders. Population, 1,127; valuation, $103,809, although the present actual valuation is estimated as high as $400,000.

1881.—EDEN, in Hancock County, occupies the northern and eastern portions of Mount Desert Island...In the north-west is Western Bay; in the north is Thomas Bay, which receives the waters of the largest stream on the island, North-Eastern Brook. North of this are Mount Desert Narrows, separating the island and the mainland. The principal eminences are Newport [Champlain] Mountain (1,060 feet in height), McFarland's Mountain (764 feet), the White Cap (925 feet), Mount Kebo (405 feet), Interlaken Hill [Brewer Mountain] (462 feet), Great Hill (748 feet). Dry [Dorr] Mountain and Green [Cadillac] Mountain (1,522 feet), four miles S. S. W. of Bar Harbor, are partly in Eden. "The view from Green Mountain is delightful...We know not what view in nature can be finer than this, where the two grandest objects in nature, high mountains and a limitless ocean, occupy the horizon. The name of Eden is truly appropriate to this beautiful place." Twenty miles out on the ocean is seen Mount Desert Rock, with its light-house beaming a fixed white light. In the west are numerous mountains of the island, with bright lakes interspersed, while the Camden Mountains are seen in the distance. It is claimed that Mount Katahdin, 100 miles to the north, and Mount Washington, 140 miles west, can sometimes be seen from this point. Whittier, in *Mogg Megone*, has a passage on this locality.

Granite, sometimes porphyritic in character [containing large crystals], is the prevailing rock in town. The soil varies from loam to gravel, with some marsh. Wheat, corn, oats, potatoes and barley are all raised to some extent. There are two saw-mills for long lumber, two shingle and two clap-board mills. Agriculture and the fisheries are both carried on to a considerable extent; but the chief employment of the people is catering to the wants of summer visitors. Bar Harbor, the principal village, is situated on the east side of the island. It has a fine sea view, extending across Porcupine Island, in Frenchman's Bay, to the rolling hills of Goldsborough. There are beaches near the village; and a high rocky islet [Bald Porcupine] near by is the summer residence of General Fremont.... About two and a half miles north of Bar Harbor is the little seaport of Hull's Cove. Here is a neat crescent beach, where the Gregoires dwelt, the grand-daughter of a Gascon noble, Condillac [Cadillac], to whom the King of France granted Mount Desert in 1688. About two miles north of his place, across the promontory, is Salisbury Cove, a port for small vessels. The Via Mala is a long passage in the neighboring cliffs. A short distance eastward from this is the little hamlet of Sand Cliff; and near it are the Ovens, a range of caves in the porphyritic cliffs. All over the island are found elm, birch, maple, cedar and the evergreens, in large tracts and scattered groups.

The first English settlement of the town was in 1763, by two families named Thomas and Higgins. Eden was taken from Mount Desert and incorporated in 1796. The name was probably adopted in honor of Richard Eden, an early English author. There is also a tradition that its natural beauties suggested its name. There are Baptist, Episcopal and Union churches in the town. The public library contains about 1,200 volumes. A high school is sustained for a portion of the year. Eden has thirteen public school houses, and its school property is valued at $8,000. The valuation of estates in 1870 was $196,499. In 1880, it was $177,534 [after the 1873 depression]. That rate of taxation in 1880 was 16 mills on the dollar. The population in 1870 was 1,195. In the census of 1880 it was 1,629.

From A History and Description of New England, General and Local, *Vol. I, by A. J. Coolidge and J. B. Mansfield, Boston, 1859; and* A Gazetteer of the State of Maine, *George J. Varney and B. B. Russell, Boston, 1881.*

Hull's Cove and Salisbury Cove

1888

M. F. Sweetser

Hull's Cove is a hamlet of about a score of old-fashioned and snug little farmhouses, scattered along the treeless fields that lie about the foot of the quiet bay. As you enter it, from the south, you see one of the oldest houses on the island, a manorial looking structure of red brick, on a sea-viewing eminence. The village has one or two small stores, a post-office, one or two boarding-houses, an anchorage for small vessels, and a place where schooners have been built, when the Cove was a well-known fishing-port. On one side is the great old brick mansion erected by the Hamor family, from bricks made here. The village was named for Capt. Samuel Hull (a brother of Gen. William Hull, the victim of Detroit), who settled here soon after the Revolutionary War. The first town-meeting was held at his house in 1796. Near the northern extremity of the hamlet, on the left, and a little way secluded from the highway [and now hidden by buildings], you may see the white monuments in the old village-graveyard, just out side of which are the graves of the De Gregoires, the last heirs of the French Sovereignty of Mount Desert. Among the generous grants of the Kings of France was one made in 1688 to Antoine de la Motte Condillac [Cadillac], a brilliant officer of the marine corps, and sometime commandant of Mackinaw and Detroit, and Governor of Louisiana. This royal largess consisted (in part) of the island of Mount Desert; and the gallant old Gascon used to delight to sign himself, "Lord of Donaquee and Mount Desert in Maine." After over twenty years of life in his lonely Western and Southwestern fortresses, Condillac returned to France, in 1717, and died soon afterwards. In the year 1786, his granddaughter, Madame Marie Therese de Gregoire (*née* De La Motte Condillac) and her husband, Barthelemy de Gregoire, came over from France, and set up a claim to this princely estate. Thomas Jefferson interested himself in their favor, and the Marquis de Lafayette joined also in his good offices, through M. Otto, the French ambassador to the United States. The General Court of Massachusetts, sitting at Boston, reported favorably; and by a special act naturalized the De Gregoires and their children, Pierre, Nicolas and Marie. And so this interesting family came into possession of 60,000 acres of land, including such parts of the island (and some of the adjacent mainland) as were not occupied by actual settlers. John Bernard's attempt to buy them out for £2,500, failed of success [Bernard had a grant to the southern half of the island]; and De Gregoire led a quiet life among his fishermen neighbors, with the occasional variation of an orgie on rum and molasses. From time to time a

An idyllic view of the main road heading north down to Hull's Cove, showing the well, sawmill and bridge over the creek, from the 1886 guide, Mount Desert with Pen & Pencil. *(Maine Historic Preservation Commission.)*

French monk visited their secluded home, and abode briefly with these lonely compatriots.

In 1792 De Gregoire sold to Henry Jackson, for £1,247, 16*s*. a vast tract of land on the island and the main, together with the Cranberry Isles and the Duck Isles. In 1794 he sold two-fifths of the original domain to Perez Morton of Boston and Sieur Joseph de la Tombe, the French Consul at Boston. These transactions, and others of similar purport, are recorded in the *Bangor Historical Magazine* for May, 1886. The princely domain ceded to the De Gregoires "to cultivate mutual confidence and union between the subjects of His Most Christian Majesty and the citizens of this State," thus dropped away little by little from the recipients; and about the year 1810, the two beneficiaries died, and were buried in the little cemetery at Hull's Cove, where their graves are marked by a white wooden cross, just outside of the enclosure. The lady lived three years longer than her husband, abandoning the old homestead (whose cellar is still pointed out to curious tourists), and dwelling with the Hulls. [The site is now hidden behind the Colony Motel.] After her death a belt of gold was found upon her body [so they say]....

...Point Levi is the picturesque promontory north of Hull's Cove, elevated in the centre, and sloping gradually to the shores, with many admirable building sites, overlooking Frenchman's Bay, Bar Harbor, and the great mountains. This tract of 85 acres has recently been acquired by city invaders, and laid out by landscape-gardeners and civil engineers. The roads cover a mile and a half, and are overlaid with beach gravel, and make beautiful curves and gradients, through shadowy groves and over sea-viewing hills.

Near the centre of this territory is the new cottage of Dr. Guy Fairfax Whiting, of Washington, with its decagonal stone tower and loggia. On the highest point rises the handsome new house of C. Wycliff Yulee, son of the late Senator Yulee of Florida, overlooking Bar Harbor, the mountains and the bay....

...Emerging from Hull's Cove, the northward road ascends a hill, and in retrospect we have a charming view of Bar Harbor and its surroundings. It is a matter of two and a half miles from Hull's Cove by a pleasant road through the woods, with occasional broad views over Frenchman's Bay, to the little cottage where people alight to visit The Ovens. A few minutes walk leads down the little glen to the shore, where a boatman stands ready to carry you around in front of the cliffs, if the tide happens to be high. The best time for the visit is about two hours after low tide, when one can descend among the haunts of sea-urchins, star-fish, sea-anemones, and other strange forms of marine life. The Ovens are a line of shallow caverns, worn by the sea in the bases of the tall cliffs. They can be visited at low tide, along the pebbly beach, which is nearly 100 feet wide; and at high tide boatmen carry visitors along the quiet waters in front of them, and into the largest of the caverns. The cliffs are of disintegrating porphyritic or slaty rock, rich in its coloring, and usually dripping from all the brightest points....

...Salisbury Cove lies about a mile and a half beyond Sands Point, and is the chief harbor in the town of Eden, giving anchorage and wharves for large vessels. It opens out on Eastern Bay, which is here over a mile wide, with the long settlement of Lamoine on the other side. There are a score or two of houses around the cove, near which is the best farming land on the island; and there is also a small Baptist church, and a rural tavern. The Cove was named for Ebenezer Salisbury, one of the first settlers of Eden, at whose house the early town-meetings were held; and the town-house of Eden still stands here, with a little burying-ground near it, in which are the graves of Salisbury, Hopkins, Young, Doane, and other pioneers. At Salisbury Cove there are two country stores, a public hall, a post-office, a mill, and several carpenters, coopers, shipbuilders, and farmers.

From Chisholm's Mount-Desert Guide-Book, *M. F. Sweetser, 1888. Maine Historic Preservation Commission.*

The middle-aged de Gregoires spent their first years in North America attempting to fund a gentrified life in Boston through sale of their lands. When this idea did not work, they came to live in Hulls Cove. Going home was not an attractive option; France during the revolution was not a healthy place for aristocrats. The couple finally sold their land in return for care during their remaining years.

The de Gregoires' resting place is marked by a simple granite stone with a cross and the words "1811, de Gregoire" carved in relief. The stone has weathered and settled. At first glance it looks like a small granite rock at the very edge of the eastern side of the cemetery. It is easily missed.

The collection of long barns on the north side of Route 3 once housed William Pierson Hamilton's fine horses. In 1941, the Hamiltons bequeathed "The Farm" to Jackson Lab. The lab kept dogs used for behavioral research in the former stables, and set up temporary quarters here after the main lab burned in 1947. During World War II, lab staff planted gardens. At one point, they tried using mouse manure, with inedible results.

Before the mid-1930s, Hamilton Pond was a wetland. Hamilton had it built to attract ducks for fall sport.

Working at Hamilton Station

1920s TO 1930s

NAN COLE

One of the most colorful summer residents over a period of years was William Pierson Hamilton, former partner in J. P. Morgan enterprises. Although a tremendously wealthy man, he alternated from lavish spending sprees to cycles of penuriousness. He purchased an enormous tract of land at Salisbury Cove, where he built massive stables and paddocks—all painted barn red—and became a breeder of champion horses. At that time Hamilton Farms was the largest employer in town. Mr. Hamilton hired caretakers, gardeners, architects, men to give him daily massages, valets, maids, and housekeepers galore.

As new buildings were erected at Hamilton Farms, gardens were designed and planted and macadam driveways were built. At one time, there were about thirty men working on a road through the property. Each day, on the dot of 1 P.M., a huge bell was rung, the signal for every man on the crew to lay down his tools and take a siesta for an hour or two. This was the hour for Mr. Hamilton's daily nap, and he ordered everyone on the place to do the same to insure peace and quiet. When Mr. Hamilton awoke refreshed, the bell sounded for the men to resume work.

[At times], the economy side of Mr. Hamilton would take command, and he became penny-pinching to an alarming degree. He would roam around proclaiming that money was to be saved and not spent, and demanding that all expenses be reduced drastically. During this phase, he would sell some of his horses and fight over all the bills—with or without cause. Frequently he fired most of his employees summarily, but the local ones, accustomed to his cycles, simply waited for the mood to change when, almost invariably, they got their plush jobs back.

From "A Native's Memories of Old Bar Harbor," Nan Cole, Down East, *September 1970.*

Researchers inspect intertidal life during the early days of the Mount Desert Island Biological Laboratory.

The lab began in South Harpswell as the Tufts Summer School of Biology in 1898. It moved to its present site on Emery Cove in 1921. The land was donated by the Wild Gardens of Acadia Association at the suggestion of George Dorr.

Today the lab's four hundred members conduct basic research on a variety of cold-water organisms, with an emphasis on investigating processes that relate to human biology. Lectures and tours are offered throughout the summer. Several historic buildings are part of the lab complex, including the old town school house, which now serves as a lecture hall. (Courtesy of Mount Desert Island Biological Laboratory.)

Northeast Creek and Eden Village

A family encampment of the Ceramic Period (2,800 to 400 years B.P.) at nearby Fernald Point on Somes Sound. It is likely that small groups of prehistoric people stopped by Northeast Creek once in a while during this time. They left little evidence of their presence.

The typical Ceramic Period dwelling was an asymmetrical conical wigwam about twelve feet in diameter, covered with animal skins. Most had gravel or sand floors and a stone-lined hearth. Some were partially buried, sometimes in piles of shells, presumably for warmth in winter. (Painting by Judith R. Cooper, courtesy of Abbe Museum, Bar Harbor.)

Today, the village of Eden is a small cluster of houses on a busy highway full of people in a rush to be somewhere else. To reach the past here, it is necessary to stop, shut off the engine and leave the road. A pull-out parking place next to Northeast Creek is provided by a generous landowner. It is possible to explore the creek and Thomas Bay by canoe or kayak, adopting the viewpoint of the prehistoric people who once lived in this spot.

The settlers who arrived in the mid-1700s were especially interested in the fodder that the salt marshes and fresh meadows could provide for their oxen and cows. Salt-meadow grass (*Spartina patens*) makes excellent hay and contains essential trace minerals. The wild meadows were more or less ready for harvesting. Turning the forests of Mount Desert Island into hayfield was hard work and took time. Most of the island's soils are acid and poor. Grass or other crops might do reasonably well for a year or two after a fresh clearing and burn, but building up hayfields that produced good crops of nutritious grass took years of contributions from the animals that grazed upon them.

The first people and those who came after undoubtably shared one of Northeast Creek's other crops: cranberries. In 1839, the managed cranberry bogs produced 500 bushels. Paddling up the creek to pick a basket of cranberries is still a pleasant thing to do on a fine fall day.

Before History

Samuel de Champlain apparently sailed up Frenchman Bay to the Narrows, where he noted the width of the channel. He did not mention meeting anyone along this shore, but he was sailing past places that had been occupied by small groups of people periodically during the past 2,000 years or more.

Champlain probably sailed over former encampments as well. Sea level was about six feet lower 3,000 years ago. At that level, Mount Desert Island was a peninsula and the shore was much farther to the east.

Abbe Museum curator Rebecca Cole-Will suggests that Northeast Creek is a logical site for a prehistoric encampment. It is a sheltered, gently sloping shore with plenty of fresh water and food nearby.

Although archaeological evidence in the Northeast Creek area is very scanty, excavations at sites of similar age in the region provide a picture of what people's lives were like.

Archaelogists refer to the period from about 2,800 to 400 B.P. (Before Present) as the Ceramic Period for the most identifiable items left behind by the people. Maine's native peoples began using pottery later, and abandoned it earlier, than other groups living in New England. By the time Europeans arrived, the natives no longer made pots, but used birchbark containers and baskets. It may be that heavy breakable clay pots did not suit people who traveled by birchbark canoe (including regular portages), but no one is sure why pottery was abandoned.

The archaeological record is biased strongly toward animal foods, explains Cole-Will, since animal bones are preserved much better than vegetable remains. People certainly ate many berries, fruits and other plant foods, but no one knows exactly what they were. Charred seeds and other minute plant parts that persist in shell middens (kitchen dumps) are difficult to find and harder to identify, but archaeologists are working on the problem.

The Ceramic Period people hunted with spears, and in later years, with bows and arrows. They fished, and kept weirs. Abbe Museum researchers identified remains of the following at Fernald Point: cod, haddock, pollock, sculpin, goosefish, dogfish, flounder, sturgeon, hake, wolf-fish, sea raven, ocean pout, striped bass, alewife, grebe, ducks, geese, great blue heron, great auk, various other alcids, owls, bald eagle, hawks, deer, moose, bear, mink, sea mink, beaver, otter, muskrat, raccoon, hare, eastern cottontail, fox, dog, porcupine, gray seal, harbor seal, and porpoise. Two of these, sea mink and great auk, were extinct by the late 1800s—hunted out by trappers and hungry sailors. The Fernald Point people also ate clams, mussels, sea urchins and whelks but apparently no lobsters.

Bones have growth rings similar to those of trees. It is possible to determine the season in which an animal died based on variation in the rings. In addition, some animals come near the coast at certain times; for example, sturgeon and dogfish in spring and summer, and sea ducks and cod from fall through early spring.

The idea that Maine's coastal Indians were "the original summer people" is an enduring bit of folklore, but it apparently was not true during the Ceramic Period and probably before then. It probably was true after European contact, since the French and English came in summer looking to trade valuable items for furs. Indians did not live on the coast in substantial numbers after the epidemics and wars of the 1600s. They did come to Mount Desert to sell their crafts to the summer people in the late 1800s. (See pages 87–89.)

Close examination of discarded animal bones found in Mount Desert middens reveals that from about 2,800 to 1,200 B.P., people lived on the island mostly during the coldest months, from late fall to early spring. This makes sense from a food-getting standpoint: the winter coast of Maine still offers a feast of sea birds, waterfowl and shellfish, but sadly, many fewer fish. By about 1,200 B.P. animals that are present only in summer appear along with cold-weather species, especially cod. It appears that people fished for cod in late winter and early spring, stayed throughout the summer at least into early fall, possibly year-round.

A dearth of appropriate tools and other indirect evidence indicates that the people who lived east of the Kennebec did not begin farming until much later in the Ceramic Period than their southern neighbors. It is likely that the corn, bean and squash varities available were too tender or ripened too late for eastern Maine's cooler, shorter growing season.

The people of Mount Desert Island may have traded for their vegetables. The island was on a coastal trade route that reached at least to Pennsylvania, New York and Nova Scotia. Islanders traded for valued items such as chert, which made especially fine blades and decorative and useful items made of copper. They possessed ocean-going canoes and traveled throughout the islands and along the coast.

No one is precisely sure who the Ceramic Period people were, although it appears that they are the ancestors of the Native Americans now living in Maine. Practically no evidence of their cultural and spiritual traditions has been found.

In the early 1760s, Cape Cod and nearby areas suffered a serious drought. France and England has just agreed to peace, allowing people to travel to eastern Maine in search of fresh and salt meadow hay, and in some cases, a new place to live as well.

One of the island's first roads went from the fresh meadows of Northeast Creek to the settlement on Somes Sound. The island residents felt the marshes were theirs, especially since they had put considerable effort into improving them. The problem was that no one had clear title to any land, since the wars between England and France had just ended, and it was not at all certain that they would not begin anew. People who needed hay simply went and got it, ignoring theoretical niceties such as land ownership.

Joseph Chadwick, in his *Journey Through a Part of Mount Desert in 1768* says "The contention among the people living on the main for the marshes of Mt. Desert is so warm, that they begin on the 15th of August to forelay one another. Cutting the grass so out of season is a great damage to the marshes." He describes Jones Marsh and the North East Marshes and the marshes between Salisbury and Hulls Cove as having been improved by Mr. Jones; and says "that there were ten loads of hay cut on Jones, fourteen loads on North East, and twenty-five loads on the meadow back of Hulls Cove."

Something had to be done, and the government–after hearing from its citizens–finally did it, granting the Mount Desert settlers title to the meadows.

A Petition

1768

THE INHABITANTS OF MOUNT DESERT

To His Excellency Governor Bernard,

We the inhabitants of mount desart Humbly Craves your Excelency's Proteccon against the In-Crossing of the Naboring inhabents made upon us Consarning hay for we cannot git hay on ye island for the keep our Stoks, other People Cut the hay before it gits its Groth so that they Spoil the marsh & if we Cut and haystack it for Sleding it is Stole so that we cannot have ye Provilige of the marsh that we have Cleared Rode too, there fore we bege that your Exelency will consider us & put a stop to this Incrossins, otherways we Shall Not be Able to keepe our Stocks & the marsh will be totely Spiled. Last Summer the People Came from the Township of No. 6 and Cut part of the North east marsh where we had a rode this five years before we knew thereof & carried off some hay after we Raked & Staked it, also other hay which we Cut & Staked was Stole. Last hay season it happened very Luckey for us that Coll. Goldthwait Came here just about the time of Cutting the marsh & we are of Opinion that if he had Not Come hear mos of the Settlers on this island must have lost or Kild their Stoks for want of hay. The Settlers of No. 4 & No. 5 & No. 6 west of mount desart River & No. 1 & No. 2 east of mount desart River Chefly Depend on this island for hay; we would further inform your Excelency that Vessels hands and others make a Practis of Coming to this island and Cutting Lumber Such as Staves, Shingles and Clap boards and other Lumber which will much discourage further Settlers. So no more but we make bold to Subscribe our Selves your Excelency's most humble Petitioners.

Abraham Somes
Andrew Tarr
Stephen Gott
Benjm Stanwood
James Richardson
Stephen Richardson
Daniel Gott
Daniel Gott, Jr.
Thomas Richardson
Elijah Richardson

From Eben Hamor's report on the families of Eden, courtesy of Jesup Library.

In 1790, the town fathers voted to establish five school districts on the northern half of the island, including one at Northeast Creek. Two years later the three families on the south side of the creek petitioned for another school, leaving four families attending the first.

A bridge was needed. On April 6, 1795, the town voted to build one, and in the long-standing tradition of municipal improvements, specified that the road committee "Git it bult to the best advantage as Cheepe as they can."

In 1881 the village of Eden had a post office, school house, a couple of stores and a mill. The mill was on the bay side of the highway. What appear to be remains of the dam are still evident.

Record Crowds at Eden Fair

1927

Bar Harbor Times

All attendance records were broken at the thirty-eighth annual fair of the Eden Agricultural Society held at Eden Park last Wednesday and Thursday. The fair followed the usual lines and the products of Mt. Desert Island farms were featured in all departments. Cattle, sheep, swine, poultry and pet stock were shown in the sheds and outside the exhibition hall. Fruits, vegetables, poultry products, dairy products, canning products, cooking products, green house fruits, fancy work, paintings and drawings, flowers, and the exhibits of the Boys and Girls Agricultural clubs crowded the hall to capacity....

Miss Beverly of the Red Cross was in charge of the Baby Show which was one of the big features of the fair. Twenty babies gave the judges the hardest task of their lives or would have done so had the prizes been for beauty. As it was they were an all prize aggregation, Miss Beverly says....

The prize winner in the three to six months class was Oliver, son of Mr. and Mrs. Walter Russell of Salisbury Cove. In the seven to eleven months class Isabelle, daughter of Mr. and Mrs. Dallas Hodgkins of Eden was the winner. In the twelve to fifteen months class Alberta, daughter of Mr. and Mrs. Leslie Dunton of Salisbury Cove was the winner.

The merry-go-round did a capacity business on both days and hundreds of children enjoyed the sport of riding the wooden horses around the ring. The midway was lively as usual with a variety of refreshments on sale and many games to attract the crowds. The Bar Harbor Band kept things lively at the track and between heats of the races there was always something going on for the amusement of the spectators. Singers, dancers, acrobats and wrestlers followed one another in entertaining the big crowd opposite the judges' stand. The stables were filled with race horses and the usual crowd of horsemen made their headquarters near the horse sheds.

Two magnificent registered Belgian mares and a four-months-old filly were exhibited by Thirlstane Farms [owned by William Pierson Hamilton] and were one of the outstanding attractions of the fair. The mares were Lourane Bell and Queen de Furnes, each weighing over 2,300 pounds and moving with the speed and action of many animals half their weight....

From the Bar Harbor Times, *September 21, 1927.*

Horse pull at the Eden Fair. (Courtesy of Bar Harbor Historical Society.)

The Eden Fair ran from 1889 until the late 1920s on the fairgrounds near Hadley Point.

In a recent Bar Harbor Historical Society talk, Eden resident Charlotte Ingalls recalled the day her father, a dairy farmer, was stopped at the top of the ferris wheel, trapped in a position that offered a perfect view of his cows happily strolling to freedom through a break in his fence.

Town Hill (West Eden) and the Emery District

Bambi, Allison Salsbury's pet deer, stops in at the Town Hill store to cadge a snack from owner Jeff Hall and his son Jack in the mid-1940s.

Allison Salsbury's father was Lyle Smith, the island's first game warden. Bambi followed Allison on the school bus, and faithfully accompanied her mother every time she went to light the fires at the old Grange Hall that stood across from the store. Salsbury recalled that one day a salesman came into the store shaking his head and saying, "Am I crazy, or did I see a deer coming out of the Grange?" The Halls assured him that he was fine, it was just Bambi. The neighbors became accustomed to the deer stopping by. One woman finished mixing up a batch of molasses cookie dough, went away for a moment to fetch something, and returned to find that Bambi had ambled in through the open kitchen door and helped herself to the giant wad of dough, which hung in a drooping mass from her mouth. The cook good-naturedly ceded dough rights to the deer. Bambi lived a grand life until a poacher shot her at age three.

Before supermarkets, Bar Harbor and the outlying villages were served by well over a dozen small local grocery stores.The predecessor to the present Town Hill Store burned in 1908. Before the turn of the century, the store and post office were located across the way, on the southern side of the Crooked Road. (Courtesy of Tim O'Brien.)

The rolling hills of Town Hill and the Emery District are an excellent place for a person interested in visualizing old landscapes to practice "seeing the fields for the trees." Until the last few decades, gardens and pasture covered much of the landscape. Town Hill residents now living remember when the bays and mountains were clearly visible from the top of the hill.

The region's many small farms provided fresh milk and vegetables to the town and the summer colony. Several farms are still active, including the late Peggy Rockefeller's cattle-breeding operation on the Crooked Road. The island's last dairy farm, also on the Crooked Road, changed over to horses in the mid-1980s. Many farms are gone. Scrub and woods have take over the abandoned gardens and fields with surprising speed. Quite a few places have been developed for house lots.

Most of the best farmland on the island is located along the loop formed by Route 3 and the Crooked Road. It is better for the simple reason that the gentle hills are covered with fairly deep soils containing some organic material. The glaciers left thick deposits of mixed material. More sediments were deposited when the sea flooded the depressed landscape after the glaciers' retreat. Relative sea level was nearly 300 feet higher, which is why marine clay–former sea bottom and mudflats–occurs in many places several feet below ground, inland of and above the present shoreline.

Settlement of Town Hill

1889

BAR HARBOR RECORD

MR. EDITOR.—I have been a reader of the *Record* from its first number until the present time, and think it one of the best weekly papers published in Eastern Maine and I have often thought, while reading the news from other places in the county, that Town Hill seemed to be "left out in the cold." For this reason, if you will adopt me into the family of *Record* correspondents, I will endeavor to report, occasionally, anything of importance that may occur at this place.

First, as to its location and name. Town Hill is situated in the western part of Eden, on what might be called an isthmus that separates the tide waters of Some's Sound from those of Clark's Cove and connects the eastern and western portions of Mount Desert Island. It is only a little more than two miles across this isthmus, from the head of Clark's Cove on the north-west.

The highest part of the hill is about 200 feet above mean high water, and affords a fine view of the mountains which extend in the form of a semicircle from the south-west to the south-east parts of the island. Gouldsboro mountains in the north-east and Blue Hill in the north-west can be plainly seen from this place, and also Some's Sound, Bluehill Bay, Jordan's River and Frenchman's Bay. In fact one gets some of the finest views from this hill that can be obtained at any place on the island. This is admitted by our summer visitors, who call the drive over Town Hill the best inland drive they find on the island.

The whole top of this Hill and part of the sides, embracing an area of 456 acres, was once owned by the town of Eden, hence the name Town Hill. It was not called West Eden until a postoffice by that name was established in about the year 1850. This tract of land is in the form of a boot, the toe being at the shore between Clark's and Northwest coves, the sole extending southeasterly along what is known as the "French Line," the heel being about half way from "Molly's Beach," so called, to the head of the Sound, and the leg standing over the top of the hill in a northeasterly direction to within about one-half mile of Northeast Marsh. This land was surveyed by James Peters in July 1812, and divided into nine lots, numbered 1, 2, etc., beginning at the northeastern point.

—T. H.

From the Bar Harbor Record, *February 14, 1889.*

In a later issue, T. H. explained that Joseph Mayo, Jesse Higgins and David Higgins came from Cape Cod to Town Hill at about the time of the Revolutionary War. These men settled along nearby coves, raised large families and "although they did not settle on Town Hill themselves, their sons and daughters did...."

Most of these families spent their lives where they first settled. They were "a hardy resolute set of men and women, who went into the wilderness, built themselves homes, working and faring hard for the benefit of their posterity as well as for themselves."

Local News from Town Hill

1889

BAR HARBOR RECORD

AUGUST 15.—The steamer *Mount Desert* carried an interesting couple from Northeast Harbor to Southwest Harbor last Wednesday. Mr. B. W. Kittredge, of West Eden, ninety years of age, made his first trip by steam in company with his wife who is eighty-two years old. Though Mr. Kittredge, in his youth, saw the first steamboat running on the Hudson, he had never traveled by steamer or railroad before during his long term of existence. The couple have been married sixty years, and it was pleasant to hear the old gentleman tell a friend, who offered to assist him down stairs from the saloon, to help the "old lady," for he "guessed" he could get along quite well alone. The old folks are well and hearty, and are taking advantage of the fine weather to visit their old friends in other parts of the island.

AUGUST 22.—President Harrison passed through this place last Saturday, the 10th inst., on his way from Somesville to Bar Harbor. We had but twenty minutes notice of the event but in that short time Mr. McKay and Mr. Rich managed to hoist a United States flag on a pole, not very high nor a very large flag, it is true, but it was the best they could do on so short notice; and get a few ladies and gentlemen together, who paid their respects to the President by waving handkerchiefs and swinging hats when he passed....

From the Bar Harbor Record, *1889.*

Farmland on Mount Desert Island

1894

EDWARD L. RAND AND JOHN H. REDFIELD

Another interesting feature of the Mt. Desert flora is shown by the comparatively small representation of introduced foreign plants, especially of weeds of cultivated ground. Excluding garden escapes and a few plants naturalized by intentional introduction, we find that the number of weeds is very small in comparison with that of similar areas in New England. The reason is a very simple one—the slight development of the Island for agricultural purposes—an explanation that is fully sustained by the facts.

In earlier time very little attention was paid to farming, doubtless because the physical character of the Island is not of a nature favoring agriculture except under limited or somewhat expensive conditions. The surface is mostly mountainous or rocky, the soil is usually thin and poor, and has often disappeared as a covering—a result of reckless wood cutting and the consequent forest fires. Taken as a whole, the north of the Island contains the best farming land; the south, for the most part, is too near the dominant granite range to furnish deep soil or level ground save under exceptional conditions. Moreover, under these unfavorable conditions there was nothing to encourage farming as a means of support, for there was no market for garden products. It is not strange, therefore, that fishing, lumbering, shipbuilding, and other pursuits, were the more profitable employments of the early settlers. All agricultural operations were conducted on a very limited scale, and for the most part involved nothing more than the cultivation of small vegetable patches for home purposes. These patches were seldom well cared for, and were rarely cultivated in the same spot for more than a year at a time. Of late years, however, it has been found profitable by many landowners to raise vegetables to supply the summer demand at Bar Harbor and the other summer resorts of the Island. Consequently, there has been a more systematic cultivation of the ground both for agricultural and for horticultural purposes.

From Flora of Mount Desert Island, Maine: A Preliminary Catalogue of the Plants Growing on Mount Desert Island and the Adjacent Islands, *Edward L. Rand and John H. Redfield, University Press, Cambridge, 1894; Thorndike Library, College of the Atlantic.*

In the late 1800s, the town of Eden had sixteen school districts, each with a schoolhouse within reasonable, if legendary, walking distance of its students' homes. West Eden (Town Hill) had its own school from the mid 1800s until the mid 1940s. Like its surviving sibling in Hulls Cove, the former schoolhouse hosts community events. The village improvement society has kept the main building's interior nearly intact. The ell (built about 1915) houses the Bar Harbor Fire Department's Town Hill Substation. (Courtesy of Tim O'Brien.)

School Days in the Emery District

1795 TO 1934

BAR HARBOR TIMES

It is an interesting fact that while most schoolhouses take their name from the community in which they are situated, the reverse is true in at least one instance.

...On February 22, 1796 the legislature of Massachusetts passed an act dividing Mount Desert into two towns, one to be known as Eden. Under the new division there were six school districts in Eden. Later several more were added. Of these, Emery District was apparently the first and was designated to include land beginning at what is now the De Laittre farm and running to the Robbins place, taking in territory now known as the Young's District. This complete district was the school territory. As most of the land included—about seventy-five percent—was owned by Joel Emery, it became known as the Emery School District, still so called.

The legal voters in each district met yearly and elected a school agent. It was the duty of this agent to hire the teacher or teachers needed in his immediate district; it was his privilege to board said teacher during his or her sojourn, thus receiving some monetary return for the importance of his position.

At the time of which I am speaking, about 100 years ago, there were two terms of school yearly, eight weeks in the spring, and eight in the fall. The recent winter weather gives sufficient reason why, in those days of lack of transportation, a winter term was omitted. It was customary to have a woman teacher in the spring and a man in the fall, thus showing no partiality....

The requirements for eligibility for teaching in those days were few and simple. Any pupil who had conquered Greenleaf's Arithmetic, parsed and analyzed thru Kerl's Grammar, learned the boundaries and capitals of the several states of the Union, and who could repeat from memory the counties and cities of Maine, could appear at a certain time before the Superintending School Committee and take an examination in these facts. If successful, the aspirant received a certificate enabling him, or her, to teach in the Public Schools of Eden for one year.

The first school in the Emery District was built about the year 1830. It stood just at the turn of Norway Drive, a few rods below the old Fox Farm, now owned by Paul Russell. On a plot of land from the farm of Cornelius Thompson, grand-father of Frank Thompson, a small building, approximately twenty by thirty feet was erected. There is no record of the vote authorizing this building, or of its cost; but for other school houses of that period amounts varying from $60 to $350 were allotted. The building consisted of two rooms, a small unfinished hallway, and a plastered main room. The seats were built of rough plank, and the desks were more planks, nailed up, not unlike shelves of today. The students sat in rows of eight, so that if the one nearest the wall must leave his seat, everyone of necessity rose and filed out to give him room. The teacher sat on a high platform, built much in the manner of a pulpit. Behind her desk was the solitary blackboard. The room was heated by a big stove, which took a cordwood stick.

An amusing incident which occurred at the Emery District School about ninety years ago was as follows: The school at that time was chiefly composed of larger boys, perhaps due to the fact that it was the man-teacher's turn. Most of the pupils brought their dinner, and ate it in the school-room. The teacher, however, boarded at the school agent's, who at this time was Deacon Jared Emery, and who lived next door to the school house. On that particular day the teacher went home to dinner, leaving the building full of noisy, chattering children. In a short time he returned, to find, on entering the building, not a scholar in sight. He was most mystified, and rushed in confusion to Deacon Emery's house to tell of the children's disappearance. Deacon Emery accompanied him to the schoolhouse. When they opened the door, every scholar was in his place, industriously studying. Upon investigation, it was found that the children had climbed on the wood-pile in the front entry to the overhead timbers, thence crawled to the back of the house over the schoolroom ceiling and there hid. History does not report the just punishment.

After forty years of service this building was torn down, the land reverting to its original owner, and later the school house now standing was built in its stead.

From the Bar Harbor Times, *February 21, 1934.*

Eden Street Shore

By the 1880s, summer cottages were going up all over the former pastures and clearings north of town. The changing times are quite obvious in this 1890s-era photograph of Duck Brook, on the bay side of Eden Street (Route 3).

The Hamor sawmill was the descendent of mills that had occupied the site since the mid-1700s. The building in the distance on the bay shore is Brook End, a Shingle Style summer cottage designed by William Ralph Emerson. It was completed in 1880–81 and torn down in the early 1960s. Originally built for Civil War General W. F. Smith, it was owned by Dr. Robert Abbe from 1889 to 1928. Its neighbor Sonogee (1903), once Atwater Kent's cottage, still stands on the north side of the brook although lowered by a story and converted to a nursing home. Atwater Kent's garage, with its turntable for multiple cars, can be glimpsed through the gate. (Courtesy of Bar Harbor Historical Society.)

The exposed shore and hilly, untillable land along this stretch of coast attracted only a handful of early settlers, who cleared the land and ran mills on Duck Brook and Eddy Brook.

In the 1860s and 1870s, the rusticators enjoyed hiking up Duck Brook along a simple path that rambled from bank to bank—all the way to the "Mill on the Floss," an abandoned sawmill located at the brook's Eagle Lake source.

Delightfully undeveloped Eden Street was an ideal place for the wealthy to build their private bay-view estates. And so they came. After a while, the walk up Duck Brook just was not the same anymore, even though one cottage owner kindly provided benches.

By the 1940s, many of the cottage owners were the summer colonists' children or others who had limited money and little interest in the old society. The cottages often stood empty.

The gale-driven 1947 fire tore along Eden Street, destroying nearly all of the buildings on the inland side of the road and a few on the bay side.

After the fire, enterprising individuals built motels on the favored sites. Leaning gateposts and stone stairs to nowhere are all that remain of dozens of cottages that burned or were torn down in later years. Some survivors were converted to other uses, and a few still serve as summer homes.

The Cottagers

1892

SHERMAN'S GUIDE TO BAR HARBOR

The valuation of the town of Eden (practically Bar Harbor) for 1889, amounted to nearly $5,700,000. Of this vast sum about $3,000,000 represented non-resident interests. Many of the wealthiest and most aristocratic people of Boston, New York, Philadelphia, Washington and other large cities of the Union have made themselves summer homes here; and the figures just given must convince the reader that they have not been niggardly in their outlay. In fact Bar Harbor can boast of more beautiful and costly residences than any other watering-place in America.

In Bar Harbor vernacular these residences are called "cottages," and the term is apt to mislead a stranger. On his first visit he will be likely to look around for those sylvan retreats which he has so often heard mentioned, expecting to find little, one-story cottages embowered amid the woods on the hill side or nestling in some shady valley, only discoverable by stumbling across them accidently on some woodland walk. He will be totally unprepared for the handsome, stately piles of architecture which greet him at every turn. Bar Harbor "cottages" have cost their owners all the way from $10,000 to $100,000.... It would be impossible in a work of this size to cite all the 150 or more cottages in the village, so we must confine ourselves to the mention of a few of the more noteworthy.

Eden Street, with its branches, is essentially the street of cottages: in that vicinity they are about seventy-five in number. The pretty shore to the eastward is dotted along its entire length to Duck Brook with beautiful structures reflecting the taste and wealth of their owners. Here are the Barnacles and Bagatelle, both the property of Edmund Pendleton, the author of *A Conventional Bohemian*. A little further along is the Sea Urchins, the summer home of Mrs. Burton Harrison, the charming author of *Bar Harbor Days*...Close to the road is Clovercroft, famous for the musicales given by its accomplished owner, Mrs. George Place of New York. On the shore, near the Harrison's cottage, is the residence of Rev. F. H. Johnston of Andover, called Villa Mary. On the high ground to the left of Eden Street, nearly opposite Miss Place's cottage, is Steepways, the summer home of the celebrated New York surgeon Dr. Wm. Rod Helmuth; and a little nearer the town is Prof. Geo. Harris' cottage. Further along and still higher up than Steepways, the magnificent architecture of Mizzentop, the home of Mrs. W. M. Hunt, the late Boston artist's widow, looks down on the road. Beyond Sea Urchins, on the shore, is Beaudesert, the handsome residence of W. S. Gurnee the New York banker; and, beyond it, Burnmouth, W. P. Walley's home. Near Duck Brook are Edenfield, the beautiful cottage of the late Samuel E. Lyon of New York, and Guy's Cliff where E. C. Cushman, relative of Charlotte Cushman and a wealthy resident of Newport, resides. On the high ground opposite Edenfield stands Greystone, the cottage of M. C. Lea, the Philadelphia publisher.

The Turrets, owned by J. J. Emery, under construction about 1893. This cottage, and its neighbors Sea Fox and Sea Urchins, are now part of the College of the Atlantic. The Turrets' exterior has been restored, and it houses a natural history museum, classes and offices. The public is welcome to visit the museum and grounds. (Courtesy of Maine Historic Preservation Commission.)

The high ground on the western side of Eden Street is opened up by two roads, Cleftstone and Highbrook, on which are situated some very handsome houses. On Highbrook Road is Stanwood, Secretary Blaine's beautiful cottage; and, near it, is Mossley Hall, the home of the railroad magnate W. B. Howard of Chicago. On that part of this hill known as Abby's Retreat, stand Avamaya, the summer residence of Capt. Geo. M. Wheeler, Corps of Engineers, U. S. Army, and Ban-Y-Bryn, Mr. A. C. Barney's cottage....

From Sherman's Guide to Bar Harbor, *W. H. Sherman, 1892. Courtesy of Maine Historic Preservation Commission.*

Marian Lawrence was born to William and Julie Cunningham Lawrence on May 16, 1875, in her mother's parents' home in Boston. Her father, an Episcopal minister, later became Bishop of Massachussetts and was an early advocate of protecting lands now in the national park.

In addition to being a fine observer and writer, Marian Lawrence was a talented artist and an independent spirit. In 1906, she married her cousin Harold Peabody. Her daughter Gertrude was born nine years later.

Despite Marian's mother's fears that "Bar Harbor was a rather wild place where girls from New York and Philadelphia walked up mountains 'swinging their arms,'" the Lawrence family began spending summers in Bar Harbor in 1886, when Marian was eleven. After two years of renting, they built their own cottage, Ingleside, on the north side of Kebo Road.

According to Marian's reminiscences, the family usually arrived on the ferry accompanied by "four horses, a cow, a dog and a bird–and usually a baby with all the necessary paraphernalia that goes with one." They also brought along a "little yellow rumble" (a small cart), but kept their large buckboard on the island. Mr. Rich, their caretaker, met the boat. He drove the maids to the house in the small cart while the Lawrences took the buckboard. The expressmen traveled ahead with the family's "many trunks."

Marian Lawrence began her diary in 1886. The following excerpts are from 1901, when she was twenty-six.

Summer Memories of Bar Harbor

1901

MARIAN LAWRENCE

Tuesday, July 2:...Took the 10 o'clock train for Bar Harbor after early start from Medford. Train in two sections and very crowded. Found that George Dorr had the seat next mine so I took the one behind mine, and what did he do but take mine so he was still next to me. When the conductor came along Georgie said to him, "Can't you arrange it so that I can sit here next this young lady?" The conductor looked at our tickets and said, "your seat is next hers now, she is sitting in the wrong seat." So my little plot failed. But Georgie wasn't bad at all. I was at his mercy as I had nothing to read, but he lent me books and magazines. He also said, "Now, won't you have something to drink? You shall have as much as you like and and just what you like and when." He pressed me so I tried several drinks I didn't like at his suggestion and then had a lot of gingerale as I was so very hot and thirsty—and I began to be glad I had met Georgie as the cold drinks were very comforting. So I was shocked and surprised to find, when the porter came with the bill, that I was to pay for all my drinks and Georgie went on reading while I did it right before his face! He never left me for a minute either on the train or on the boat...A gorgeous clear fresh evening as we ferried over beautiful Frenchman's Bay, and I felt as if I had never left Bar Harbor which really seemed lovelier than ever. Glad to be in my cool, breezy, bright, sky parlor again....

Marian Lawrence at about age twenty. (Courtesy of Gertrude Lawrence McCue.)

Monday, July 15th: 92 degrees on our piazza—very hot for Bar Harbor. Carrie and I lunched at the Morris's and the two Fabbri men and Mr. Cushing were there. I sat next Sandro [Alessandro Fabbri] who is certainly attractive. He said he saw me in the railroad station in Florence this spring! After lunch we had wonderful sail. We went in Dave's sloop and raced the Fabbris in their new fast Crowninshield "Rockabout." They beat us badly but they had to haul out a big balloon jib to do it. They sailed all around us making jeering remarks through a megaphone.

Tuesday, July 16th: Still very hot. Carrie and I made party calls and ended up at May

Automobile: Bar Harbor banned automobiles from 1903 to 1913. Reputedly the first auto was built on the island by Paul Hunt in 1896.

Bogue Chitto: This shorefront cottage built for John A. Morris in 1888 was opposite the present park entrance. The Morrises and Lawrences were good friends, and Marian sometimes stayed at Bogue Chitto. The name means "Brook of Shadows" in a Louisiana Indian dialect. The house was demolished in the early 1960s.

Corsair: J. Pierpont Morgan's third immense black steam yacht. Morgan came regularly to Bar Harbor, but never owned a house, staying instead on his yacht.

Cornice, The: This fanciful name, taken from The Corniche in Italy, referred to Eden Street (Route 3) along the Bluffs. The original road ran up over Paradise Hill, and apparently there was some heated discussion at town meeting about moving it down to the cliff face, since it was felt that horses would be terrified by the exposed drop-off. At the time of this story, the road dipped down closer to the water at the Bluffs than it does now.

Cutunder: An open or canopied four-wheeled carriage, sometimes privately owned, but usually for hire. They were the island's taxis.

Dorr, George: (1853–1944) A fellow Bostonian and "Father of Acadia."

Fabbri, Alessandro (Sandro): (1878–1922): One of three brothers. Developed the Naval Radio Station at Otter Point during the First World War.

Horse Show: A three-day equine extravaganza held from 1900 to 1912 at Robin Hood Park, on grounds that are now part of the Jackson Lab. Colonel Morrell, an avid horseman, owned the grounds and championed the event.

Phaeton: A light four-wheel carriage with open sides drawn by one or two horses, usually driven by the owner, not a coachman.

St. Saviour's Episcopal Church: Built in 1878, this church still stands on Mount Desert Street. Bishop Lawrence delivered guest sermons on occasion.

Vanderbilt, Mr. and Mrs. George: Their cottage, Point d' Acadie, occupied Odgen Point next to Cromwell Harbor. The house survived from 1868 to 1956, but the Vanderbilts left Bar Harbor for Newport after automobiles were allowed in town. Mrs. William Jay Schieffelin was their daughter.

Sherwood's for a swim. Carrie is much amused by the way the girls go in here. Pretty Miss Hoy wears a large hat with a sky blue taffeta bow and feather, a dotted veil, turquoise earrings and bronze high heeled slippers, but swims well in spite of it. They are all amazed at Carrie's tight rubber cap and her prowess in the water....

Saturday, August 17th: Am staying at Bogue Chitto for a few days where my room looks out over the bay—a window on either side of my bed from which I could almost drop a stone down into the water far below, just like the real Sorrento only much more homelike and cheerful. I always watch the sunrise right out of the water, so still and clean and rosy and golden. Oh! this place!

Sunday, August 18th: Most perfect day ever. Drove into church [in Hulls Cove] with Dave. Papa preached and the church was jammed. Spoke to a lot of people on the lawn afterwards. Met an automobile on the most dangerous part of the Cornice! After a beautiful sail over to Sorrento Dave and I paddled around Hulls Cove in the canoe. Beautiful sunset, not a ripple on the water. Spent the evening lying in the hammock on the porch listening to Dave and Angela playing violin and piano. Typical August evening, soft gentle breeze, the sky dotted all over with stars while the searchlight from the *Corsair*, lying just outside, darted hither and thither, a silent, mysterious streak of light. No lapping of the waves below, and the sighing and swishing of the firs and birches, with the plaintive music, sent me off on a very sad line of thought as I lay and watched the stars shoot across the heavens. I thought of how selfish and useless I was and of the happiness I seem somehow to have missed.

Tuesday, August 20th: Many chances to play tennis, but declined all; also two lunches, but went to Mrs. Wadsworth's where were Sylvia, Natalie B., Mrs. Ingalls and Miss Scott. Then to the Horse Show. Crowds there and it was a pretty sight this lovely afternoon. Leaned on the rail with Dyer H. and watched the judging of the tandems and saddle horses. Many coaches lined up filled with lookers-on. Evening, danced at the Charlie Wrights with Sylvia, Miss Biddle, C. Winslow, Gummey Sears, Phoenix, Mr. LeBrun, Mrs. McMillan and Victor Cushman. Mrs.Wright is so pretty!

Wednesday, August 21st: Lovely but hot. My "tennis morning," consisting of the Boylston Beals, Mr. and Mrs. James Rose Todd, Frank Rogers, Dyer Hubbard, Charlie Winslow and Cosby was very pleasant and successful. Mr. Kassen came and seemed to enjoy it, took a great fancy to C. Winslow who was most polite to him. It was a good looking crowd! Elsie, Mrs. Todd and C. Winslow are all beauties, and Rogers, Dyer and Cosby are all very good looking. Then I went to a lunch of girls at Dr. Stokes! He was the only man. He informed me "the seven most attractive girls" were coming, and he certainly put on a most beautiful party. A little "Buttons" opened the door and presented a silver tray on which were seven unaddressed envelopes and in each a tiny card with a clever drawing like a miniature and under it was "1., I love, 2. I love, 3. I love, I say...." Then we went in to lunch and matched our numbers to some lovely painted dinner cards with only a number on them. In this way he avoided having to give the seats of honor which he possibly thought might make the rest feel badly! At each place and down the middle of the table were lavender sweet peas of different shades and we each had a large horseshoe of them tied with yards of lavender ribbon and each a lavender glass vase shaped like an orchid with another bunch in each. So every guest carried off with her the vase, bouquet, horseshoe and two dinner cards! Two men waited and the food was delicious, the cold bouillon in lavender cups. Afterwards he drove us all out to the Horse Show where he had reserved seats for us in the Grandstand. The show was very good with lots of Entries in every class. A perfect day in the valley of two mountains, a gay crowd of people on coaches, carriages and afoot, a band playing and the beautiful horses prancing up and down the track made a scene of color, life and gayety. One of the prettiest turnouts was a spanking pair of William C. Whitney's. They were a beautiful brown, business-like, glossy team driven in a spider phaeton by Helen Barney who drove so well and looked so straight and pretty and stylish in a linen suit with her golden hair shining! The little groom was in whipcord too, so it was all of a color except for touches of shiny metal and clean white. This was the popular turnout and received ovations of applause as it went by the grandstand at a fast trot, back and forth in absolutely faultless style. Another pretty feature was the coaching event. They trotted up and down in front of the judges' stand sedately, all shining and clanking and very smart—with the grooms jumping down to hold the horses for the judging and then suddenly Col. Morrell's arm shot up—his long whip flung out with a sharp crack and off he went at a gallop. The others after him, the grooms just barely jumping aboard, and away they went twice around the track on a dead run—dashing by us with a loud roar and a cloud of dust—very pretty and exciting to see....

Thursday, August 22nd: Lovely, drove out to the Morris's and had some good tennis.... P.M.: Stayed in and worked on my dress, which is a concoction devised by Cousin Jessie and me. I was sick to death of the three evening dresses I brought up here and was bound to have something new for the Vanderbilts' Ball which was the event of the season. A lot of the Philadelphians weren't asked to this party and of course, none of the Westerners. Everybody was asked to dinner first and mine was at Mrs. Markoe's and those at it were Miss Biddle, Miss Schieffelin and Mrs. Markoe who had Frank Harrison on her right, then I came and George Willing, Jim Markoe, Tom Ridgway and Lawrence Houghton who I was much surprised to see and who talked to me after dinner. He was in his nicest mood and we went on together to the Vanderbilts. After shaking hands with Mr. and Mrs. V. at the entrance to the ballroom, which was filling up rapidly, we danced and had a grand waltz with the floor all to ourselves at first. How I did enjoy it! He is so good-looking and waltzes beautifully. Then we spoke to Cousin Estelle, who with Cousin Jim, had come over from Islesboro for it. Then Brooks Fenno came up and Frank Rogers, and the latter and I had another lovely waltz, as he also is a good dancer and again we had the floor to ourselves and Sandro F. was still looking on in a corner—Strangely, the Fabbri men don't dance. After a few more turns with different people the Cotillion started. L. Houghton had asked me but I had been engaged for some days to Boily Beal for it. It was such a pretty cotillion! Just enough couples to go once around with the Hungarian Band in costume at one end of the hall against some evergreens and the "stags" at the other end. Creighton Webb led and was very nice indeed to me but I don't think he does it as well as Phoenix. Well! Suffice it to say I had a perfect time. All my partners were tall and danced beautifully, but the best of all in that respect was George Vanderbilt himself. Ernesto Fabbri and L. Houghton sat by me much of the time and Dave, Ashbell Barney and Larz Anderson also kept coming up and gave me some of my six lovely favors. Dyer Hubbard danced with me several times and Schuyler Schieffelin and Willie Schieffelin and many I can't remember now. Hasket asked me for a supper and we got a table.... At about 2 A.M., when we were about half-way through supper the lights suddenly all went out. It really was quite disagreeable to be plunged into inky, pitchy blackness, a lonely and awful feeling in spite of hearing people all around. Hasket murmured something about its being "lucky I was between two cousins." After perhaps three minutes, which seemed much longer, we became conscious of a faint glimmer and saw a waiter bringing in a candelabra. He was soon followed by more waiters and even Mrs. Vanderbilt carrying more candles. How Mrs. V. ever got out in the darkness and how they found candles I don't know! Finally they got all the tables lighted. Mr. Vanderbilt's table and ours each had one candle stuck in a bottle which gave an informal camping out effect. The band had a student lamp and that was all the light in the hall. I was glad of darkness myself because my dress was so torn by that time that trails of chiffon rags were hanging around me in all directions. The stiffness had gone from the

(From Mount Desert with Pen and Pencil*, 1886, courtesy of Maine Historic Preservation Commission.)*

tulle in my hair and around my neck and in fact I was a sight! The lights came on again just after I had said good-night but it was after 3 A.M. and I was dead tired. Our poor cut-under man who had probably been there all night only charged 50 [cents] apiece to take us home!

Friday, September 6th: Such a perfect afternoon. Ap [her younger brother] and I went canoeing. The bay was like an opal—rose, lavender, purple and green. No impressionist could have got the clear brilliance of it. Driving to the house our cut-under man seemed very agitated and finally he said, "I s'pose you know that President McKinley has been assassinated!" It gave me "quite a turn" as they say and I felt hot, then cold, and after crying "What!" could think of nothing more and he knew no more.

September, 14th: Got up at 5:30 in the pale misty gold sunlight. Looked a last good-bye off the upper balcony. The sun was throwing a shimmery golden path on the sea and dissolving the misty veil over the islands which was floating off in thin streaks. It was warm for September and so peaceful, the bells of the Church were tolling slowly and the flags raised and hanging at half mast so that we knew the President was dead. Driving to the wharf the air smelled so deliciously clear and clean after the rain and everything in the woods was dripping. Sailing across the bay I took a last look at Bogue Chitto with the sloop still at her mooring and as Bar Harbor receded in the distance it looked like a dream island rising from the sea, the same pale blue as Capri seen from Naples but a far more beautiful shape! There's nothing to compare with it!

From the journals of Marian Lawrence Peabody; courtesy of Gertrude Lawrence McCue; Bar Harbor Historical Society.

Bar Harbor

Bar Harbor sprang into prominence in the 1860s. Within a couple of decades, it grew from a small village to a vastly popular summer resort with hotels accommodating thousands.

The early hotels were not plush. The rising bell rang at 6:30 and breakfast appeared at 7:00. Fried and boiled meats dominated the menu. When the guests protested, they were reminded "Wal, you came here for a change didn't you? Now you've got it."

After awhile, some of the visitors decided to build their own summer places. In 1890, a reporter for *Harper's Bazar* recalled: "Some fifteen years ago, in the early days of Mount Desert summer travel, I met on the beach at Newport, Rhode Island, a shipwrecked sea captain from Bar Harbor, who talked in eloquent astonishment of the rapid changes coming over the ownership of real estate in that region. 'It does jest beat all,' he declared. 'Folks will come along from New York or Philadelphy and they'll kinder take a fancy to a man's farm. They'll end up givin' him more for it than he ever thought o' askin' for it; and they'll pay him more for livin' on it in winter to take care of it than he ever made off of it.'"

Bar Harbor in the early 1880s was a booming place—then it was discovered. The most influential members of East Coast society adopted it as their latest summer retreat. These new people had almost unlimited money, and no shyness about spending it, especially when it came to the extravagant estates and social events.

The "old summer people" bemoaned the arrival of high society. In the late 1880s, painter Ellen Robbins sold her cottage and left, observing, "If I were to come again next year, I should expect to see the rocks and trees all decorated with lace flounces and bows of ribbons."

In the 1890s, there were at least 10,000 visitors, summer residents, seasonal shopkeepers and others in town on any given day in July and August. They came by rail and sea.

High society devised its own amusements. Mountain hikes, flower walks and "rocking" parties were out; fine horses, tennis parties and unbelievably elaborate balls were in. The Kebo Valley Club was "the centre of amusement for the fashionables." In the early 1890s it had a theater, restaurant, race track, baseball field and several tennis and croquet lawns. A golf course and Greek temple to the arts were added in the following decades.

The golden age lasted until the 1930s, when incomes and lives changed dramatically. The summer colony declined through the Second World War. The fire of 1947 destroyed much of the town of Bar Harbor, including many summer cottages, putting an end to hopes that the summer colony might be revived. The townspeople recovered from the fire and turned their energies to new ideas.

Getting Around

Walking is the best—and easiest—way to explore most of Bar Harbor. Many of the shore-front summer cottages can be seen better from the water, however. A small boat is perfect for this pursuit, since there are numerous ledges and shoals along the shore.

Postcard courtesy of Maine Historic Preservation Commission.

1. Bar Harbor, Frenchman Bay and the Waters Beyond
2. The Shore Path
3. Oldfarm and Compass Harbor
4. Neighborhoods
5. Mount Desert Street
6. The Hotels and the Village Green
7. Downtown Business
8. West Street and Devil's Half-Acre
9. Bar (Rodick's) Island

(Note: Bar Island is in the town of Gouldsboro)

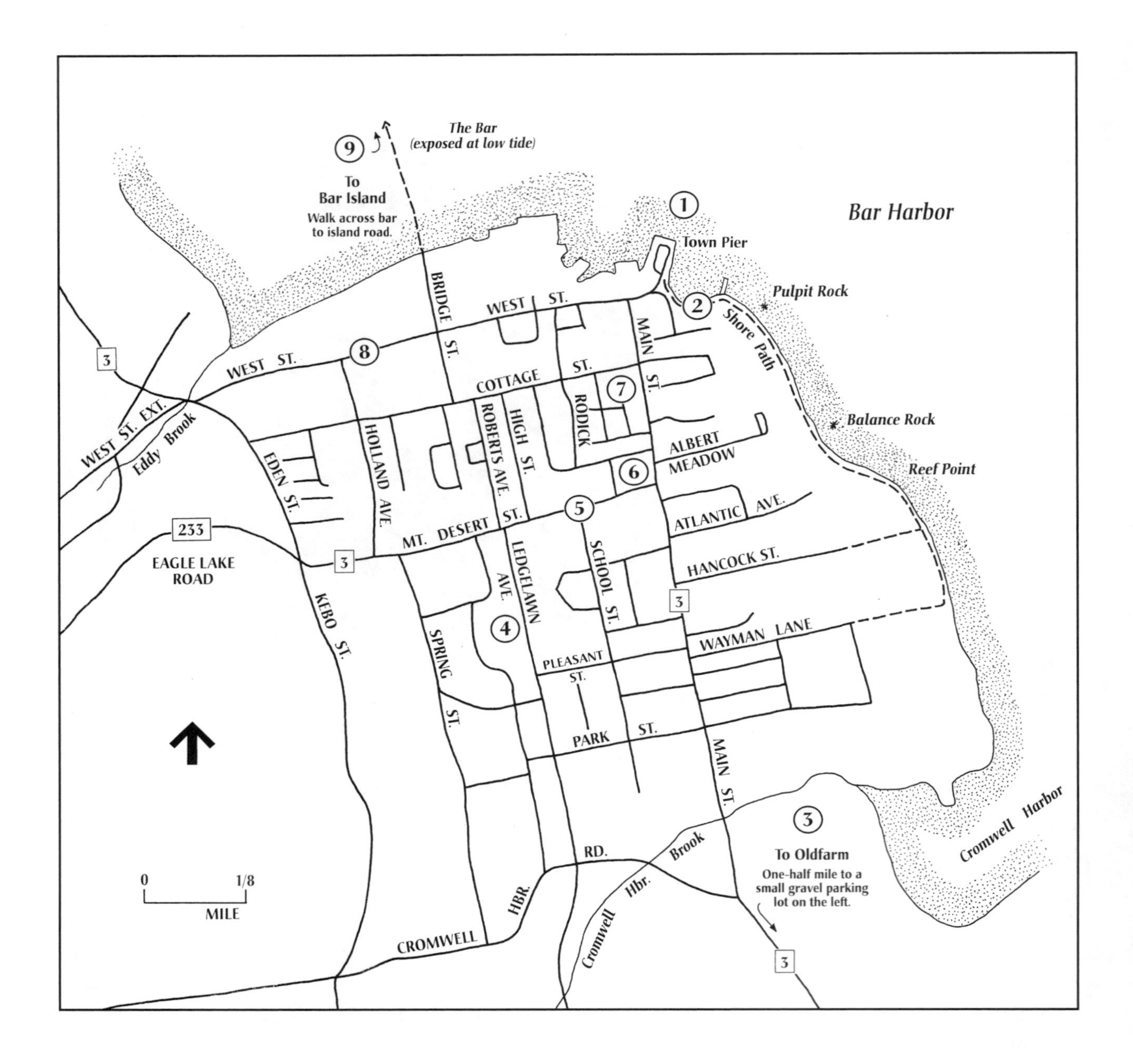

Bar Harbor, Frenchman Bay and the Waters Beyond

ABOVE: The Portland, Mount Desert and Machias Steamboat Company's City of Richmond *and* Lewiston *at the pier in the early 1880s. The 234-foot* Lewiston *ran from 1867 to 1886 on the "inside route" from Portland to Machiasport. In 1881 she was joined by the 227-foot, 900-ton* City of Richmond, *which operated until 1893, when the spectacular 263-foot, 1,634 ton* Frank Jones *replaced her. The speedy 162-foot* Mount Desert *("Old Mounty") is arriving from Rockland on the left .*

AT LEFT: The pier in the mid-1870s.

(Both courtesy of Maine Historic Preservation Commission.)

Until a generation or so ago, most people espied Bar Harbor for the first time over water. Until automobiles became reasonably trustworthy—and for a while afterward—boats, sometimes combined with rail, offered the most efficient transport Down East. Steamship service began in the 1860s. From the mid-1880s to the 1920s, a trip to (or from) Boston took less than a day by steamer, or by steamer and railroad combined. Only those "who could not abide the sea" traveled by land.

By the turn of the century, Bar Harbor was packed with wharves, floats and boats of all sizes. Both the lower and upper harbors were often full. When southeasterly swells rolled in, which they continued to do despite the breakwater built in the 1890s, the boats moved to the upper harbor, seeking shelter behind Bar Island.

The summer correspondents never failed to remark upon the bracing, uplifting qualities of the maritime air. In 1888, M. F. Sweetser observed that "This activity, this desire to row and walk and drive and to become acquainted, was all due to the air. It has a peculiar quality. Even the skeptic must admit this. It composes his nerves to sleep; it stimulates to unwonted exertion. The fanatics of this place declare that the fogs are not as damp as at other places on the coast. Fashion can make even a fog dry. But the air is delicious.... It is better than the Maine Law. The air being like wine, one does not need stimulants."

Traveling to Mount Desert

LATE 1860S

BENJAMIN DECOSTA

As regards the accommodations for travel, comparatively little has been said, though they will be found quite ample. They are subject to more or less change from season to season, and are at the same time improving. New resorts are continually being found out, which necessitates new means of communication. For Mount Desert direct, the favorite route from Boston is by rail to Portland, and thence by steamer to Southwest and Bar Harbors: though such as have an unconquerable dread of the sea can proceed by rail to Bangor, and reach the island by the stage route. But thus they miss one great charm, namely, the ocean views of Mount Desert, which, to be thoroughly enjoyed, must be seen from every point of approach.

...For such as live to eat, and are curious about the matter of lodgings, there can be little more than the general remark, that, both as regards quality and expense, the same variation is found on the New England coast that is characteristic of the city of New York. Slender consolations, indeed! At any moment, the feast may be turned into a famine. It will be the business of Jenkins, who has fared sumptuously (and freely) at the one, to warn you, specially, of the other. After the elegant entertainments of Portland and Appledore (Isles of Shoals), the tourist will experience a steady decline; on the way down the scale reaching the average at Mount Desert; and touching bottom with the necessarily frugal fare of Grand Menan. All, save epicures, will find the real feast spread out of doors, free of cost to every comer....

Wandering along the coast, we found ourselves, in course of time, at the Isles of Shoals, where we took passage in a trim-looking schooner for Mount Desert. We sailed in the morning on a fresh southerly breeze. It was not long before we had a fine view of Agamenticus, which rises to a height of several hundred feet, sending out its greeting from afar.

...The Skipper here gave the coast a wide berth, and laid his course due north-east, shortly running down the land, though not before we had gained a glimpse of the distant peak of Mount Washington. The wind held fresh until sunset, and by nightfall the schooner was off Penobscot Bay, when the light-house on Mount Desert Rock opened its bright eye.

Our progress during the night was slow, but when morning dawned we were not far from the isle of our dreams. I was aroused from my slumbers by Old Sol himself, who, like some rude linkboy thrusting his torch in one's face, rose from the sea and sent a broad beam in through the little cabin window into my berth, hitting me square in the eye. Thereupon I resolved to rise. But Mr. Oldstyle, fully determined to have the first glimpse of the land, was ahead of me; and while I was pulling on my boots, disappeared up the companion-way in his smart, swallow-tailed coat with a long spy-glass under his arm. Aureole, a young gentleman of our party, who, under the influence of Neptune, was very quiet the day before, followed him, having now got his "sea-legs" on; and before I could get on deck I heard him engaging in the following brief colloquy:

"What land's that, Skipper?"

"Mount Desert, I reckon," was the reply, putting the accent on the last syllable of "Desert."

"How far off?"

"Six or eight miles, ma'be."

"When are we going to get there?"

"Don't know."

Thereupon I felt it high time to inquire into the real state of affairs; and accordingly I hurried onto deck, and found that there was a dead calm, the mainsail hanging perpendicular from its gaff, our little craft appearing altogether

> "As idle as a painted ship
> Upon the painted ocean."

Yet it was a splendid morning; and, besides, there lay our enchanted isle, towering up out of the calm sea, veiled in a thin mist, and gilded all over with the golden glories of the rising sun.

In order to find a scene that will equal this, we must sail far away into the Pacific Sea. At a distance, the island appears like a single mountain, of great height, green around its sides, and bare at the summit, which, on this occasion, gleamed upon us through mists like a pinnacle of gold.

We sat long gazing upon this beautiful prospect, not even desiring to come nearer, lest the vision should be dispelled. Yet with the sun came a light breeze, and as it approached in the distance, rippling the surface of the still sea, the Skipper unlashed the helm, and stood ready to steer his craft into port. And when the breeze came, it barely swung out the schooner's boom, though at last we managed to get steerage-way, and sailed slowly, wing and wing, and with a sort of classic pomp, the gull wheeling and the porpoise diving, and both showing a sort of welcome by escorting us on our voyage.

In due time we entered the Harbor, went ashore, and found comfortable quarters.

From Rambles in Mount Desert: With Sketches of Travel on the New-England Coast from Isles of Shoals to Grand Manan, *B. F. DeCosta, A. D. F. Randolph & Co., New York, 1871.*

Coming to Bar Harbor on the Steamer

1894

F. Marion Crawford

The first impression made by Bar Harbor at the height of its season upon the mind of one fresh from a more staid and crystallized civilization is that it is padding through a period of transition, in which there is some of the awkwardness which we associate with rapid growth, and something also for the youthful freshness which gives that very awkwardness a charm. The name of Mount Desert suggests, perhaps, a grim and forbidding cliff, frowning upon the pale waves of a melancholy ocean. Instead, the traveler who crosses the bay in the level light of an August afternoon looks upon the soft, rolling outline of wooded hills, on the highest of which a little hotel breaks the skyline, upon a shore along which villas and cottages stretch on either side of a toy wooden village, which looks as though it were to be put away in a box at night, and upon the surrounding sea, an almost landlocked inlet, in which other islands, like satellites of Mount Desert, are scattered here and there.

As the little steamer crawls up to her moorings the groups of people waiting on the pier stand out distinctly, and the usual types detach themselves one by one. The clusters of hotel-runners and expressmen are lounging listlessly until they shall be roused to clamorous activity by the landing of the first passenger; in knots and pairs, those serenely idle people of all ages, who, in all places and seasons, seem to find an ever-new amusement in watching the arrival of trains or boats, are as deeply interested as usual; the inevitable big and solemn dog, of nondescript breed and eclectic affections, is stalking about with an air of responsibility.

And yet the little crowd is not quite like other gatherings on other piers. Girls in smart cotton frocks are sitting in shining little village carts, with grooms at their horses' sleek heads, wedged in between empty buckboards that look like paralyzed centipedes, the drivers of which wear clothes ranging from the livery of the large stables to weather-bleached coat of the "native" from Cherryfield or Ellsworth, who has brought over his horse to take his share of the "rusticator's" ready money during the short season. There are no hotel omnibuses, no covered traps of any kind, as becomes a holiday place where winter and rough weather are enemies not meant to be reckoned with; everybody seems either to know everyone else, or not to care if he does not, and there is an air of cheerful informality about the whole scene which immediately makes one feel welcome and at home.

From Bar Harbor, *Francis Marion Crawford, Charles Scribner's Sons, New York, 1894.*

The saloon of the Maine Central Railroad steamer Sappho, *which carried passengers from Mount Desert Ferry at Hancock Point to the large MCRR pier in Bar Harbor from 1886 until World War I. The 140-foot propeller-driven boat was built specifically for the railroad ferry run.*

On August 6, 1899, Sappho *and her sister* Sebenoa *were waiting at Mount Desert Ferry when a trainload of passengers eager to see the warships in Bar Harbor overloaded the pier. It collapsed, killing twenty. (Courtesy of Maine Historic Preservation Commission.)*

The Maine Central Railroad steamers Sappho *and* Sebenoa *at the wharves next to an unknown schooner in the late 1880s. The steamer arriving in the background is the* Mount Desert, *and the black yacht is J. P. Morgan's* Corsair. *The 91-foot, 89-ton* Sebenoa *was built in Bath in 1880. She had a beam of 18' 6" and was screw-driven. She developed a wicked roll in unprotected waters, an ability she shared with a significant number of similarly designed steamers. (From* Scenery of Mount Desert, Indelible Photographs, *1890; courtesy of Maine Historic Preservation Commission.)*

An Afternoon on the Water

1886

THE DAILY HERALD

The members of the Press Association have serious reasons for regretting the change of their program on yesterday. Instead of going on the twenty-two mile drive as had been proposed, they rashly undertook the sail in the *Sebenoa,* around to Northeast Harbor and up Somes Sound. The day was rainy and a strong breeze was blowing and before half the trip had been accomplished, the breakfasts of most of the party had been given up to the old ocean. The sail was fraught with incidents both ludicrous and dangerous.

As Judge Baker was leaning over the rail, regarding with deep interest the hue of the water underneath, the steamer gave a roll and the portion of the rail on which he was holding being detachable, it came away in his grasp and he was thrown against the wall of the saloon. The return roll threw him into the opening in the rail, and but for the aid of Mr. Geo. S. Rowell and others, he would have gone overboard.

Mr. Forbes, of the *Oxford Democrat,* was standing on the forward deck with some of the other members, but as the breeze freshened one by one they "sought the seclusion that the cabin grants." Not so Mr. Forbes, he was too much overcome by the enchanting motion of the steamer to remove from his pleasant position. So he continued there, striving with his eagle eye to pierce the thickness of a Mount Desert fog, until the gallant vessel, taking a tremendous header, drenched him completely with salt spray. He then concluded that there were more desirable positions to be had, and gloomily followed his friends to the cabin.

Mr. Joseph A. Homan, of Augusta, has quite a reputation among the members of the association for the manner in which he renders the old song "The Battle of the Nile," the ninety-five verses of which are all alike. But he was so much overcome by his enthusiasm on the trip that he did not feel equal to giving it in the manner which the occasion demanded, and was seated quietly in the cabin, evidently deep in thought—when Mr. H. K. Morrell staggered in and exclaimed: "Homan, can't you sing the Battle of the Nile?" Hardly had he uttered this when a tremendous lurch threw him across the apartment. Homan straightened up and very gravely replied: "I don't know; I see you've got the pitch."

Amid such scenes the party reached Somesville, all on board being subjected to fearful pangs of the *mal de mer*.

Arrived here such of the party as could eat, obtained dinner at the Central House. The question then arose, how were they to get home. Return by boat was not to be thought of. All were sick, part of the ladies were indulging in hysterics, and the others had not sufficient vitality left to participate in that exercise. The difficulty was finally solved by telephoning to Bar Harbor for the Green Mountain stages, in which they arrived at the "Atlantic" late in the afternoon.

From the Mount Desert Herald*, July 16, 1886.*

Carrying On

EARLY 1900S

MAINE CENTRAL RAILROAD

Arriving at Mount Desert Ferry, the terminus of your journey by rail, you are transported in one of the splendid steamers of the Maine Central Railroad across Frenchman's Bay to Bar Harbor and the landings "around the hills."

How sweet and pleasant and refreshing is the first breath of the ozone-laden air you get as you step from the train to the steamer! It seems as if your lungs could drink in all of the free winds that sweep across the bay from Mount Desert.

And with what eager anticipation do your eyes turn toward Mount Desert! Here, at last, is The Land of Heart's Desire!

You first make out what seems a solitary mountain, darkly blue, cool as an iceberg, lifted up above the coast. By what chance has this freak of nature heaved or lodged itself against these shores? Upon getting closer, the mass expands into a crown of barren summits, more or less pronounced, one of which, standing as it does at the head of the chain, easily overtops the rest, becoming the fixed landmark of the island. It is everywhere conspicuous by its height and bare, grayish white crags. This is Green [Cadillac] Mountain.

Bar Harbor is the first landing. The steamer passes Bar Island and the Porcupines, fir-clad islets, before rounding her way into Bar Harbor's wharf.

The distant roofs and gleaming walls of the town seem charming amid masses of dark evergreen growth illumined by the white stems and quivering foliage of innumerable birches.

Viewing more closely this city of artistic homes and gardens by the sea, the scene discloses glimpses of dainty verandas, of tiny emerald lawns, of awninged windows and flower-boxes, not so far away as to make summer comfort a mere elusive dream.

People come eagerly, smile broadly on finding themselves here, continue to smile during their whole stay, and *in fine*, evince more of the pure joy of living than in any other haunt of holiday diversions.

The water side of life at Bar Harbor is a chapter apart: the bay and harbor are, from June to October, as full of movement and change and color as a Broadway theatrical spectacle. When the squadrons of two nations [United States and Britain] are anchored in the bay and harbor with two bands clashing simultaneously two different national hymns, and all the water intervening and circumjacent is dotted with yachts and boats of lookers-on, it seems that the center of gayety must truly be at Bar Harbor, leaving the rest of the animated world to enjoy its leavings.

From a Maine Central Railroad promotional brochure, undated; courtesy of Bar Harbor Historical Society.

There was no market for lobsters until the mid-1800s. People sent the children down to the shore at low tide to look under the rocks and grab a few for dinner.

The first Boston lobster smacks arrived in eastern Maine looking to buy lobsters in the 1850s. They offered just a few cents apiece. An average lobster weighed about five pounds, and larger ones were common. The smacks kept their cargo alive in wet holds full of seawater that flowed through holes in the hull.

There were no limits to the size or amount of lobsters that could be caught. Twenty or more pounds per trap was typical. The larger ones were sold to hotels, restaurants and fish markets, or to the lobster smacks. By the 1880s, the smaller ones went to Maine's many lobster canneries. Lobster fishing, once the province of old men and boys, suddenly looked good to ambitious young men.

Lobster traps of a century ago were larger than today's regular traps. They had two heads, or tarred-twine net openings, (one at each end) that allowed the lobsters access to baitfish hung inside. Some lobstermen tended their traps from rowboats, which they rowed standing up and facing forward. Others preferred small sailboats which were rowed with a single long oar whenever the wind died.

By the late 1800s, the lobster population had dwindled alarmingly despite protective laws and minimum size restrictions that had been enacted in the 1870s. In 1895, the state settled on a minimum measure of ten and a half inches (total body length), and the canneries closed for good.

A Brief Stop at the Lobster Cannery

1881

HARRY HAZEL

After a tortuous course among buoys, and around spits and headlands, and almost boxing the compass in its various windings, our steamer ran into Southwest Harbor, the rival of Bar Harbor for attracting tourists and summer sojourners; and its pretensions are not altogether assumed, as its hotels, numerous cottages and more humble huts, strongly indicate. The extensive lobster and chowder factory, built upon the principal landing-pier, must however be a drawback to the place as a summer resort as long as it occupies its present position. The atmosphere is pregnant with a compound scent from the cooking of lobsters, fish and clams, intermingling with the less savory odors from this marine slaughter-house. We saw cords of lobsters, green, cold and kicking, from the traps; and other cords of lobsters, red, steaming hot, and still, from the hissing caldron; we saw the former consigned alive to the "damned pot" with pitchfork, and pitched out again with this same implement; we saw good looking damsels dissecting the crustacea and tearing the flesh in bits for the cans of commerce; and if the boilers and pitchforks brought to mind the orthodox demon of Hades, the dissectors forced upon us a passing thought of some of the attributes of the fabled Harpies. Among the cords of live and dead lobsters visible in this lobster-slaughtering establishment we saw not a single half-grown specimen; they were baby-lobsters, all, weighing we should judge from eight ounces to one pound; and yet they were thought fit to sacrifice at the altar of Avarice. No wonder is it that this delicious crustacea is growing smaller and...less with each returning year. Before the canning business was engaged in, lobsters weighing less than two pounds were rarely exposed to the market, and those from three to seven pounds were most frequently to be found there.

At precisely fifteen minutes before seven ...the plank was drawn aboard from the pier at Bar Harbor. Amid a bustling throng of humanity on the pier our hundred [newspapermen] landed, delighted with that sunny day's voyage, made with restful ease, and without a single untoward incident to mar our pleasure....

From "Castine to Bar Harbor," Harry Hazel, Mount Desert Herald, *July 21, 1881.*

The turn-of-the-century lobster sloop-boat Dolphin *earned her keep during the summer shedding season by hauling tourists. Fall was (and is) the best time to lobster. (Courtesy of Ralph Stanley.)*

Yachting on the Bay

1894

F. Marion Crawford

A sunny summer day. It is not clear who the small steamer is, but she may be the Ruth*. The walking beam portion of the large sidewheel steamer's paddlewheel piston drive mechanism is clearly visible. The masts on both steamers are for sails. Until the early 1880s it was common for Maine coastal steamers to carry a couple of sails; they could be used to dampen the roll in a sea or during steamless emergencies. Some of the livery rowboats shown may have been built in a shop at Eddy Brook that offered Whitehalls and other popular designs. (Courtesy of Maine Historic Preservation Commission.)*

The truthful chronicler is forced to admit that the climate of Bar Harbor has two drawbacks—high wind and fog, one usually following the other. Out of a clear sky, without a cloud, while the sun grins away derisively overhead, a southwest gale will often blow a whole day, filling the village streets with stinging dust and the whirling disks of vagrant hats, and making the little fleet of catboats and launches in the harbor duck and strain at their moorings; turning venturesome girls who try to walk into struggling pillars of strangely twisted drapery, and even in the heart of the warm woods tearing at the crowded trees so that they sigh and creek as they rub their weary old limbs against one another. The second day is gray and cloudy, on the third it rains, but still the wind blows, a nervous wind that makes one long to pick a quarrel with one's best friend. And then the wind drops as steadily as it rose, and the next day all discomfort, past and to come, is forgotten for awhile in sheer delight of beauty. For the air is still, and the sun shines gently on a dull green sea over which little shivers run now and then, and far in the offing there is the gray line of a fog-bank. Slowly it comes in with the southeast wind, stealing along the surface of the water, now closing softly around an island, then rising from it like a wreath of smoke, here piled into a fleecy mass, there turned to silver and scattered by a sunbeam, but coming on and on, creeping up and up, until the trees on the Porcupines have their feet in the clouds like Wagnerian heroes; and presently they are also hidden, and the whole harbor is swathed in a soft cloud, from the depths of which come now and then the muffled, anxious whistles of the little steamers which ply about the bay—the *Silver Star*, from Winter Harbor; the *Cimbria*, from Bangor; and louder and deeper, the hoarse note of the *Sappho* as she feels her way across with passengers from [Hancock Point].

When the oldest inhabitant is asked how long a fog may last he will shake his head, shift his quid, and decline to commit himself. There is a legend of a young man who came in on a yacht some years ago, duly prepared to enjoy himself and the scenery. His skipper groped his way to an anchorage in a mist so dense that he could not see fifty feet ahead or astern; the luckless young man went about for nine mortal days, swathed in a soft, smothering blanket; on the tenth day he sailed away, still in a thick fog, and swearing mighty oaths. Even when the fog lies over the bay the air may be quite clear inland, and after a drive among the hills it is a curious sensation to come back to the shore. In the wooded uplands all is sunny and cheerful, but when the village is reached a cold breath is stealing through it as though the door of an ice-house had been left open, and on turning down a side-street toward the sea a gray wall of mist blots out trees and shore alike.

To anyone not familiar with it, catboat sailing in a thick fog does not suggest itself as an amusement. It has a strong attraction of its own, however, for the breeze is usually steady, and the entire obliteration of familiar landmarks gives an element of uncertainty and adventure. The course must be steered by compass, and it is necessary to have accurate notes of local bearings. If the harbor is at all crowded, the little boat feels her way out slowly, close-hauled, as carefully as though she were alive, but once in the freer water the sheet is started, and she slips forward into infinite mystery. Every sense is strained to take the place of sight, which is baffled and almost useless in the thickly pressing veil that now and then grows thinner for a moment, only to close in again more densely. The sharp lapping of the water against the sides of the boat, the wash of the rising tide upon some island, the shrill scream of a gull overhead, the whistle of a launch astern in the harbor—all these make to themselves echoes, and by and by the far-off beat of a side-wheel steamer throbs with great palpitation in the stillness. Boats which ply for profit or sail for pleasure are apt to make noise enough in a fog; but the fishermen give themselves less trouble, and slipping along, ghost-like, one may be suddenly aware of a larger and darker phantom ahead, to which it is wise to give a respectfully wide berth, without insisting too much upon the privileges of the starboard tack and the possible right of way, when the water is over-cold for much swimming. There does not seem to be any particular reason for ever turning back, when one is not bound for any visible point, and you may dream your dream out before you come about and run free for the harbor again. The fog is, if anything, thicker than when you started, and it is no easy matter to find your berth; but the boat seems to "kinder smell her way," as an old sailor once remarked in a like case, and at last she bumps gently against her mooring-buoy.

...Men who know what they are talking about say the Frenchman's Bay is apt to be dangerous for small craft, on account of the sudden squalls which come over the hills and drop on the water like the slap of a tiger's paw, and it would certainly be harder to find a place in which there can be at the same time such an amiable diversity of winds. It is not at all uncommon to see two schooners within a couple of miles of each other, both running close-hauled or both before the wind, but on the same tack and in opposite directions.

From Bar Harbor, *Francis Marion Crawford, Charles Scribner's Sons, New York 1894.*

Regular steamer service to Bar Harbor ended in the early 1930s, but the Eastern Steamship Line decided to offer weekend cruises from New York to Bar Harbor for a fare of $13.50 on the 408-foot, 10,000-ton, 607-passenger liner Iroquois. *The trips were fairly popular.*

It was very, very foggy at 3:30 A.M. on Sunday, July 13, 1936, when Captain Hammond decided to take the Iroquois *home to New York. He misjudged the strength of the ebbing tide and ended up on Bald Porcupine Island. (The shore is dimly visible; the breakwater is to the left.) She was floated off at high tide.*

The breakwater was begun in 1889 on a year's contract, but by October the crews had managed to place only 9,500 of the 42,500 tons of stone needed. The Bar Harbor Record *noted that "the oldest vessel in the United States is at present engaged carrying stone for the breakwater. She is the two-masted schooner* Good Intent, *Captain Ira Webb, of Rockland...." The breakwater was never finished. Spring high tides and storm seas easily top it, and most boats head for more protected harbors in foul weather. (Courtesy of Bar Harbor Historical Society.)*

A German Princess Visits the Bay

1914

MARIAN LAWRENCE PEABODY

August 4, 1914: Harold [Mr. Peabody] got up and stepped out on the porch and then called out, "By Jove, there's a big ocean liner in the harbor." I rushed out and sure enough there was a ship so huge that her four smoke stacks towered above the church steeples and she seemed longer than the whole town. At first, we thought the ports must be so full of ships that they were obliged to use new harbors. We called out to the newsboy to find what ship it was and he called back that it was the *Crownprincess Something*, and immediately our excitement knew no bounds.

Since the first of August, the *Kronprinzessen Cecilie* had been dodging battleships of different nations and finally got wireless orders to return to America. Since they had left, France had declared war and England was on the verge, so they could not go to Canada.... They had used no lights and no wireless after the first of August. All the ports and decks were covered with canvas. The funnels were painted like a White Star liner, and, of course, her name was painted out. As silently as possible and without a light, they had rushed through dense fog for two days and two nights in spite of the excited remonstrances of the passengers, some of whom offered to *buy* the ship so they could do what they liked with it.... None of the passengers were told where they were going except Mr. Ledyard Blair who had talked to the Captain and mentioned his steam yacht and sailing it up and down the coast between New York and Bar Harbor. So the Captain had asked his advice in this dilemma which resulted in Mr. Blair offering to [pilot] the big ship in Bar Harbor.

When, therefore, the passengers saw the chain of mountains in the distance, they thought they might be headed for the Azores or Newfoundland. Mrs. Hinkle and her daughter were on board and said, "How much this scenery looks like Mount Desert!" and then added tearfully, "How I wish it were!" For two nights and two days Mr. Blair and the Captain were on the bridge and accomplished the very difficult task with the greatest skill. What a responsibility for Mr. Blair to take and what a thrilling adventure—like a Stevenson tale with millions in gold bullion in the ship's hold!

On July 28, 1914, the elegant liner Kronprinzessen Cecilie *sailed from New York for Southhampton and Bremerton. She was nearly across when she was ordered to flee to the neutral United States. She was carrying more than 1,000 people and $14 million in German gold bullion. She stayed in Bar Harbor from August until November. The* Cecilie *was reborn as the troop transport* Mount Vernon. *(Courtesy of Bar Harbor Historical Society.)*

Sandro Fabbri heard on his radio that the big ship was coming in so he went out in his motor boat at sunrise and took pictures of her and of the passengers landing and going through the formalities and all the excitement. He got the films off on the noon train and sold them to a New York moving picture house for $600 and they were shown that evening before the newspapers had done anything! It was the first money he had ever earned, he said!

We were among the first people to get on the ship and that was because the Saundersons took us out in their launch and Anne had made a voyage with the Captain and asked for him. He was a fine-looking old German as tall as Harold and twice as straight and broad. Captain Pollack, though looking desperately tired, was very genial and polite. The poor stewards also were very tired and worried-looking and said, "Oh, if you are from the land, do tell us the news of our country. Has England declared war?" When we said, "No," they breathed sighs of relief. Most of the passengers had left but those in steerage were all still on board and seemed cheerful and resigned. They must have been so thankful to be in a safe and beautiful American port. It must have seemed like heaven after their terrifying voyage. We had a glass of German beer with the Captain and then left as there was much confusion on board and we felt in the way.

From the journals of Marian Lawrence Peabody, courtesy of Gertrude Lawrence McCue; Bar Harbor Historical Society.

Naturalist Notes from Frenchman Bay

1933–1934

ARTHUR STUPKA, RANGER-NATURALIST

AN EARLY WINTER

December 1933: By mid-November our winter had come to stay, and before the first of December, the Moon of the Long Night, a considerable amount of snow had fallen. December proved to be one of the coldest twelfth-months on record, the temperature going on below zero on at least six days. On the 28th, the mercury tumbled to ten degrees below zero, on the 29th it was a record of twenty-seven below, and on the 30th the reading was twenty-two below in Bar Harbor. Snow fell on at least ten of the thirty-one days. Flocks of Crows and Herring Gulls, driven by hunger, kept flying low over the town, occasionally settling in the streets and yards where some food was to be had. Heavy freezing over the intertidal region inflicted considerable hardship on these beach-combers.

HARDY BIRDS

January and February, 1934: A lone robin has spent this bitter cold winter in and about the haw hedge which grows on the Acadia National Park Office grounds, while an unusually approachable blue jay has been seen time and again at Sieur de Monts Spring. In Bar Harbor, in small pools of open water just off the wharf, flocks of buffleheads and golden-eyes defy the piercing winter blasts which sweep over the frozen expanse of the bay. Although under ordinary circumstances they are fairly approachable, these ducks, especially the attractive little buffleheads, appear almost wholly unconcerned about one's presence when strong biting winds send the mercury far below the zero mark. On February 9, with the mercury around twenty degrees below zero, I was able to come within a few yards of some buffleheads which were resting in a little pool of open water.

THE NATURALIST'S SEA CRUISE IN FRENCHMAN BAY

July and August, 1934: Twice a week, during the months of July and August, the Naturalist's Sea Cruise, a popular event on the Acadia National Park Nature-Guide Program, left the wharf at Bar Harbor on a two-hour cruise around the nearby islands in Frenchman's Bay. From Bar Harbor the motor launch headed southeast following the eastern coast of Mount Desert Island as far as the rocky promontory of Great Head. From there the course lay northeast passing Egg Rock Lighthouse at the very mouth of the bay, continuing around the steep eastern coast of Ironbound Island, then heading westward close to the southern margins of the Porcupines, and back to the starting point. Sixteen cruises, averaging thirty-four persons to a party, were taken in the course of the season.

The geology of Mount Desert Island and the nearby islands was stressed during the first half of the cruise while the latter half of the brief voyage was devoted largely to sea birds in the vicinity of Ironbound Island. Since living things are always of greatest interest to the general public, the sea birds attracted the most attention. To see the little Black Guillemots (locally called "Sea Pigeons") winging their way rapidly over the waves, their bright coral-red feet trailing behind, gave rise to many exclamations of delight. Occasionally troops of Double-crested Cormorants left the high perpendicular cliffs along the southeastern face of Ironbound—a kind of mysterious dignity enshrouding the flight of these dark, long-necked, silent birds. Noisy Ospreys enlivened the trip with their high-pitched cackling, frequently flying close to the boat. A number of pairs of these large fish-hawks nested on the islands in the bay, and some of these bulky conspicuous nests were always pointed out by the nature-guide. Herring Gulls were always seen in greater or less number, a large number of them congregating on the Hop Island where they nested in early summer. Great Blue Herons, Sandpipers, noisy Common Terns, Crows, Bald Eagles, and a few other species were observed by some of the groups.

At times a school of sleek black Porpoise would be sighted, and, in mid-August, three or four of the groups were favored by seeing a Humpback Whale in the immediate vicinity of the Porcupine Islands. The big cetacean first made its appearance on August 10 and was seen thereafter on thirteen consecutive days. At sunset, on August 14, two launches bearing seventy-five members of the Appalachian Mountain Club—a special Naturalist's Sea Cruise party—came upon the whale near Bald Rock and watched it spout and breach—a memorable exhibition.

From Nature Notes*, Arthur Stupka, Acadia National Park, 1933–34; courtesy of NPS, Acadia National Park.*

The Shore Path

The Veazie Cottage housed the Mount Desert Reading Room social club from 1881 until 1887, when it was taken away and replaced by a new building designed by William Ralph Emerson (see page 57).

The club began in the mid-1870s, as the Oasis, in a small building downtown. It was a private men's club, offering culture, literature and a place to get a drink of something more inspiring than lemonade. Its membership included all the right people. From the turn of the century to the first world war the Reading Room hosted many of the best social functions, even admitting women–for the festivities. The cottagers turned their backs on the Reading Room in the early 1920s, preferring to drink their cultured beverages at home. (Courtesy of Maine Historic Preservation Commission.)

For many years the village shore walk went from the pier to Cromwell Harbor.

In 1881 the *Mount Desert Herald* noted the growing tendency among some owners of real estate along the bay shore "Lover's Walk" to close off the traditional path, "forcing the public to walk over jagged rocks and sharp stones." The *Herald* felt that this was "in bad taste, although it may be the legal right of the cottagers to do so."

Shorefront property owners J. Montgomery Sears (The Briars) and Thomas Musgrave (Edgemere) began building a better shore path that August. Four years later Mrs. George Bowler of Devilstone and Mrs. Jones of Reef Point built an access path from Hancock Street to the Shore Path

In its protest against the closing of the Shore Path, the *Mount Desert Herald* mentioned that people enjoyed both views from the path: the busy harbor and lovely bay on one side, and the fine summer cottages and beautiful gardens on the other. A fair number of the cottages have been torn down during the passing years, but a significant number have been restored and several now serve as inns.

The Shore Path still remains open to strollers and picnickers through the generosity of the owners of the shorefront properties. For more than a century, the path has been maintained by the Village Improvement Association.

Romantic Notions Along the Shore Path

1892

Sherman's Guide to Bar Harbor

For those who appreciate the beauties of Nature and yet like to mingle with their fellowmen in the enjoyment of them, there is no more pleasing walk than the Tow Path [Shore Path]. This favorite promenade extends from the steamboat wharf southward along the shore of the bay to Cromwell's Harbor. It is only a foot-path; no carriages can pass. And it is well that it is so, for an innovation in the shape of a driveway would destroy the romantic beauty of the scene.

Let us look at some lovely evening in July. the moon has risen above the hills across the Bay, and sheds a broad band of silvery light over the waters which break in tiny waves at our feet. Ever and again, like some white-winged phantom, a sail boat crosses this wake of light, to vanish immediately in the gloom which seems so dark in contrast to its brightness. Shadowy objects flit to and fro on the dark bosom of the Bay, probably canoes freighted with loving couples enjoying the calm, sweet silence of the night.

Away off in the distance, to the south, shines the warning light in the tower of Egg Rock lighthouse, like a brilliant star on the horizon; while to the north are the many twinkling lights of the yacht fleet at anchor in the harbor. Before us looms a black mass rising out of the waves, the steep, bold cliffs of the Bald Porcupine. All is silence upon the water save now and again some light refrain from the boating parties, or the strange weird cry of the loon, like the shriek of some lost soul going out with the tide.

Ashore, where we are walking, life abounds. The path by the rocks is illumined here and there by streams of light from the windows of the cottages nestling among the trees; and strains of music, from the musicians within, fall upon our ears. This is a favorite walk with lovers, and we meet many in all stations of life from the cook and coachman to the dude from Rodick's and the season's belle. There is plenty of company here, and one never tires of watching the tide of humanity as it flows by. By daylight the beach is the resort of nurse maids and their charges gathering shells and pebbles and wading in the little pools left by the receding tide. Many beautiful cottages are built along this shore, and the well-kept grounds extend to the edge of the path. Here and there, among the trees, we come across pretty lawns on which tastefully dressed men and women are engaged in a tennis tournament. Everyone we meet seems bent on pleasure, and everyone seems to know that this is a good place to find it. And so say we.

From Sherman's Guide to Bar Harbor, *W. H. Sherman, 1892; courtesy of Maine Historic Preservation Commission.*

Careful footwork on the Shore Path. The tower was located at the bend at Reef Point, and belonged to the summer cottage built for Thomas Musgrave in 1881. (Courtesy of Maine Historic Preservation Commission.)

Edward and Evalyn Walsh McLean received their Shore Path estate, The Briars, as a gift from her father in 1909. There was apparently plenty of family money to keep the young McLeans in alcohol, fancy cars and fancier jewelry (including the Hope diamond). They died in the 1940s; the Briars survived until 1968. Their former bowling alley and servants' quarters, now homes, remain along the Shore Path exit to Wayman Lane.

The crowd waits in front of the Mount Desert Reading Room for President Taft to come ashore on the steel pier. The pier was built in the late 1880s and was demolished in the 1930s. It was used by the Reading Room club until it closed in the early 1920s, then by the Bar Harbor Yacht Club until it dissolved in 1932. Two posts remaining from the steel pier are visible at low water, near the shore seaward of the present pier. (Courtesy of Maine Historic Preservation Commission.)

A Proper Greeting for President Taft

1910

NAN COLE

[President William Howard Taft] was the first President—since [1889]—to visit us while in office, and his coming created a great furore in Bar Harbor that week.

Mrs. Evalyn Walsh McLean, always a leader in any social project, decided to decorate the salon of the presidential yacht *Mayflower* in honor of the distinguished guest. At the time my brother Chet [Chester Wescott] was working in the uptown store of Mount Desert Nurseries and happened to be on duty when Mrs. McLean entered to inquire the price of American Beauty roses. She was quoted a price of "$1 an inch." Without hesitation Mrs. McLean ordered 100 dozen of the longer stemmed roses, and Chet nearly fainted, because there were only four dozen in the shop! However, he got in touch with the manager, who immediately phoned New York to fill the order. When the *Mayflower* dropped anchor offshore Chet, with his fragrant cargo, went out in the launch that transported the reception committee. He was about to climb the gangplank, when a hand on his shoulder restrained him, and a Secret Service man wanted to know what he was doing there. Chet explained, pointing to the ten eight-foot boxes in the launch. He was ordered to fetch them aboard, open the boxes and spread out the roses for viewing on the floor of the salon. He complied and, after a thorough and satisfactory inspection, the decorating was allowed to begin.

From "A Native's Memories of Old Bar Harbor," by Nan Cole, Down East, *September 1970.*

Landscape gardener Beatrix Jones Farrand and her husband Max Farrand made their home at Reef Point, the 19th-century cottage once owned by her mother. The grounds were typical shoreline: sand and clay interrupted by rocks and forested with spruce. The family kept it that way.

Farrand recalled, "In the early days visitors to Reef Point were puzzled by the lack of a trim lawn stretching unbroken to the sea. Occasional delicate veiled remarks indicated a question as to whether the dominant trees and shrubs implied a spirit of economy, while others asked more openly why the type of planting had been chosen."

In later years, Beatrix Farrand began to landscape the grounds, learning through her mistakes which plants would grow in the harsh coastal location. In 1939, she and her husband Max opened Reef Point gardens to the public for educational purposes. In 1955, near the end of her life, Beatrix Farrand decided to end the project. The house was torn down, and the moveable plants transferred to other gardens.

Today the grounds are occupied by new houses, but the elegant rustic fence designed by Farrand still shelters the plants within. White spruces grow along the shore and the rocks continue to erode in the face of the sea. The path from the Shore Path to Hancock Street runs along the boundary that once separated Reef Point from its neighbor Devilstone, a continuing gift from the property owners.

Many of Beatrix Farrand's plants can be seen at the Asticou Azalea Gardens and Thuya Gardens in Northeast Harbor.

Shorefront Gardening

1947

Beatrix Jones Farrand

Even in one little lifetime the aspect of the shore has changed. Some of the big volcanic walls have split and fallen, overturned by thrusts of ice in the fissures, and battering of the sea on softer strata. Part of the easterly point has collapsed and walls are needed to halt the hunger of the waves. Many more millions of years passed before the land took on its present expression and became clothed with vegetation, but the aspect of today is formed by the underlying rocks and the soil made by their disintegration and the deposit left by the ice sheet.

Building of the soil is a long process often needing centuries for accretion, therefore the present thin coat must have been accumulating for many years before it became fertile enough to support the growth of trees and shrubs which in their turn fed and protected the ground in which they grew....

In the early days of human settlement there must have been an Indian village near Reef Point, as a stone implement was found near the shore in a heap containing many clamshells. When the white settlers came they made winding paths through the evergreens which grew thickly in spite of shallow soil, as the moist sea air and cool nights were to their liking. Their present owner found a grove of big red spruces straggling over the eastern half of the acreage; most of these have followed their predecessors, but even today a few survivors show the size of the old seaside forest. Many old trees have yielded to a younger generation, and white spruces have replaced the old reds on nearly the whole waterfront, but the reds are still holding their own on the west.

Sixty years ago, fertile topsoil was almost entirely lacking. The roots of the big spruces spread over the ledges and under their branches a meagre covering of evergreen needles was varied by occasional streaks of red or white sand. In the course of half a century soil has been built up from almost nothing to a covering neither rich in composition nor generous in depth but at least sufficient to nourish many different ground-covers. Ferns, bunchberries and goldthreads have replaced the thickets of rust-infected blackberries and spindly half-starved roses.

As the soil gradually improved under kindly treatment experiments were started in planting a few alien shrubs. At first failures were far more frequent than successes as the owners were both self-willed and unobservant and did not heed the plainly indicated opportunities before them. Slowly they learned that it was safer and wiser to cast aside their own fancies or preferences and to adapt their plans to what lay before them awaiting proper use. The plants which now predominate are those which prefer acid rather than alkaline soil. This series is one of the loveliest in the plant world. The range is from the ground hugging bunchberry or dwarf cornel, bearberry and goldthread to the tallest of the rhododendron family, with heaths and huckleberries among those of middle height....

From the Reef Point Gardens Bulletin, *Beatrix Farrand, November 1947; courtesy of College of Environmental Design Documents Collection, University of California, Berkeley.*

Oldfarm and Compass Harbor

George B. Dorr's mother and father built Oldfarm in 1876 at a cost of about $50,000. According to Dorr, his mother loved gardening and entertaining, and was extremely good at both. He carried on the family traditions, with events such as this play staged on the lower lawn.

This photo was taken at location "A" on the sketch map (page 61), probably before 1920. The spruce in the center foreground, to the left of the main stairs, remains as a head-high weathered stub. The lawn where the playgoers gathered is completely overgrown. The sturdy spreading lower branches of the older trees, especially the pines, show that they spent their youth in the sunny open, not in the shade of a forest understory. (Courtesy of NPS, Acadia National Park.)

Oldfarm was the home of George B. Dorr, the "Father of Acadia." From 1901 until his death at ninety in 1944, Dorr used his inherited fortune and influence with friends in the right places to acquire land for Acadia National Park.

A constant parade of well-known and well-spoken guests kept Oldfarm a lively place, especially during the summer. Dorr stayed at Oldfarm throughout the year, and went swimming in the cove regardless of the season. He created a network of paths that wandered throughout his estate, and connected it to nearby summer cottages, as well as to trails at Sieur de Monts and the surrounding mountains.

Before he died, George Dorr gave his beloved Oldfarm to Acadia National Park. The 1947 fire passed close to Oldfarm, but did not touch it. The house was torn down in 1951.

The buildings are gone, but many clues to Dorr's life here remain. It is possible to trace the outlines of the house and gardens, and follow many of the old paths on the grounds. Some of the old garden plants (or their progeny) survive, despite neglect and "poachers." The stalwart may wade in the ruins of the saltwater swimming pool. Dorr's neighborhood paths are now inaccessible on private land, but the trails located on land given to the park are open to all, thanks to his generosity and foresight.

The main house at Oldfarm was built to last. Naturally weathered granite, taken from a nearby quarry opened specifically for the purpose, formed the lower story. Cut granite was used only around the windows and doors. The upper stories were wood-framed with redwood shingles. The piazza and terrace were paved with bricks laid so well that they remain tight and nearly level after almost fifty years of exposure. On the northern side of the house, granite stairs and graded paths lead to the water through a landscape that once was tended carefully, now gone wild. Rhododendrons thrive in the light shade of the woods just below the piazza.

This photo, taken in the early 1900s, shows the view from location "B" on the site map opposite. The terrace walls and piazza floor are easily seen today, but the outlines of the house have been erased almost completely. It is possible to trace the foundation by locating the stairs and their associated thresholds. Presumably, the large stones that once made up the steps were taken for use elsewhere.

Most of the plants in the photo are still alive, and are much larger. From left to right: The cedar trees that tower overhead were once the large shrubs shown next to the foundation and to the left. The somewhat ungainly pine, minus a couple of branches, still grows to the right of the drive. The deciduous branches at the far right of the photo belong to a cucumber magnolia, Magnolia acuminata, *a tender species that miraculously has survived. (Courtesy of NPS, Acadia National Park.)*

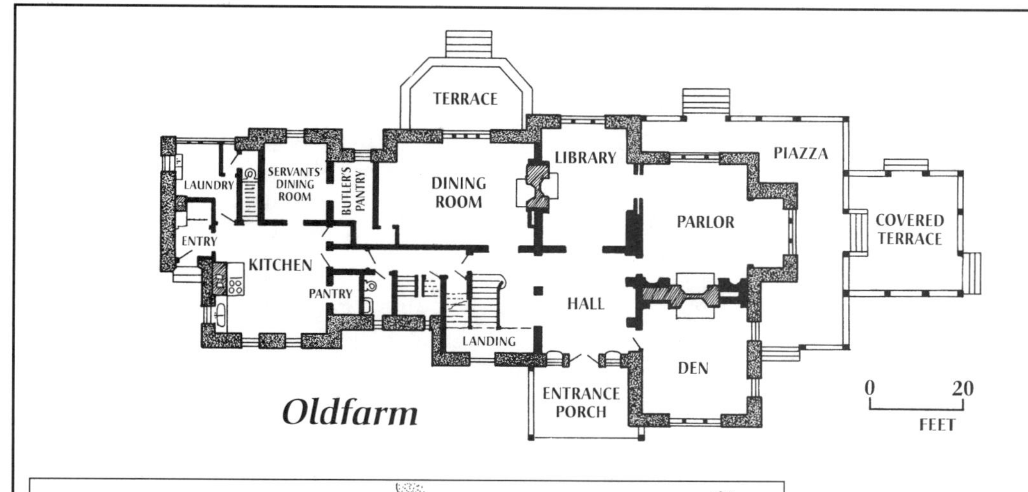

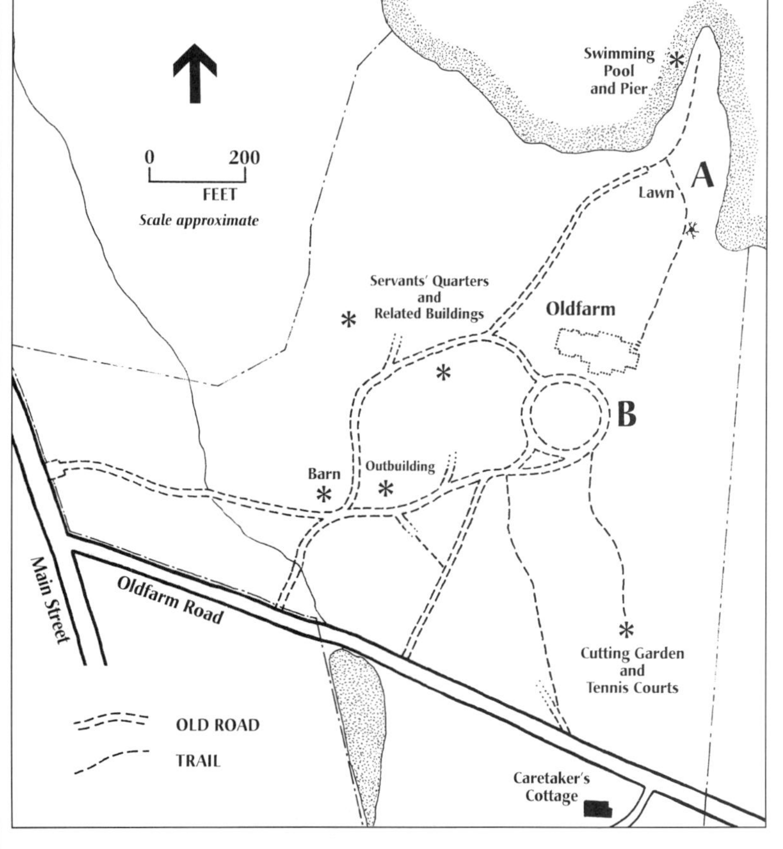

Note

Oldfarm has an abundance of old roads, old paths and new trails that can be more than a little confusing to the landscape detective.

This sketch map shows the major old roads and several important trails. The best way to start exploring is to walk along the former front drive from Main Street to the remains of the main house. Use the house foundation as a reference point for investigating the rest of the estate.

Map based on sketch map courtesy of NPS, Acadia National Park; 1903 map courtesy of Bar Harbor Town Planning Office. Floor plan based on original Dorr plan, courtesy of NPS, Acadia National Park.

At first glance, Oldfarm appears to be a typical popular park, with the usual enhancements: parking lots, gateposts and well-worn trails. To find hints of the estate that occupied these grounds for seventy-five years, it is necessary to look closely and consult the map. Even so, the smallest clues are important.

Oldfarm offers botanical detectives plenty of challenge. Many of the trees, shrubs and flowers are non-native species planted by Dorr or his mother. Quite a few of these species grow wild elsewhere in North America, since the Dorrs preferred a "natural" landscape, but did not want to restrict themselves to plants native to Maine. There are also truly native plants, some that were part of the estate's landscaping, and others that sprouted later.

Generally speaking, most of the smaller trees have grown up in the years since George Dorr's death. Some of the "trees" are in fact plants that would have been kept trimmed to shrub size.

Gardeners will find some old friends at Oldfarm, especially around the cutting garden.

It is not easy to find signs of Oldfarm's buildings. The structures were torn down, and their foundations filled and flattened. The east terrace of the main house is probably the best place to start, since its walls remain. To find the servants' quarters requires real imagination, since the best clue is the large, unnaturally flat area covered by weedy young trees, just to the west of the service drive. The barn is a similar problem, but the landscape offers a suspiciously rectilinear flat area, an exposed section of water line and another flat rectangular area. A tangle of vines now climbing the trees may have once climbed the barn. The caretaker's cottage, or Superintendent's House, as it is also known, is owned by the park. Its future is uncertain, but it may be renovated for offices and housing.

George Dorr offered Oldfarm to President Franklin Roosevelt for his personal use as a retreat and command post during World War II. Roosevelt regretfully declined, but suggested that the government could accept the estate. The following is taken from Dorr's letter offering Oldfarm to Acadia National Park.

Some Thoughts Concerning Acadia National Park, Planning for Its Future

George B. Dorr

1940

Oldfarm, one of the earliest, and best-situated summer homes upon Mount Desert Island, was for many years the scene of generous hospitality, till those who made it so, my father and my mother, passed on, leaving to me the spirit of that hospitality, to which, extended to a wider, national field, Acadia National Park, in its origin, is due.

The site occupied by this home is that of one of the earliest cultivated farmlands on the Mount Desert Island, with the woodlands and wild lands associated with it, is, owing to the bold, rocky character of the coast beyond, the last tract of farmland character capable of being cultivated upon the western coast of Frenchman's Bay or the coast beyond until Seal Harbor and the island-sheltered entrance of Somes Sound is reached. It also fronts directly upon the last good harbor for small vessels along that whole stretch of coast, lying closely outside the extensive sheltered basin of Upper Frenchman's Bay created by the breakwater extended by the Government, at great expense, from Round [Bald] Porcupine westward toward the Bar Harbor shore, with passage-way left open for smaller craft.

George Dorr was blind in his later years. He lived in the caretaker's cottage on the south side of Oldfarm Road. His friends worried, with good reason, about his tendency to buy land with no concern for his own needs. Dorr was essentially penniless when he died. (Courtesy of NPS, Acadia National Park.)

The original Oldfarm grant acquired by my father extended back from the Compass Harbor shore and the Storm Beach point beyond for a measured mile, ending on the all but precipitous slope of Champlain Mountain, the easternmost mountain in the Mount Desert Island chain, which, with Bear Brook and Beaver Dam Pool at its base, was one of the earliest gifts of land, made by myself, which now constitutes Acadia National Park.

This Oldfarm Tract, which, in its entirety, I inherited from my father, is one of extraordinary interest and variety, with its harbored shore, its cultivated farmland, its bold granite heights above the cottage I now occupy, its tiny lake, Compass Harbor pond, and the stream which winds its way down from it to the harbor....

...While extended as the Park now is, it has, even yet, no frontage upon any harbored shore until Somes Sound is reached, midway of Mount Desert Island. The Oldfarm tract I now offer will fill this want, and in the most complete and satisfactory way.

The house itself, Oldfarm, built by day labor under my father's, my mother's and my own direction in consultation with the architect and builder, is, owing to the good care taken of it, in as good condition now as it was when it was finished, sixty years ago, and no repair of it is needed, within or without. It occupies a magnificent situation above the shore and harbor and is completely furnished, having been rented to friends of mine at intervals throughout the years. This furniture is included in my offer. Private roads, avenues and foot-paths connect the house widely and directly with the lands now already included in the National Park, and it seems more natural and right to have the Park extended across the public way to Compass Harbor and contact with the sea and to the house that was my own.

From George B. Dorr's papers, courtesy of NPS, Acadia National Park.

Looking over the backyards in the late 1870s or early 1880s. The white Union Congregational Church (with steeple), graveyard and new St. Saviour's Episcopal Church face Mount Desert Street. The building in the foreground is near the Rodick House. A traveler's valise holds the window open, and the crop looks to be potatoes.

St. Saviour's and the graveyard still occupy the same places; the old Union Church was replaced in the late 1880s by a stone "Tudor-Shingle Style" edifice that burned in 1942. (See page 71.) The present church resembles the old meeting house. (Courtesy of Maine Historic Preservation Commission.)

The grand hotels and magnificent summer cottages, together with their migratory inhabitants, were a presence that was impossible to ignore. Village life went on quietly in the background, unheralded by popular writers. The guidebooks speak glowingly of the fine summer season and proudly list the best accommodations and finest estates. Normal village activities were not what the summer visitors wished to read about—or to see.

In 1888, M. F. Sweetser did note the following: "By winter all the fashionable world has bidden farewell to this region; and the Bar Harbor villagers are left to enjoy their sociables and hops and masquerades and sleighrides, their hunting of deer among the mountains, and of sea-fowl along the shore, and their trout-fishing through the thick ice of Eagle Lake. As many as 1,500 men are sometimes kept at work here all winter long, on sewer and water-main excavations, new hotels and cottages, grading, and other avocations connected with the summer city."

The township of Bar Harbor had a population of 1,195 in 1870; 1,629 in 1880 and 4,379 in 1900. Today it is just over 4,000.

There is still a perception amongst summer visitors that Bar Harbor goes into hibernation after the last T-shirt is sold on a chill day in fall. Now, as then, this is not quite the case.

A Perspective on the Neighborhoods

1894

F. MARION CRAWFORD

Wandering through the streets of the little village one is struck again and again by the sharp contrast between what may be called the natural life of the place and the artificial condition which fashion has imposed upon it. In some of the streets almost every house is meant to be rented, the owners usually retiring to restricted quarters in the back, where they stow themselves away and hang themselves up on pegs until they may come into their own again. Here and there a native cottage has been bought and altered by a summer resident, and over the whole there is the peculiarly smug expression of a quarter which is accustomed to put its best face foremost for a few months of the year. But in the back lanes and side streets there are still the conditions of the small New England community, in which land is poor and work is slack during the long winter, so that although there is no abject poverty in the sense in which it is known to cities, there is also little time or inclination for the mere prettiness of life.

From Bar Harbor, *Francis Marion Crawford, Charles Scribner's Sons, New York, 1894.*

Summers in Bar Harbor were full of grand society balls attended by the rich, famous and well-connected. Local residents were not on the guest lists; they were the help. To retaliate, a group of businessmen decided to hold their own "society" affair in the dead of winter. Since the summer people seemed to think of the native population as "hayseeds," the ball's participants naturally adopted full rural regalia. The first Hay Seeder Way Bak Ball in February 1895 was a thorough success, and quickly became a much-anticipated annual event.

The first Way Bak Balls were held at the Hep's Music Hall. At the turn of the century, the ball moved to the Casino, the town's all-purpose meeting hall. The Casino, which was torn down in the 1970, stood at the corner of Cottage and Bridge Streets.

The Way Bak Ball celebrated its centennial in 1995. Recent dances have been held in the Masonic Hall on High Street, but not much else has changed.

The descendents of the forty original Hay Seeders issue the coveted invitations, complete with creative spelling and the poem of the year. Couples wearing their least fancy calicoes and overalls dance the traditional contras till the late hours, and refresh themselves with lemonade, unassuming whiskey, rat-trap cheese, doughnuts and salt cod.

The Casino at the corner of Cottage and Bridge Streets. (Courtesy of Maine Historic Preservation Commission.)

A Real Old Fashioned Dance at Music Hall

1895

BAR HARBOR RECORD

Every dancing man in town got an invitation last week, written on brown paper, sprinkled with hay seed and enclosed in a yellow envelope, inviting him to attend the Hay Seeder's ball in the Music Hall, Monday evening.

Every invitation was accepted and promptly at 7:30 the grand march formed at the sound of a melodious cow bell, led by Samanthy and Ike. Samanthy wore a sunbonnet and a calico gown, but Ike was attired *a la mode* of half a century ago, with long white hair and whiskers. About a hundred couples fell in line, but all eyes were on the leaders who in their natural characters proved to be Messrs. Frank Leighton and Fred A. Foster.

The Misses Bunker and Hodgkins were attired as ballroom belles of our grandmother's day and very quaint and pretty they looked, with their hair arranged in smooth, glossy bands, large silver combs, big earrings, and full-skirted gowns.

A written description of the dance order, made with crayons cleverly handled by Joe Stevens, would never do it justice, so arrangements will be made to have it reproduced if practicable in the *Record* at an early date. It was the crowning glory of a well-conducted affair.

The hall was decorated with sheaves of grain, pumpkin jacks, farm products and farming implements of every kind. From stone jars, labeled Old Rye and Medford Rum, was served lemonade to drink with the molasses doughnuts and ginger snaps.

The entertainers, Messrs. Charles Allen, Alonzo Ash, E. N. Benson, A. G. Bulger, John Conners, Frank Conners, J. E. Clark, D. L. Drew, J. E. Foster, Charles Green, T. C. Higgins, C. L. Higgins, S. N. Higgins, A. L. Higgins, B. S. Higgins, E. C. Parker, Andrew Rodick, S. H. Rodick, G. E. Rodick, Nathan Salisbury, B. E. Whitney and V. G. Wasgatt wore boutonnieres of ripe wheat.

Monaghan's orchestra played for the old-fashioned dances which were kept up till a late hour, and the ball was professed to be the social success of the year.

From the Bar Harbor Record, *February 22, 1895.*

Keeping an Eye on Things

1906 TO 1916

NAN COLE

In the 1890s and the early 1900s, [Papa] was employed by most of the prominent rusticators, and was on a first-name basis with many of them. His friends—both those at home and from away—called him "Uncle George Wescott"; his workmen dubbed him "Dod-burn-it George," in honor of his habitual exclamation of irritation....

...May and June were Papa's busiest months, when he helped to construct Italian gardens, rebuild stone walls and do needed repairs inside the cottages before the arrival of their owners. I loved going with him, wherever he was working, so I could glimpse how the other half lived....

...Because I was a child, I was at liberty to enter many of the kitchens, where the servants would treat me to cakes and cookies and also to tidbits of gossip that they never seemed to surmise that I understood—so long as I kept quiet. Also, I was often called onto the porches of the owners, who plied me with candies and chatter. The latter was relayed to my diary, but both my back-door and front-door familiarity whetted a natural inquisitiveness so that, as I grew older, I became a deliberate spy, sometimes armed with binoculars.

Most of the houses on our street [High Street] were rented to rusticators. A judge of the New York Supreme Court lived beside us, and directly opposite lived a friend of his whom I will call Mrs. Rice. She was one of my favorite people, and also was very neighborly with my parents, so that there were more of wonder than of malice in my reports to my diary about her relationship with the judge.

They loaned servants back and forth, whenever either household entertained, and every pleasant afternoon, the judge drove Mrs. Rice in his surrey out to Jordan's Pond for tea....

...Weather permitting, I slept on my sleeping porch, directly opposite that of Mrs. Rice. She never slept on her porch, but invariably spent her mornings there, usually in a negligee trimmed with white maribou. At 10:30 daily the judge joined her there. They both had coffee, and then the judge read aloud to her.

I knew them both for at least twenty years, and heard a great deal of malicious gossip about their association. I took my cue from Papa who, when I was very young, said that the judge and Mrs. Rice had a true platonic friendship and, having looked up the word, I still agree that their strange relationship was so innocent as to confound the gossips. But I've always wished that I knew what the judge—who later bought our house for Mrs. Rice and created a sunken garden within the foundation walls of our old stable—chose to read to his lady friend during a lifetime of boudoir trysts.

Although we local people had become nonchalant about the presence of famous personages among us, every one was agog with anticipation when the news spread that Alice Roosevelt was coming to town. This was in 1906, when Teddy Roosevelt was our extremely popular President, and his daughter Alice's lighthearted escapades intrigued the entire nation. There were rumors that some of the numerous social gatherings devised for her entertainment were gay affairs—particularly a large and boisterous reception held at the swimming club—but not even our reliable grapevine came up with any occurrences out of the ordinary.

However, Alice Roosevelt was a friend of Countess Cassini, who, at that time, was renting a cottage near our house. One day I saw her carriage drive up, and Alice alight to call on the countess, so I made haste to put on clean clothes and to begin my childish snooping by parading back and forth in front of the house.

Eventually, I was rewarded. The two ladies came out onto the piazza, lit up cigarettes—the first I had ever seen being consumed by the gentler sex—and, the better to enjoy them, put their feet on the veranda rail while they smoked. I have never decided which was more childish—my snooping, or gestures by which the two ladies flouted the conventions of the time, doubtless feeling very devilish with their feet up and wreaths of cigarette smoke proclaiming their independence.

Ten years later—in June of 1916—I returned to snooping to see Mrs. John Jacob Astor's wedding to William Karl Dick. As a young bride she had been aboard the *Titanic* when it struck an iceberg. Her husband helped to assist her, along with many other women and children, into the available lifeboats, nonchalantly smoking cigarettes until he—and over 1,500 others—went down with the ship. After four years of widowhood, Mrs. Astor was forfeiting a $500,000 trust fund to marry Mr. Dick.

The wedding was held at St. Saviour's, and I hid behind a tombstone of the adjacent Congregational Church graveyard. Twice policemen drove me away, but I sneaked back through the hedge for a fleeting satisfaction of seeing the wedding party come out of the back door, thus eluding the hordes of reporters at the front.

One of the vagaries of the very wealthy that never failed to intrigue us natives was the contentment of some of them with conditions that were far from luxurious. The Mellon ladies, sisters of Andrew Mellon, spent their summers for many years at Geranium Cottage, attached to the Malvern Hotel [at the corner of Mount Desert and Kebo Streets]. The Mellon cottage—and the ladies always stipulated that they be given the same one—was hardly a decorator's dream, albeit clean and comfortable. The bedrooms were equipped with old-fashioned white iron beds, bureaus and a desk painted white, with a few matching chairs. However, the cottage also boasted of very good mattresses, handsome oriental rugs over the wall-to-wall straw matting, two living rooms with fireplaces, and a front piazza with ordinary rocking chairs.

There the Mellon sisters were content to rock, sniffing the fragrance of a profusion of flowers within the stone wall enclosure—for which my father was responsible—that isolated each cottage. The sisters spent their afternoons making calls or attending teas. In return, they gave small tea parties and received callers. A kitchenette in their cottage enabled their breakfast to be prepared there, but for other meals they went to the hotel dining room. They returned eagerly for many years, until their ripe ages no longer permitted them to enjoy this simple routine. I am sure that the Mellon sisters never knew that the hotel staff identified them as Miss Honeydew and Miss Casaba behind their backs, more in affection than with malice.

From "Personal Glimpses of Bar Harbor's Lush Era," Nan Cole, Down East, *July 1969.*

Quite a Day

1920s

Sylvia Kurson

It all came about quite naturally. Brick Bragdon was my next-door neighbor and what-are-we-going-to-do-today friend. Her father was caretaker for the Auchincloss estate. Every morning except Sunday, he tramped the three miles from his house to his job, spent the day seeing to whatever needed doing inside or outside the cottage, then tramped the three miles home in time for supper. When the notion was put to him that he might take Brick and me along with him one Saturday, he reared up and balked. But Brick went at him with her only-daughter blandishments, and when his good wife let fire with "Now Henry, you get her out from under my feet for one blessed day!" he succumbed, shaking his head dolefully at the prospect.

And so we packed up our vittles in an oilcloth bag and went forth like a tandem of squaws following an unwilling brave.

The Auchincloss cottage looked like a fairy castle in the snow, ivory white against blue white, framed in the dark of firs. Whether it was as beautiful as I remember it, I don't know and it doesn't matter. What we saw seemed a palace to two ten-year-olds conditioned to stand in awe of summer visitors' wealth and rich possessions. To enter that palace, even through the cellar door, was to enter another world where magnificent people lived magnificent lives beyond our wildest imaginings.

We stamped the snow off our overshoes. Brick's father policed the operation, grunted eventual satisfaction, unlocked the door, and led the way into a basement room as big as the town roller-skating rink. There was little to see: a tall woodstove with an outsized pot belly, a jumble of flowers and flat boxes, one kitchen chair with a sagging cane bottom, and mounds of raffia piled up around it. But to our bemused eyes, it was a place arrayed in mysterious splendor.

Brick's father went about his business at once. He chunked the stove, put a match to it, finished the match on his corncob pipe, and settled into the chair. "Now, you young'uns stay put over there," he said, pointing to a piece of the wall and floor just within reach of where he was sitting, "and behave yourselves. There's work to be done, and I aim to do it."

We sat on the cement floor, backs against the wall, so caught in the wonder of where we were that we didn't know we were cold until the fire took hold and thin heat crept toward our toes. Then we began to smell cold getting warm, dry bulb dirt, and the corncob pipe. We shifted our bottoms and let out our breaths. We were beginning to feel at home in the palace.

Mr. Bragdon worked. We watched and marveled at the easy way he was doing queer things with the raffia, almost as if he was puttering with tangled fishing lines....

Because the winter days were short, he was ready early for the lunch he'd brought in a lard pail. He had one of his own home-cured stripped fish, some soda biscuits, and a quart jar of stewed tea. We'd brought sugar doughnuts, molasses cookies, and apples—a feast more exotic in that setting than jellied eels and escargot. To this day I can taste the smoky saltiness of the stripped fish and the brown sweetness of that stewed tea.

That would have been a great plenty of goodness, but there was more to come. Almost before the last crumb had been disposed of, Mr. Bradgon's eyelids began to go up and down with a jerky motion. Brick poked me with her elbow, a signal I recognized immediately as a prepare-for-action alert, and I gathered myself together, ready to spring.

When the eyelids stopped going up, and long puffing noises came from behind the bushy mustache, we started stirring, a little at a time—one leg, the another, then both. A moment's wait to be sure of safety. A final decisive jab, and we were off on a wild voyage of discovery up the cellar stairs, through the door at the top, into a kitchen bigger than the whole ground floor of Brick's house or mine.

"Look at that, would you! And that! And that!"

But there was no time for loitering. We raced madly through two dining rooms, three sitting rooms, room after room of sheet-covered furniture, our breaths leaving wakes of mist behind us. If there'd been time to realize what we were seeing, we might have felt some uneasiness about being where we had no business to be—it was all so quietly private, so smug against invasion, so invested with the strangeness of difference.

But time was running out, and there was too much left to explore. Without the exchange of a single spoken word, we knew what we meant to do—go through every last room in the whole house. Unless we did, we'd never be sure we hadn't missed the only other eye-popping revelation.

So on we raced, up another flight of stairs, through enormous bedrooms and baths, up to the top floor where the rooms dwindled in size and looked more like our own.

In the last room we were brought up short. The moment had come to turn back, but in that moment Brick's eyes fastened on a stray coat-hanger lying on an iron bed. Should we? She looked at me for affirmation.

"Too big. It'd stick out of your coat."

Her face crumpled. Then she nodded slowly, recognizing the sad truth for what it was. We would have to leave empty-handed with no booty-proof to show off to our friends.

Back to the cellar was downstairs all the way. We made it with moments to spare. When Brick's father woke up, we were sitting like the good children he'd told us to be, backs against the wall, legs stretched out straight on the floor, waiting demurely for further orders.

"You young'un's about ready to call it a day?" He sounded relieved that the sky hadn't fallen in, and less disposed to expect the worst.

"Well now, you've had quite a day I'd say," and something like a smile flickered across his face.

We had all right—more of a day than he could ever suspect.

From My World on an Island: Growing up in Bar Harbor, *Sylvia M. Kurson. (Down East Books, Camden, Maine, 1982.)*

Margaret and Parson Anson Williams lived on Pleasant Street near Ledgelawn Avenue. Like many Bar Harbor women, she faced the fire at home, then was forced to leave town by the best means possible.

At three o'clock on the afternoon of October 23, a roaring northwest gale drove the fire from Hulls Cove toward Bar Harbor. The evacuation signal sounded at four, prompting about 2,500 people to gather at the ball field.

The fire stayed south and west of Eden Street, then consumed the Malvern Hotel and nearby buildings at the corner of Kebo and Mount Desert Streets. Fire crews made a stand there, and the fire continued down Spring Street, paralleling Glen Mary Road and Ledgelawn Avenue. Hard work by fire fighters kept the fire on the south side of Cromwell Harbor Road and west of Main Street. It then tore south over Strawberry Hill and the mountains beyond, touching the sea south of Sols Cliff. The fire reached Great Head less than three hours after the evacuation signal sounded.

As the fire advanced, it became obvious that the ball field was no place to be. Planned evacuation routes to Seal Harbor and Ellsworth were cut off. The people on the ball field retreated to the pier, where military ships picked up 400 despite heavy seas. Most people evacuated to Ellsworth as soon as a road was cleared.

Three persons died, and more than 170 houses burned. Several of the remaining large hotels and sixty-seven summer cottages were also lost. Total damages were estimated at $23 million.

The Big Fire: Mrs. Williams's Account

OCTOBER 22 TO 25, 1947

MARGARET WILLIAMS

The fire siren had sounded continuously all through the night, calling for more helpers, and each time we listened for the signal of 7-7 blasts, which would mean that we must evacuate Bar Harbor. Finally, at about 4:30 A.M., Anson got up, dressed, and said that he was going to the fire station. So I gave him breakfast and, flinging on his hat and coat, he was gone, saying, "Keep the radio on; you may have to be evacuated."

I stood in a daze for a few minutes after he left. I knew that the last and worst chapter in this horrible fire was approaching fast, and I was terrified. But Anson's final warning gave me something to think about. If there was a chance of my being evacuated, I would have to take a few things with me.

I went upstairs to our clothes closet, and began nervously flipping through the things on the hangers. My thoughts wouldn't jell; I couldn't decide on anything. This garment should be taken; no, it was too bulky; this one, then; no, it was too light-weight. In desperation I went downstairs, warmed the leftover coffee and sat down in the living room with a pad and a pencil, trying to calm myself sufficiently to make plans.

I felt that I must take a good suit of Anson's; he had gone in rough clothes, and there might be many duties for him as a minister when it was all over. I prayed there would be no dead to bury, but there certainly would be Sunday services somewhere, and pastoral calls to the sick and those whose worlds were suddenly blotted out by the loss of their homes and all their possessions. He would also need a change of clothes including shirt, tie, socks and a good pair of shoes. I went upstairs and packed that much; the suitcase was almost filled.

I opened the cedar chest where one of my sons had stored some of his belongings. On top was his wife's lovely wedding gown. How often I heard Harriet say, "If we ever have a little girl, I'd like her to be married in my wedding dress." I hesitated a long time, but sentiment got the best of me, so I carefully rolled the dress in tissue and put it on top of the other things I'd packed. I closed the suitcase firmly; there was room for nothing more. For myself, I chose my best suit to wear when I left, and things to go with it; put a few small pieces of jewelry in my largest purse, plus our two address books and some mail which would have to be answered sometime.

The day seemed endless. I straightened the house, and wondered if it would be the last time I'd ever dust the furniture, adjust the window shades and curtains, and water the house plants. As I went through the house, I thought of some of our treasures that I would miss.

There was the small collection of old glass that had been given to me by a dear old lady in Norridgewock. In the china cupboard was my set of Spode, a service for twelve, always used when we had guests. Then I came to the Frenchboro bowl, now filled with some red berries and, as always, it held the spotlight; even when it was empty, the bowl drew the eye as soon as you entered the room. When I got to my new spinet, I felt a great desire to take that, too. I had wanted the piano a long time before we had been able to buy it, and I was so proud of it, and had such pleasure from playing on it. Then, I thought, "How selfish you are! Here people are being burned out, many already with no homes, clothing or household goods; injured, maybe, and you're moping over your piano!"

The heat, which I could already feel from the raging fire, made the day oppressive, and I had a sensation of being stifled. When the telephone rang, I jumped as if it was strange to hear it. It was Beth, the wife of Reverend Bousfield, the superintendent of the [Maine Seacoast] Mission. She called to say that they were going to Lamoine and would save a place in their car for me if I hadn't made other plans. I accepted gratefully and put the suitcase and a briefcase filled with important papers near the front door for convenience. A short time later my next-door neighbor, Mary Hadley, phoned. Her husband Ben, superintendent of Acadia National Park, had just called her and said, "Mary, get Mrs. Williams, your mother and Mabel and get out of town. This thing is out of control." I told her the Bousfields had already asked me. Finally, in mid-afternoon, the long-expected 7-7 blasts sounded. It was almost a relief at last to know something definite. I wondered where Anson was.

National Guardsmen watch over household belongings taken for safekeeping to the ballfield. (Courtesy of the Bangor Daily News.*)*

When the doorbell rang, I expected to see Reverend Bousfield. Instead, there stood the tallest soldier I have ever seen. He asked me if I was alone and, before I could explain my plans, he seized me and took me, protesting every step of the way, to a huge Army truck parked by the walk. On the way, he said that he'd been ordered to pack people in the truck and take them to the athletic field, where the evacuees where gathered. Before he left the porch, he opened the front door clear back and also the storm door, leaving the house open to the terrific gale. He said it was to prevent the heat from concentrating, and blowing the house up. I kept telling him that I already had a way to go, and that the people would be expecting me to be at home. Apparently, he didn't hear a word; he'd been told to evacuate the women and children, and he was doing it. I was bodily lifted up into the truck and taken to the field. As I looked back at our house, I saw flaming shingles blowing over it from other houses already on fire. I never expected to see our house or possessions again; it was sure to be burned to the ground.

The wind all but took my breath away; it was a wind of gale force anyway, and added to it was the wind which the fire itself made. Together, they meant widespread destruction and danger. When we got to the athletic field, one of the officers in charge saw that I was very upset, and said, "What's the matter here?"

I said, "I didn't want to come down here."

He asked, "Where do you want to go?"

"The Mission House."

"Where is the Mission House?"

I told him [on West Street]; also that people were coming there to take me to Lamoine, and that I should be there when they arrived. The officer turned to the driver and said, "On your next trip, take this lady and drop her off wherever she wants to go." He dropped me at the Mission House and I found I was to go first to Seal Harbor with Mr. and Mrs. Worchester, there to be picked up by Mr. Bousfield and taken with them to Lamoine.

Our car was the last one out before the road going to Seal Harbor was closed. The ride was terrifying. There was a long line of cars, approximately 700 I learned later, and they were bumper to bumper. The roadway was pitch black as all of the electric lights were out, but you could see flares of the fire overhead. We had to have the car windows tightly closed as the sparks and flaming bits of material were hitting the car everywhere, and we were afraid they'd get inside. We simply crawled for three miles, closely packed in with luggage and coats, very hot, our eyes and heads full of smoke, and everyone tense for fear the fire would come up on us from the rear and we'd be burned to death in this creeping caravan.

After what seemed an eternity, we finally reached Seal Harbor. From there we could see the red glare of the fires very plainly, and of course the smoke was dense. Mr. Bousfield arrived and picked me up and we continued on to Lamoine.

I tried to contact Bar Harbor the next day, but all the phones were out. Where was Anson? I tried not to show it, but I was frantic. I disciplined myself time after time, saying, "You must believe that he is all right," but it was useless.

The next night I was thrilled when the phone rang and it was Anson, saying he was tired, bruised and scratched, but all right. He said our house was not burned; nothing hurt. I still had my spinet!

On Saturday morning, October 25, Mr. Bousfield said that he was going back to Bar Harbor, and asked if I'd mind going to the Mission House to get some dry clothes for some of the firefighters. (In the Mission House we kept a lot of clothes which were donated for the island parish, or to use as we saw fit.) So, armed with a commandant's permission to return—the city was now under martial law—we went back to Bar Harbor.

It was terrible sight. It was like a dead city: there was not a sound; not a store was open; you saw no one you knew; there was no other car but ours; no motion except the soldiers patrolling to prevent looting. Houses everywhere were burned to the ground: five of Bar Harbor's hotels, sixty-seven summer cottages, and 170 permanent homes. Many were still smoldering. There were hundreds and hundreds of feet of fire hose in the street. The air was full of burning paper, cinders, smoke, and over all was the awful smell of burnt things.

When I got to our own home, I saw that every pane of glass in both the front door and storm door had been broken into bits by the gale. The house was full of smoke and pieces of ash, but nothing was burned, even though the fire had come to within a hundred yards of it. After getting the clothes at the Mission House it was almost dark, so I went home and was just lighting some candles, when I was startled to see a head poking though the broken glass of the door. I was relieved to see that it was a soldier. He looked suspiciously at me, and said, "Lady, do you live here?"

"Yes, I do," I replied.

"Do you live alone?"

"No, but my husband is away helping with the fire."

"Are you afraid to be alone?"

"No," I said, and then he stalked off.

The Army was doing a good job of guarding Bar Harbor!

On Saturday morning, I saw Anson for the first time since we'd been separated. It was wonderful to see that he was safe and well. He was dreadfully tired, and he was certainly scratched and bruised, but we were lucky to have each other, and also our house and belongings. It made our sympathy even greater for those who had lost so much.

From "The Big Fire," Anson and Margaret Williams (as told to Mary Wilkes Haley), Down East, *October 1962.*

Note: Margaret's husband, The Reverend Anson Williams, tells his story of facing the fire at Duck Brook beginning on page 105.

Mount Desert Street

Mount Desert Street in 1919, six years after automobiles were allowed in Bar Harbor. The auto debate went back and forth from the turn of the century until it was resolved in the auto owners' favor by the State Legislature in 1913. Generally speaking, the summer people were against and the locals for, although as time went by many summer people, including George Dorr, reconciled themselves to the inevitable coming of the auto and began to think about its possibilities. Other summer residents proved as anxious to have a stable of first-class automobiles as they–or their parents–had been to have a stable of fine horses and carriages.

The stone Congregational Church of this era was designed by Shingle Style architect William Ralph Emerson and built in 1888. It burned in 1942. According to Bar Harbor Historical Society curator Deborah Dyer, the bell went rolling down School Street when the tower gave way. (Courtesy of Bar Harbor Historical Society.)

Mount Desert Street is the heart of the community. It is also a street lined with historic buildings, many of which are listed on the National Register of Historic Places. These architecturally important buildings are not museums; they live. Exuberant children crowd into the library for morning story hour; the faithful hear the words of God and sing the old hymns in the churches; and travelers settle in for a quiet stay at the inns.

Many of Eden's early inhabitants rest in peaceful communion in the old Congregational burying ground. Some of their names will be familiar from the stories in this book.

Mount Desert has long been a busy street. It was the summer colonists' favorite intown driving road, an excellent place to display one's finest horses and most elaborate carriage. The street scene on Sunday morning must have been quite impressive.

Most of the houses along the street were owned by or rented to summer people during the late 1800s and early 1900s. Each end of the street was taken up with large hotels.

By the late 1880s, electric lights glowed through the cottage and hotel windows. Bar Harbor's first electric lights were turned on July 12, 1884. Two years later the *Mount Desert Herald* noted that street lights were in use, "struggling bravely through the heavy fog."

Mount Desert Street and Slightly Beyond

1888

M. F. Sweetser

Mount Desert street leaves Main street opposite the Porcupine Block, about 500 yards from the wharf, and runs nearly due West. On the lower corner (towards Cottage Street) is the Grand Central Hotel with wide lawns fronting on both streets. A couple hundred yards from the corner is the only store on this street [Kittredge's]; and just beyond it on the same side (the north) is the beautiful Congregational Church. Opposite the church School street begins and runs south through the new extension to Strawberry Hill Road. On the right hand side of School street, a short distance from Mount Desert, is a handsome brick church built by the Methodist Society. Still further south on School street is the Hamilton Hotel, a small, transient house; and beyond that, the public school building. On the corner of School and Mount Desert streets is the Public Library.

A little further along Mount Desert street is the handsome stone church of St. Saviour, the Episcopal place of worship. Moving westward, we pass High street on the right and come to Ledgelawn avenue on the left hand. The latter is a comparatively new street, and running south, opens up a great number of fine building sites in that part of the village. It is wide and well built, and its eastern side is occupied by numerous pretty houses. On that side, about three hundred yards from Mount Desert street, is the Baptist Church, a handsome edifice; and a few rods nearer Mount Desert street, on the opposite side, stands the Unitarian Meeting-House, a quaint building. On the western side of the avenue is Miss Mary Shannon's beautiful estate Ledge Lawn, which also borders on Mount Desert street, and, further along, on Spring street parallel to Ledge Lawn avenue. The house on this estate is situated on a rocky eminence overlooking Mount Desert St.

A few rods beyond Ledge Lawn avenue is the St. Sauveur Hotel, on the north side of Mount Desert street; and next to the westward stands the Lynam House. From thence to its junction with Eden street, the north side is entirely occupied by cottages.

On the south side of the street, beyond the Lynam House, are two small lanes leading south to a wooded eminence on which are built the summer residences of Dr. Robert Amory, Dr. A. L. Mason and Mrs. James S. Amory, all of Boston. Between the entrance to these lanes and Eden street, are several cottages, the apartment houses known as the Parker Cottages, and the Belmont Hotel. It is barely half a mile from Main street along Mount Desert to Eden street; but the fine smooth roadway makes it the popular driving street of the village.

Eden Street, beginning at the western end of Mount Desert street and trending northwesterly along the shore of the Bay at an average distance of a fourth of a mile from it, is the next street of importance, though the greater part of it lies rather in the suburbs than in the village proper. It crosses the western ends of both Cottage and West streets also, and just after it passes the latter street dips down into the valley formed by Eddy's Brook, so-called. Near this point are a few stores; but the houses on it are principally non-resident cottages....

The extension of Eden street, beyond Mount Desert street, is known as Kebo street. On the eastern side of this street, about 200 yards from the corner of Mount Desert street, stands the Malvern Hotel. Just beyond this is the Roman Catholic chapel, St. Silvia's. Overlooking the street on the west side is a high wooded hill known as Malden Hill, and on this and along the line of the street are many fine cottages....

Running west from Mount Desert street, over the high land in that direction, and almost a continuation of that street, is the Eagle Lake road, so-called. Here also are many handsome cottages ... as is also the Casino [which soon housed the clubhouse of the Kebo Valley Club], the great society resort of Bar Harbor.

From Chisholm's Mount Desert Guide-Book, *M. F. Sweetser, Chisholm Brothers, Portland, 1888.*

St. Saviour's Episcopal Church was ready for worship in 1878. It was enlarged in 1886. In that year, a Louis Comfort Tiffany three-panel stained-glass altar window was given to the church by a Philadephian in memory of his father. Many more church members have given windows in the years since. Eleven of these are Tiffany windows.

The church welcomes visitors.

Daily Life of the Streets

EARLY 1900S

SYLVIA KURSON

"Tally-ho!" comes to us on the wind of horses passing and a spectacular vision gallops by. Four or six or eight paired horses, harnesses gleaming, are couriers of a long high chariot driven by picture men in hunting pinks with white stocks and black velvet caps. Men standing, burnished horns to lips, sound the imperious "Tally-ho!"—the wondrous annunciation.

Down Main Street, from the edge of the sea toward the distant mountains, they move, proud, aloof, clothed in their lordly splendor.

It is summer, of course, and the unquenchable summer people are playing prodigal games—playing with imagination and laughter, in the mad, gay world they create.

Behind them plods the lowly sprinkler, its arms wetting down the dust in sideways arcs of spray. Decorous, useful, sensible, putting things to rights after the children finish playing.

It is still morning. If we hurry, we may catch up with the ice-wagon on one of the side streets. There is no way to know if he's still making his rounds except to scurry up one street and down another looking for where a trail of water drops has pitted the ground in a straight line toward somebody's back door. If the pitting is dark enough, the wagon has just been there. Rush, pant, tangle our feet, get there in time—and there it is, a huge rectangle on wheels, its back open, its insides spilling out sawdust. The iceman strides back from the house, tongs dangling loosely from his load-free hand.

If we stand still, look up at him, and wait mutely, he jerks his head up and down once, spreads open the tongs, sets them wide around whichever one of the great ice blocks come closest to hand and yanks it to the lip of the wagon.

We watch, transfixed. We've seen him do this before, but it is always the first time—the unfolding, the revelation.

He drops the tongs to one side and reaches for his hatchet of a pick. "Clink, clink, CHINK!" A rainbow-colored spray of ice-chips falls around and into our outstretched hands.

He slams the back door of his wagon shut, shoves a thick wooden pin through the hasp, clucks to his horse, and moves on, leaving us stuffing our mouths with frozen slivers. We suck in total bliss. Ours is the ice and the goodness thereof.

...The junk man's rickety wagon looms into view, the worn-down horse crouching under the slapping reins. "Rags and bones. Any rags and bones?" His call is less a question than a signal that business can be done, all parties willing.

The cart creaks toward us, its wheels squeaking and squealing, its freight of rags and bones, rusty wire and cracked bottles grinding and clashing, rolling crazily in dizzy pattern from side to side, from end to end of the wagon.

He lifts the sweat-stained rim of his battered old hat, nods benevolently in our direction, and rattles on.

We wave. He is gone. It is a pleasant encounter.

Cut-unders pass us by, each with two softly padded seats for four passengers under a canopy of waving fringe. They offer no surprises. Their drivers are business bound, eyes fixed on the road to their destination. They are the horse-drawn taxis. We walk.

We walk in search of the organ grinder and his monkey. The monkey is our friend even though he gets money for what we aren't allowed to do—climb all over people, tweak their noses, tug at their hair, stick out his hand for pennies and, clutching them in his little fist, scuttle off, grinning. He is our friend in a world of grown-ups who can't understand why we want to act like monkeys.

The organ on wheels has what we know but can never believe: a voice locked inside, a voice that breaks free, singing, when the crank goes round. Like a dazzle in the mind, the song begins a light-filled dream that shimmers on the horizon, bursts in a moment of impossible magnificence, and then is gone. In reality the organ is scabby, shabby, scrofulous—but not in our eyes. To us it is a box on wheels that sings the romance of a faraway country in a language much softer than our own, full of longing, full of dreaming. A miracle it is when the dark little organ grinder in the dusty purple suit puts his brown fingers around the crank, starts winding in a slow circle, and out comes the full-voiced singing. "*O sole mio, O sole mio*." We can tell what it says without understanding the words. And when the singing stops, we are glad that the pennies come showering down. The monkey claws for them in the dust. The organ grinder laughs and bows, throws a general kiss, and then is gone.

From My World on an Island: Growing up in Bar Harbor, *Sylvia M. Kurson, Down East Books, Camden, Maine, 1982.*

Librarians Adeline Bunker Rumsey (1896–1906) and Inez Suminsby (1906–1942). Inez Suminsby worked at the new Jesup Library, built in 1911 in honor of Morris K. Jesup by his wife. The first library opened in 1875. The Jesup is its fourth home.

Inez Suminsby is well remembered for demanding absolute silence, and for keeping the books in brown paper wrappers and the library itself decidely on the cool side. (Courtesy of the Jesup Library.)

The Bar Harbor Historical Society Museum is located in the basement of the Jesup Library. The museum is free and open during the summer.

The society's collection includes hundreds of photographs, including this personal favorite of curator Deborah Dyer, taken in 1914 in front of Scott's Stables on Cromwell Harbor Road. All, including the horses Thistle and Reliance, appear ready for anything, including the newly arrived automobiles. (Courtesy of Bar Harbor Historical Society.)

The Hotels and the Village Green

"[A] quiet house, though of large proportions," the 350-room Grand Central stood on the site of the Village Green from 1873 to 1899. It joined the older Bay View House, visible on the left above.

The hotels kept adding new rooms, but maintained the same primitive domestic systems: wells and "direct deposit" sewage disposal. In 1873, the inevitable happened; typhoid came to town. The outbreak started at the Bay View and was limited to just over a dozen people. The specter of Bar Harbor becoming known for fevers instead of healthful sea and mountain air drove the townspeople, with help from the state of Maine, to build a wooden flume to carry water from Eagle Lake. The water arrived in town on July 4, 1874, announced by jubilant fanfare provided by the town band. During the following decade, the town built a sewer system that emptied into the bay. About a century later, it joined the outflow pipes together and installed pumps to send everything back uphill to the treatment plant.

The town bought the Grand Central in 1899 with the notion of building a town hall on the site. This idea was vetoed at town meeting, but the hotel was torn down and some of the salvaged lumber used in the Y.M.C.A. building. In 1904, the Village Improvement Association leased the land, complete with cellar hole, and built the Village Green. (Courtesy of Maine Historic Preservation Commission.)

It requires mental gymnastics to conjure up an image of what this part of town looked like in the 1880s. Stand near the Village Green clock looking down Main Street toward the water. On the left looms the ghostly facade of the Grand Central Hotel. In front, the immense Rodick House occupies the entire block from Rodick Place to Cottage Street. Across the street are the smaller Porcupine Hotel and an assortment of shops.

It all started in the mid-1840s when Tobias Roberts opened a small tavern near the harbor and found himself with an overflow of young New Yorkers sleeping in his barn. In 1855, he built Agamont House, across from today's Agamont Park.

After the Civil War, the trickle of adventurous visitors coming to Bar Harbor increased to a steady current, and by the mid-1870s there were fifteen small, very unpretentious hotels in town. A decade later, thousands came by steamer and rail-ferry. The hotels rose to the challenge by buildings hundreds of additional rooms.

Just as the hotels bloomed, summer society began to change. New people came to make Bar Harbor their own. They built impressive summer "cottages" and did not associate with hotel guests, except those staying at the Malvern (on Kebo Street) and a few other genteel places. Practically overnight, the hotels were seen as fusty, old, unfashionable—and doomed.

Sunset at Bar Harbor

1881

Mount Desert Herald

The white-capped band, brave in blue and brass, are blowing lustily their horns on a bit of green lawn in front of the Rodick House. What a motley crowd are gathered to hear them! Here a group of young tars from the government warships lying in our harbor, with flat caps and square-collared blue shirts, wide trowsers and all the conventional rig of men-of-war's men. There a little assemblage of Indians, one of whom has thrown a big pack of birch bark from his shoulders that he may enjoy the music unincumbered, looking soberly on. Several noisy urchins are pounding pebbles in imitation of the cymbal player, and tumbling pell-mell over each other on the gravelled walk. Red legged, fancy capped tennis players; blooming country maidens, in holiday attire; queenly daughters of wealth and fashion, in faultless costumes of delicate lace and muslin; old ladies, in stiff rustling silks and elaborate head dresses; gray bearded men of business, now retired and resting a bit after the bustle of a busy life before they "join the innumerable caravan that moves to the pale realms of shade"; brisk young bucks, in knobby white suits, sucking their silver-headed canes and ogling the passing ladies; groups of merry little children, cared for by trim nurse maids in snowy linen aprons—all these, and a dozen other types of humanity, are gathered to hear the band. In the spacious parlors a few dancing couples are improving the music. But soon the last rays of the setting sun gild the many windows of the Bradley Block; the twinkling lights flash out from the stores; the hotel boys return from the just opened evening mail with great baskets of letters and papers; the band men find it difficult to read their music in the rapidly waning light; the grand flourish is heard, closing the performance; the crowd go their several ways, and darkness settles over the scene. As this lovely evening, so many others.

From the Mount Desert Herald, *August 17, 1881.*

In 1888, M. H. Sweetser described the Rodick House as "a vast building on Main Street, with 400 chambers, and famous halls for music and dancing. It is said to be the largest hotel in Maine, and is the centre of much of the joyous summer life of Bar Harbor." At the time the Rodick was painted straw color with olive trim. The interior was pale pink, flesh color and café au lait. *Main Street is on the lower left; Cottage Street at lower right.*

Rodick House began as a small guest house built by David Rodick Jr. in 1866. Nine years later, Rodick and his sons expanded, increasing the hotel's capacity to 275. In 1881, they added on again, ending up with the six-story behemoth shown above. The Rodicks ran the town water company for years, and advertised that "the Rodick House is well-supplied with Eagle Lake water, from Eagle Lake, a beautiful mountain lake of the purest and coolest water, three or four miles from the village, from which an unfailing supply of the best of water is obtained, thus insuring perfect drainage...." The hotel closed in 1892 and again in 1894, and was dispatched in 1906. (Courtesy of Maine Historic Preservation Commission.)

The Evening Pastime

1880s & 1890s

F. Marion Crawford

In the evenings when there was moonlight the sight on the bay was really charming. The meal called tea at the hotels tempted no one to linger over it, and as soon as it was over the board-walk was alive with boys and girls hurrying down to the landing-stages, the young man in light flannels, sunburnt and strong, with his companion's bright shawl flung over one shoulder, while the maiden pattered along beside him, her white frock drawn up over a gay striped petticoat, after the fashion of those days, and often her own special paddle in her hand, perhaps with her initials carved carefully thereon and filled in with sealing-wax, rubbed smooth. Then there was a scramble at the floats, and a few minutes later the harbor was covered with boats and canoes, while those who were crowded out consoled themselves by sitting on the rocks along the shore. Slowly each little craft drew away from its neighbor on the quiet water, the young man pulling lazily or wielding the paddle silently with broad strokes of his bare brown arm—the girl sitting luxuriously in the stern-sheets, or on a deer-skin in the bottom of the canoe. The sun went down toward Hull's Cove; and as the red glow faded on the upper bay and the moon rose behind Schoodic, twilight merging into moonlight, the rippling note of a girl's laughter or the twang of a banjo rang softly over the water, a white speck showed where a boat was beached on the shingle of an island, while another floated like a black bar into the silver wake of the moon.

From Bar Harbor, *Francis Marion Crawford, Charles Scribner's Sons, New York, 1894.*

"Boats to Let." (Courtesy of Maine Historic Preservation Commission.)

Especially in the early years, the hotels housed young, active people who liked venturing out into the great outdoors, particularly if the expedition involved the opposite sex. Indoor pursuits were equally important. The guests ranked the hotels by social attractions: the Rodick's lobby was known as "The Fish Pond" for its romantic angling potential; another less favored was known as "The Morgue."

To address the concerns of the fashionable or would-be fashionable, the *Mount Desert Herald* offered a regular "Fashion Notes" column. One dedicated female visitor drew the attention of the *Herald* for wearing twenty-two different outfits in four days, each carefully selected to match the time of day and activity.

Fashion Notes

1881

Mount Desert Herald

It is safer to wear feathers at the seaside this summer than it has been in former years, for the uncurled variety look as well after a fog as before.

Muslin dresses with embroidered flounces reaching from belt to hem, and kerchiefs embroidered to match, are pretty for the country or for watering places.

Rough seaside hats of white straw are trimmed with a frill of lace around the crown, and one or two very short ostrich tips, and have a heavy silk cord laid outside the lace.

Lawn tennis players wear the tied-back apron to keep the full skirt in place while they are playing. A tempestuous petticoat is a good thing in poetry, but is decidely out of place when rapid running is to be done.

The latest rowing dress is called the "Newport" and is quite pretty. It is of white linen, with almost straight skirt, trimmed with narrow ruffles, edged with outline embroidery. A broad belt and a fichu [a three-cornered cape] of the linen is embroidered to match. The latter is edged with broad, linen guipure lace. The sleeves are full at the top, cut long, and cuff shaped to the arm below. A gipsey straw shade hat and a pair of light spruce oars are the proper accompaniments.

From the Mount Desert Herald, *July 31, 1881.*

The End of the Season

1881 & 1890

Mount Desert Herald

Bar Harbor Record

1881.—Now from pillar to pillar along the piazzas of the summer hotels the useful clothes-line extends itself, and the family washing furiously flaps and flaunts where erst the lazy lotus-eater lolled luxuriantly in his hammock; the heavy lumber teams have taken the place of buckboards upon our streets; and instead of red-capped tennis players in knickerbockers disporting themselves upon the green, the busy carpenters, masons and painters are making a cheery bustle and noise all over the village. The last Indian basket-maker, and the last belated tourist have taken their departure; winter is at hand, and Bar Harbor has put off its holiday attire and settled down to a busy season of work.

1890.—The summer hotels are closing their doors now against rats, moths and boarders; chloride of lime and camphor odors fill the halls, from which the cold north winds have driven all traces of "Tea Rose," "Ylang-Ylang," and "Wood Violet." The blinds of each room are closely tied; no more do feminine fingers close them cautiously 'til just enough space is left for feminine eyes to peep through at the advancing or departing depot wagons; and no more does the masculine expletive arise on the summer night air as a fixtureless blind refuses to remain open. The office and desk seem actually to throb with silence, and dumbly protest at the absence of the glorious creature who presided over them. Neatly closed lies the hotel register, with the August blotter warmly pressed against the last name in it, which is generally that of a drummer from Lynn, or "S. B. Clipper and lady," from "Cyclone Junction, Illinois." The dining room smells of washing soap and one must admit—water-bugs, and we think how long ago it seems since the Jolly Boys sat at this table, and the Prim family at that, and the old familiar murmur of "There's rose beef, rose lamb, baked coddineggsos, cole turkey'n applesos," or "Cabernet puddin, mince pie n' ice cream" flowed acceptably into our ears. The piazzas—ah, the lonely piazzas! with spiders spinning across them, or gathering in little unmolested piles in nooks and corners. Birds hop smartly about in the driveways, and the crickets chirp dismally all the shortening September days in the grass-grown tennis court. The wind whistles shrilly around the corners, and rattles the loose blinds and windows. We hear a door slam somewhere inside, and we hurriedly turn our step toward the rising smoke of the distant city, as we listen fearfully for some ghostly voice to call out, "Hot water for seventy-two!"

—*Boston Sunday Evening Gazette.*

From the Mount Desert Herald, *September 9, 1881, and the* Bar Harbor Record, *October 2, 1890.*

The Rockaway piazza. The Rockaway was located on the site of the present Agamont Park, next to the Reading Room. (Courtesy of Maine Historic Preservation Commission.)

The Battle of the Bands

EARLY 1900S

SYLVIA M. KURSON

The lines had been drawn as soon as word got around, and it got around as fast as fire in a high wind.

"Meddlin' busybodies out to do away with our own band concerts in the village green and put a piece of the Boston Symphony into the bandstand where it doesn't belong and never will!"

"No fools like old fools for not moving with the times. Sure, our band's all right for winter, but summer's another story. The rusticators want better, and they're going to get it!"

"Over our dead bodies!"

The issue was shaping up for civil war with nothing civil about it. Carnage was expected at town meeting.

...[T]hat day we could see that trouble was brewing all over the Casino. The place was packed. There was a groundswell of muttering. The moderator would have his hands full calling for order and sweet reason.

I'd never laid eyes on half the people there. They must have come out of the back of beyond to see the show and to do battle if need be. In their winter duds—earlap caps and mackinaws and high laced boots—they look fully equipped to weather whatever storms might come. I was puzzled. Why should they care who played for the village green band concerts?

The air was thickening. People were hot and mad, ready for action.

At last it was time. The gavel came down with authority. But before the moderator could open his mouth and the meeting begin, an old man in the front row was up on his feet and going nonstop.

"About this here Boston Symphony idee. I don't know who's behind it, but I know I ain't, not by a long sight and in no manner at all."

The muttering swelling to a bass roar with a heavy drumbeat of clapping.

A voice from the balcony bellowed, "Sit down up front! Hold up. You're out of order."

"Don't care if I am. I'll speak my piece here and now." And he did. The Boston Symphony should be told to stay home where they belonged.

The moderator pounded frantically.

The meeting roared him down.

The battle was engaged.

"We want our own band. They look good and they sound good and they're ours!"

"How in God's name can you compare the two? Anyone in his right mind should jump at the chance to get the Boston Symphony. It's class!"

"Yeah, but can they play as loud?"

"Oh hell, if it's noise you want...!"

The war of nerves was turning into a war of attrition with no end in sight.

It took a matron of the Eastern Stars to arbitrate. "Mr. Moderator, with all due respect, I want to put a fair motion. I move that we have our own band play four nights a week. The Boston Symphony can have the three nights in between. That way we show we stand by our own and still give the Symphony their chance."

She was a sparrow of a woman, but her eyes and voice were strong with conviction. And she was making sense—the most valued commodity in Yankee reasoning.

They didn't rise up and call her blessed, but the muttering died down to a murmuring, and for the first time that day, the voice of the gavel was heard in the land.

The motion was entertained, seconded, and put to a vote. The article passed. Once again town-meeting democracy had prevailed.

From My World on an Island: Growing up in Bar Harbor, *Sylvia Kurson, Down East Books, Camden, Maine 1982.*

The Fountain Arrives

1909

GEORGE B. DORR

"[Mr. Philip Livingston wrote from Florence, Italy] telling me that I had been right in thinking that he would like to establish some memorial in Bar Harbor for his wife but that he had already taken steps to do this in the purchase, in Florence, of a fountain for the Village Green. The fountain arrived that spring, was unpacked in the town barn for the selectmen and ministers of the town to pass upon, it being surmounted by the figure of a naked boy; and, approved after much discussion, it was erected and is there."

From the papers of George B. Dorr, NPS, Acadia National Park.

Weighty Issues at the Band Concert

EARLY 1900S

NAN COLE

[Summertime concerts from the bandstand on the Village Green] originated with a band of local musicians, each pridefully aware both of his talent and his bandman's uniform. The dark blue suits, trimmed with gold braid, were topped by blue-visored caps, and the brass buttons on the uniforms, as well as each man's shoes and band instruments all were polished to a high luster that gleamed in the lights from the bandstand.

On concert nights, our family went equipped with a blanket to spread on the ground and each of us carried a camp stool. While grown-ups chatted with friends from neighboring towns, we children would run around and play until the music started. Then we joined our parents, and woe to any one of us who made a noise! Members of the band arrived at 7:45 and when, on the dot of 8, the conductor raised his baton, a hush fell and everyone stood for America. After a program of popular marches, the band concert ended with *Good Night, Ladies.*

I don't remember just when our local musicians stepped aside in deference to talented visiting professionals, but for many years a group of thirty members of the Boston Symphony Orchestra gave weekly concerts every summer on the Green. On one occasion, we children were delighted when, in the middle of a performance, the blatant whistle at the firehouse adjoining the Green started blasting. It completely drowned out the music, and besides, no one in Bar Harbor ever purposely missed a fire, so in a moment the Green was totally deserted. The musicians, however, were stranded in the bandstand. The players had entered the stand by means of a ladder, which, once they were ensconced, was stored beneath the platform until the concert was over. Fortunately, the fire proved to be a false alarm and the audience soon returned to find the musicians lounging and smoking while awaiting rescue.

The stand on the Village Green was graced on July 21, 1910 by the President of the United States, William Howard Taft. He was the first President—since 1890—to visit us while in office, and his coming created a great furore in Bar Harbor that week....

...[W]hen President Taft was to speak from what on such occasions was called the "grandstand," I was bothered by how the committee would get that portly President up and down the famous ladder without mishap. I was too short to see from the crowd, so I pushed and elbowed my way to the front row, not noticing that I was completely surrounded by men. President Taft was already in the stand and beginning his speech. My eyes were glued upon the heavy gold watch chain, displayed across President Taft's expansive chest, which he had a mannerism of fingering as he talked. Suddenly, I heard his genial voice saying how much he appreciated the welcome given him by "the citizens and the young lady in the front row"—which caused me to grin adoringly at him from then on! I never did learn how he got up on the stand.

From "A Native's Memories of Old Bar Harbor," Nan Cole, Down East, *September 1970.*

Sunday Morning Chase

1910

BAR HARBOR TIMES

Edward B. McLean's handsome peacock, which has spent the winter more or less quietly at the McLean estate [The Briars] on the Shore Path caused quite a bit of excitement around the village green just before church time Sunday morning a week ago, and incidentally barely escaped an untimely death at the hands, or rather the teeth of a bull dog, which made an unsuccessful grab—from the point of view of the dog—at the bird and succeeding only in pulling out a few tail feathers. It seems the peacock is in the habit of escaping from the pen at the McLean place and making more or less extended excursions about town, and he chose Sunday morning for one of his periodic flights. The attention of people on the green and nearby was attracted by the frightful screeching of the peacock and quite a crowd gathered. The bird alighted on the roof of B. S. Higgins' store on Main Street and then flew to the roofs of other buildings in the vicinity and finally alighted on the green. A number of boys and men attempted the capture of the peacock and a bull dog joined in the chase ...and finally the peacock was cornered and taken in a carriage back to his pen on the McLean estate.

From the Bar Harbor Times, *May 17, 1910.*

Downtown Business

North Main Street in the 1880s. The Rodick House fills the view at the top of the hill.

M. F. Sweetser wrote the following description in 1888: "Main Street runs from near the steamboat-pier to the foot of Strawberry Hill, a distance of not quite a mile, and is lined by the chief shops of the village, and several of its hotels. It is a busy, crowded street, with plank sidewalks and borders of irregular and huddled wooden buildings. In the Oriental stores are treasures of Benares brass and India silks; at Huyler's, delicious ice-cream soda and confections, Jacqueminot roses and pink pond-lilies; at Sproul's, ice-cream and dainty viands; at Bee's, the novels and newspapers of the day; at the Indian store, odd baskets and carvings; at Koopman's and Clothier's, rare antiques and old English furniture, Norwegian silver-ware, and other precious bric-a-brac. Here, also, are apartment hotels; rooms to let; the newspaper offices of The Bar-Harbor Record, The Bar-Harbor Tourist, *and the* Mount-Desert Herald; *the financial house of Bar Harbor Banking and Trust Company; the fashionable ladies' store of L. P. Hollander & Co. (with Jordan, Marsh & Co. just off this street); decorators, milliners, lawyers, doctors, and many other offices and stores." (Courtesy of Bar Harbor Historical Society.)*

It might be best to read the following selections on a warm August afternoon while seated on a bench at the intersection of Cottage and Main Streets.

M. F. Sweetser captured the crowd of the 1880s: "The young men, in their vivid-colored and striped blazers, or garments of white India silk, their bright-colored caps and Tam-o'-Shanters, tennis suits or yachting suits, are hardly less resplendent than their sisters, the high-bred patrician girls, dressed like Parisiennes of the Faubourg St. Germain, in trim tailor-made suits, impressive in their apparent simplicity, or fairy-like in delicate summer gowns, with marvelous pleatings, vests of India silk, panels of rich velvet, sprayings of lace, and shimmerings of white lawn. Here come Peepy Marshmallow, and Lina Van Rooster, Chicky Chalmers, and Poodle Van Ulster, and the Hon. Hare Hare; and there in the background, in their moiré and black lace, are Mrs. Gatling Gunn and Mrs. Wellman Heidsieck, and even Mrs. Stylington Ribblehurst herself."

Today's sidewalk throng bears little resemblance to the above in nearly all respects. Still, there are similarities. . . .

First Stores in Bar Harbor

1835 TO 1920S

A. L. HIGGINS

Editor, *Bar Harbor Times*
Dear Sir,

My earliest recollections of East Eden (Bar Harbor) is, that it could boast of but one store, which was supposed to have everything in it from a shoe peg to a suit of "oil-skins," including groceries.

This little store was in the basement of Agamont House, at the North end of Main Street, and was kept by Mr. Tobias Roberts, who was soon succeeded by his son, Tobias L. Roberts, and each of them in turn was Post Master of the little settlement. Mr. Roberts the senior opened the business in 1835. The second business to be opened, was the general store known as "Desisle and Company." This store was opened in 1867 by E. G. and I. B. Desisle in [a] building near the Village Green. Benjamin Kittredge and his son Richmond were the proprietors of the third store which was also of the "general" variety. R. H. Kittredge is undoubtably the oldest ex-Bar Harbor business man living today.

The next general store to be opened was one operated by my brother, the late Blythn S. Higgins and myself, as Higgins Brothers, in a building near the Village Green. This building was erected in 1868 and we opened the business in 1878.

There were several little incidents which occurred during my partnership life with my brother, on Main Street, which I will always remember with a great deal of pleasure. One morning in Autumn, and before there were any banks in Town, one of the wealthiest men in the United States, if not the World, walked into our store and surprised me as follows: "Mr. Higgins, I understand that I have an account with you, and as I am leaving for the City, I wish you to loan me $1,000, to pay my family's expenses and charge it on the account." I made no excuses, and tried to show no surprise, although it nearly took my breath away. Our customers nearly all paid by cheque drawn on home banks, and there was but little cash in the whole village. I reached into our money box and counted out $400, and hastened over to our neighbor, who loaned me $400 more, and put the $800 in his hand. He thanked me pleasantly, saying: "This $800 will answer my purpose, quite as if it were $1,000."

Kittredge's Store, along with a goodly portion of the family. (Courtesy of Maine Historic Preservation Commission.)

One early morning, about the time that the Pillsbury's Best New Process Flour came on to the market, as I was fastening a barrel head to the front of our store bearing the stencilling "Pillsbury's Best XXXX" for an advertisement, I heard a voice "Hello, I guess we had better go in and interview this fellow," looking up, three nicely dressed gentlemen, in turn, grasped my hand, and one of them was Mr. Charles A. Pillsbury...manager of the greatest of all flouring mills, The Pillsbury-Washburn Co., of Minnesota, but I never learned what called Mr. Pillsbury so very far East, and how he and his associates happened to be passing our store so very early in the morning....

...The gentleman who holds the record for the longest period of active service, in any line of business, in Bar Harbor, today, is Mr. Charles Green, at the Stove, Tin & Hardware Co., of Green and Copp Co., on Main Street near the corner of Cottage Street.

From a letter to the editor from A. L. Higgins, Bar Harbor Times*, September 1933.*

Cost of Living: Cottage Life

1890

SHERMAN'S GUIDE TO BAR HARBOR

How much does it cost the visitor to live at Bar Harbor?...

People who are about to spend their first season at Bar Harbor...have very often thought it necessary to purchase their groceries and furnishings in the city and send them down here by the vessel load; they have never done it a second time. They labored under the grievous error of supposing this to be a little, one-horse, country village, with perhaps one or two general stores where the natives assembled to smoke their pipes and discuss politics and the weather. One summer's experience has shown them their mistake. They discovered that what they had paid out for freight was just so much dead loss to them, and that they could get goods here of as fine a quality and at as cheap a rate as they could in the city. Besides this, in the matter of furniture, art goods, millinery and clothing, they found here branches of the houses which they had always dealt with at home, and they were even waited on by the same people who had already grown familiar with their tastes and had served them many times over the city counters.

And there are other articles which can be procured here much cheaper than they can possibly be had in the city. Our marketmen have their own farms where they raise vegetables and force early delicacies for the table; and the milkmen have their dairies just out of the village, and supply the cottages every morning with much better milk, butter and eggs than can be had in the city. The famous creameries have agents in town also, and Darlington and other kinds of fancy butter can be always had at city prices.

There are a dozen groceries in the village, with as complete a stock of goods as any city shop can carry; and they sell as cheap. Half-a-dozen markets cater to the cottage trade, and get their meats, fish and game from the most reliable sources. The early fruits and vegetables are here as soon as they are received in the cities. Delivery wagons go on their rounds daily; and affable, intelligent clerks attend to the wants of customers. The dry goods houses are second to none in the state; the art goods, bric-a-brac and furnishing establishments, are branches of the most celebrated city houses. You can have your cottage built, and furnished from kitchen to attic in the most expensive and elegant style, without leaving the village. You can supply your table as well as you would your town house and at as cheap a rate. Ladies can procure the services of the best *modistes* and the most fashionable milliners, and gentlemen can have their wardrobes replenished and purchase lawn-tennis and yachting costumes, just as they might at home. The boot and shoe shops carry as fine a line of goods as any town shop; and the harness dealers can fit you as well as anywhere. If you are sick there are a dozen doctors of both schools who can minister to you (among them some of the most celebrated of city physicians and surgeons who make their summer home here); and there are good druggists to fill out their prescriptions.

All other businesses are well-represented. Two florists cater to the wants of society. Elegant restaurants (which if not exactly equal to Delmonico's are patronized by his patrons and considered by them first-class) furnish the tables of the cottagers, provide waiters, cater at picnics and garden parties, and serve up private dinners in their own rooms. We have an excellent photographer; stationers who keep well supplied with the best of everything in their line; booksellers and newspaper-dealers; jewellers who do fine watchmaking and repairing; and branches from city confectioners' establishments. A dozen finely equipped livery stables furnish vehicles of all kinds for the public, with excellent horses and competent drivers. Good boarding stables give accommodation to the horses of those visitors who may have no stables of their own....

The Bar Harbor Banking and Trust Co. has an office in Mount Desert Block, Main Street; and the First National Bank of Bar Harbor does business in the Rodick Block, corner of Maine and Cottage Streets. There are four law offices in the village; and real estate brokers and insurance agents are numerous.

There are music and musical instrument shops; piano tuners can be hired who can do a good job; and orchestras or bands can be had for dances or garden parties. Other trades there are, too numerous to mention, but all doing their work and selling their produce as cheap as any of the same business in the city....

What we wish to impress upon people is that THEY CAN LIVE AS CHEAPLY AND WELL AT BAR HARBOR AS THEY CAN ANYWHERE....

From Sherman's Guide to Bar Harbor, *W. H. Sherman, 1892; courtesy of Maine Historic Preservation Commission.*

A Walk Down Main Street

1894

F. MARION CRAWFORD

In order not to be left behind every self-respecting town throughout the Western world, Bar Harbor has a Main Street, which plunges violently down a steep place toward the pier, and which is beautified for a short distance by a mushroom growth of tents and shanties, the summer home of the almond-eyed laundryman, the itinerant photographer with a specialty of tintypes, and the seller of weary-looking fruit, of sandwiches that have seen better days, and temperance drinks of gorgeous hues. Plymouth Rock also vaunts its [ready-made] pants and young ladies are recommended to grow up with Castoria. Then comes the more necessary shops—the tinsmith's, at whose door a large bull-terrier benevolently grins all day; the tailor's where one may study the fashions of New York filtered through Bangor; the china shop, where bright-colored lamp shades spread themselves like great butterflies in the window, and the establishment of Mr. Bee, the locally famous and indispensable provider of summer literature, and of appropriate alleviations for the same, in the shape of caramels, cigarettes, and chewing-gum. Directly opposite stands a huge hotel, apparently closed or almost deserted, but evidently built in the years when the gnawing tooth of the national jig-saw grievously tormented all manner of wood-work, a melancholy relic of an earlier time, when, as "Rodick's," it was almost another name for Bar Harbor itself.

No lover of Bar Harbor has been found bold enough to say that Main Street is pretty; and yet, between ten and twelve o'clock on a summer's morning it has a character, if not a beauty, of its own. Alongside of the "board walk," which takes the place of a pavement, the buckboards are drawn up, waiting to be hired; in some of them, often drawn by four horses, are parties of people, consisting of more women than men, as is becoming fashionable in New England, already starting upon one of the longer expeditions, and only stopping to collect a stray member or to lay in a stock of fruit and sugar-plums. Farmer's carts, with closed hoods like Shaker sunbonnets, are on their rounds from one cottage to another, meandering through the crowd, and driven with exasperating calmness by people who sit far back in their little tunnels, and cannot possibly see on either side of them to get out of anyone else's way. Then there are all sorts of light private traps, usually driven by women or girls bound on household errands or visits, and psychologically unbalanced between their desire to speak to the friends who meet them on foot, and their anxiety lest they should be forced to recognize the particular acquaintance on whom they were just going to call.

Along the board-walk there is a row of little shops, some of them scarcely larger than booths, the proprietors of which perch like birds of passage, pluming themselves in the sunshine of the brief season, and taking flight again before the autumn gales. In one window, a lot of Turkish finery looks curiously exotic, especially the little slippers, gay with tassels and embroidery, turning up their pointed toes as if scorning the stouter foot-gear which tramps along outside. Another shop is bright with the crude colors of Spanish scarfs and pottery; in another, Japanese waters manage to keep their faint smell of the East in spite of the salt northern air, and farther on you may wonder at the misplaced ingenuity of Florida shell jewelry, and be fascinated by the rakish leer of the varnished alligator.

By one of the contrasts which make Bar Harbor peculiarly attractive, next door to these cosmopolitan shops still thrives one of the indigenous general stores, where salt fish are sold, and household furniture and crockery, and the candy peculiar to New England stores and New York peanut stands, which keeps through all vicissitudes a vague odor of sawdust, and where one may also buy, as was once advertised by the ingenious dealer, "baby carriages, butter and paint."

From Bar Harbor, *Francis Marion Crawford, Charles Scribner's Sons, New York, 1894.*

A Worthy Exhibition

1886

MOUNT DESERT HERALD

The mammoth cow, "Lady Lyon," on exhibition in a tent on Cottage Street, is well worth seeing. She is eight years old, and weighs 2,500 pounds. She is fourteen feet from nose to end of tail, and girths eight feet four inches. The cow is of the Vaughn-Durham breed, and was raised by Taber Lyon, of Manchester, Maine.

From the Mount Desert Herald, *August 18, 1886.*

Constance Southworth spent eighteen summers selling finery to the ladies of the Bar Harbor summer colony. For three years, she sold custom-made negligees, lingerie, and gifts for new babies in her own shop. For the other fifteen, she rented display rooms in several hotels.

Dressing the Ladies of the Summer Colony

1930s TO 1940s

CONSTANCE SOUTHWORTH

In the 1930s and 1940s, many of the regular summer visitors to Bar Harbor were wealthy widows and maiden ladies, past middle age, whose mornings were spent shopping and whose afternoons revolved around luncheons, tea, and dinner parties. During the shopping hours the streets were lined with high-priced motorcars, Packards, Rolls-Royces, and Pierce-Arrows being the most popular. All were driven by chauffeurs in livery, who gossiped with their colleagues while standing on the sidewalk awaiting their ladies. The lives of these society women seemed to follow the same pattern year after year.

...Many summer visitors of that time were spoken of as eccentrics. Perhaps having wealth enough to satisfy their peculiarities and whims made them different, but for all their oddities they were usually gracious, kind and friendly. Mrs. George Forsyth of New York, whose grandniece became the wife

of John Jacob Aster, called at my shop nearly every morning to make a purchase. But the next day she would return that article for exchange. Since she bought, returned and made further purchases all in one week, it took a bit of bookkeeping to catch up with her. She wore, hanging from her belt, a pedometer, because her doctor had ordered her to walk a certain distance each morning—and she would not walk a whit less nor more. Mrs. Forsyth caused me further inconvenience: she never drew a check after the fifteenth of the month because to do so made confusion between her checkbook and her monthly bank statement.

She was friendly with two cousins of former Secretary of the Treasury Andrew Mellon. Miss Mary F. and Miss Matilda Mellon, though possessed of great wealth, were very careful buyers, always being sure to receive their money's worth. I remember how hard I tried to sell Miss Matilda a simple necklace of seed pearls for a gift she wanted, at a cost of five dollars. She herself wore a fortune in Oriental pearls and her hands were covered with diamonds and sapphires. Having answered several tiresome questions about the wearability of these particular seed pearls, I was relieved to hear Mrs. Forsyth finally say in commanding tones, "Matilda, for heaven's sakes, buy them."

Mrs. Markoe of Philadelphia was a widow well along in years, who took pride in entertaining the head of the Bank of England every summer. It was well within her income to have owned a splendid car but she chose Chevrolets, an open one for fine weather and a closed one for inclement days. In the thirties a Chevrolet was not an attractive car, and certainly it was one of the lightest. Mrs. Markoe wore hats similar to those favored by Queen Mary of England, and underneath the hat she always wore a square of lace on the top of her head. A heavy woman, she sat on the rear seat of her car on the opposite side from the chauffeur, as was the custom, and the Chevrolet showed a decided list to starboard. When Mrs. Markoe had been bounced around for a spell, her hat rose higher and higher to reveal four points of the lace square covering her hair or, perhaps, the lack of it. Still, in other respects she lived in grand style, and everyday table service at her house was formal. She and I had a mild argument one day when she wrote me a check for ten dollars on a bed jacket whose price was ten dollars and a quarter. When I called her attention to this, she replied, "I know, but I never pay uneven amounts. It's so much easier to keep my accounts straight that way!"

Many ladies took little interest in their accounts. Some employed secretaries who were adept at figures, but many of these, unable to handle business matters, were engaged only in issuing and replying to invitations. The great majority of society women approved their bills and then sent them on to Morgan & Company or similar banking houses for payment. I remember Mrs. Charles Pike's telling once that she never minded how much she spent as long as she could have checks drawn for her, but she never carried cash.

...In the Depression years it was difficult to understand the attitude of those people whose incomes were not substantially cut, but were reduced just enough for them to imagine they felt a pinch. Miss Edith Bowdoin, a sweet, gentle lady, said to be worth 90 million, wrote to me that "it was so hard to make ends meet these days." She dressed in the style of the Gay Nineties all her life; shirtwaists, handmade in Paris, long pleated skirts with nipped-in jackets. Her suits were made by Pockers, who advertised that they "made suits for Gentlewomen." Deaf, and embarrassed by her infirmity, she seldom went out socially. Rumor was that she caught pneumonia when quite young while stargazing on a cold night, and that this brought about her deafness. She carried with her a large box for batteries, to which was attached a long horn; this was her old-fashioned hearing aid, and to my knowledge, she never used a more modern instrument.

When Miss Bowdoin rode in her Pierce-Arrow touring car, she wore a veil over her hat and wrapped herself warmly in an old golf cape. I made a burnoose, copied after the great cloak of that name worn by the Arabs, but without the hood. Of black broadcloth or tweed, it was especially convenient and warm for motoring, since few cars were heated then. When not in use as a cape, a burnoose could be folded in a square for packing or used as a robe. But as long as I knew Miss Bowdoin, I could never persuade her that this useful garment would be preferable to her worn and bulky golf cape.

Inordinately fond of animals, Miss Bowdoin owned a beautiful chow dog. An aristocrat among dogs, certainly, he was so haughty he appeared to be completely devoid of affection even for his mistress. A special seat was built into her cars for him, and she was said to have spent $5,000 for a New York veterinarian's services one summer when the dog was ill. Much of her time she motored about, placing pails along the roadside beside brooks and streams so that animals might drink while traveling.

...I soon learned that no matter how busy I might be I must drop all other work to receive Miss Bowdoin. Once when I called on her and before we went to her lovely cool, green and white drawing room, she rang for the butler to take the dog upstairs via the elevator. I had come to show her some scarfs with deep fringe or tassels, then popular, and had color swatches of 30 or 40 shades. Miss Bowdoin ordered so many one season that she had to employ a maid just to catalog and pack them.

Little Miss Cope of Germantown, Pennsylvania, spent a lifetime of summers on Mount Desert Island. When I knew her, she was in her nineties, a tiny lady always dressed in blue or gray wool. She loved buying pretty things, and would walk around the shop feasting her eyes and often clapping her hands with pleasure. Her Quaker chauffeur and companion encouraged her to buy, saying, "This would become thee."

... My strangest experience came one day when a well-known New York lady walked into my shop. I soon noticed that she was attracted to a wrapper in two shades of green, that was hanging on a form. "Would this wrapper fit my daughter-in-law?" she asked. I was then forced to ask, "Do I know your daughter-in-law?"

"Well, maybe not," she admitted. "She summers on Long Island. But do you think this would fit her?"

Trying to be helpful, I inquired, "Is she my size?"

Thoughtfully, the lady answered, "No, she is larger than you but smaller than I."

Since I wore a size 12 dress and my potential buyer would have burst the seams of a size 42, I came to the crux of the matter by asking for her daughter-in-law's bust measure.

Whereupon the lady charged to the door, I following her, and, once on the sidewalk called in a loud voice for Gustav, her chauffeur. He left the cluster of chauffeurs with whom he was talking and came running towards his lady. But he had only run a step or two before his lady, in tones audible for a full block, called, "Gustav, Gustav, do you know my daughter-in-law's bust measure?" The chauffeur, rocked back on his heels by the question, features purple with embarrassment, apologized, stammering, "No, no, Madam, I—I—don't believe I do."

From "End of an Era," Constance Southworth, Down East, *September 1978.*

West Street and Devil's Half-Acre

A family selling their wares at the Indian encampment near Hamor's wharf and sawmill at the foot of Holland Avenue. For many seasons in the mid-1800s, the Penobscots and Passamaquoddies came to Bar Harbor to sell their crafts and other products like furs and gull feathers to eager buyers in the summer colony. They advertised in the Mount Desert Herald: *"The camp is open on pleasant evenings until half-past ten o'clock, and will be found both quiet and orderly.* Perfectly safe for anyone to visit. *Goods purchased at this encampment will be delivered to any part of the village free of charge." The Indians stayed at Holland Avenue until 1888, when they were asked to leave. Various alternate sites were suggested for them, including the Porcupine Islands. They finally settled near the present ballfield in a spot that became known as Squaw Hollow. George Dorr bought the land at Squaw Hollow in 1910. (Courtesy of Maine Historic Preservation Commission.)*

West Street is, and was, a road with a split personality. For most of its distance, it is a quiet street lined with trees, summer cottages, year-round homes and inns. It becomes busier and more commercial as it heads down to the harbor.

Until the 1890s, West Street ended at Holland Avenue, which continued on to the water. The growing community of summer cottagers petitioned to have it extended to Eden Street.

The shore at Holland Avenue was known as the Devil's Half-Acre and was the site of a thriving summer craft cooperative operated by Penobscot and Passamaquoddy Indians. Their land was sold for summer cottages in 1888.

Many of the summer cottages along West Street have survived, including the Bowdoins' cottage La Rochelle, now home of the Maine Sea Coast Mission. The residential part of the street is listed on the National Register as a Historic District.

The waterfront end of West Street was always busy. The coal, wood, garbage and other working wharves were jammed along the remaining navigable water west of the steamboat and livery boat wharves. The West End Hotel, a laundry, baths, the Rodicks' ice-houses, a bowling alley, the electric plant and a variety of unassuming homes and businesses filled the available space along the street. It is rumored there was also at least one establishment of entertaining women nearby.

This selection is taken from a summer novel by Mrs. Burton Harrison, the owner of Sea Urchins on the Eden Street shore. She writes from her particular viewpoint, and undoubtably arranged her story for dramatic effect. It may not be immediately evident, but the narrator of this story is a small dog.

A Visit to the Indian Camp

1887

MRS. BURTON HARRISON

Having failed to reach the Indian camp ...we walked there the next day. Nothing worthy of note occurred until we encountered, in a cove where a small fresh-water stream flowed to the sea, a most agitating cow. I observed my mistress gather her skirts around her and look to the right and left, as if seeking some easier method of reaching the path beyond where the cow stood...[and] when my mistress finally made up her mind to pass the enemy, I observed her close her eyes. We followed suit, and when safely up on the steep hillside above, I turned and barked furiously at the creature....

...It was a pleasant walk across the bluff leading to the Indian camp. So many wild-roses grow there, amid thickets of sweet-fern and vanilla grass, that the air was embalmed with odors. Approaching the settlement in the rear, we saw more of their inside life than in front, where all is swept and garnished for customers. Old women hovering over pots and kettles; girls up to their elbows in dye-stuff; old men mounting birds, curing seal-skins, or hanging upon lines the dyed splits to be woven into baskets; dogs and babies without number...My mistress told the boys they must look respectfully upon these tribes, since they were lords of the soil long years before the mushrooms of summer aristocracy sprang up in Maine. During the Revolution the Penobscots were allies of the colonists, she said, and for their services were allowed to keep a large tract on the Penobscot River. But, like most old grandees in this America of ours, they have parted with their estate, and are struggling on to-day in the effort to make a living. That they are brave, patient, and law-abiding in the communities where they wander now as aliens, none deny. In religion many of them are Catholics, attending on Sunday the little Church of St. Sylvia [on Kebo Street], nestling beneath the crest of Malden Hill in Bar Harbor. I remember we met an Indian maiden once upon her way from Mass, in her fashionably-made polonaise [an 18th-century dress with a split skirt and elaborate underskirt] of ruby velvet, and Gainsborough hat and plumes, she looked like a bird-of-paradise in a barn-yard, beside the island girls.

With these Penobscots unite certain Passamaquoddies in the business of supplying Bar Harbor visitors with their wares. Their dwellings, half tent, half booth, are erected to leave a well-swept carriage road between the lines, and here, every day during the season, come throngs of people from whom an unsuspected philosopher like myself is able to derive a good deal of quiet fun. To see the young ladies, for example, going the rounds trying their accustomed coquetries of shopping upon those Indians! Little shrieks, pouts, conversation meant to edify the man behind the counter, flirtation with attendant

Open for business. Joseph Lola, second from the left, advertised as follows in the 1886 Mount Desert Herald*:*

At the
INDIAN ENCAMPMENT,
near Hamors Wharf, Bar Harbor
Season of 1886.
A large assortment of Indian Wares of all kinds.
Baskets of every description.
A very fine assortment of Sea Fowl Feathers.
Toy Canoes, Bows, Arrows, Etc.
Please call and examine our wares.
JOSEPH LOLA, PASSAMAQUODDY INDIAN, CAMP NO. 100.

(Courtesy of Maine Historic Preservation Commission.)

swains, are so much wasted ammunition. Lo! the poor Indian looks down on them utterly.

Within the booths are draperies of red and blue and orange calico, or bunting. Broad shelves serving as counters, present a charming medley of harmonious colors. Baskets of every shape and tint are piled into glowing masses. Seal-skins and deer-skins, pipes and sticks fashioned from distorted roots, canoes and paddles great and small, snowshoes, lacrosse-bats, bows and arrows, moccasins and caps—what do not their skilful fingers put into captivating guise to witch away the money of the idler? Then there are the gulls' breasts and wings, stuffed owls, pearly grebe plumage, and, their latest novelties, wood-baskets and flower-pots of birch-bark, etched with a frieze of native scenes.

Lola, the queen, is a sovereign of generous proportions, living in a circular tent, around which are planted vines of the California cucumber, and sun-flowers. We found her that day sitting on a low split-bottomed chair, knee to knee with a gossip in shawl and bonnet, suggesting Betsy Prig. Fast as her hands could fly she was shaping a waste-paper basket of deep, soft yellow, braided with vanilla grass....

...My mistress bought of Lola a flat basket to hold handkerchiefs, then passed on to a tent where the proprietor, a stately old fellow, wore a clean gauze undershirt, with bran-new slop-shop trousers.

At his feet sat the prettiest little maid, with ripe red lips, and dusky hair tied up in a knot of crimson! They had dressed in a petticoat of yellow stuff and a dark-blue jersey. Spite of the visitors who came and went, she kept busy with the playthings in her lap—a china doll, some shells, some bits of silk and ribbon packed in a small tin box....

...In another tent we found a pretty young woman, helping her husband to dispose of the sweet grass baskets, for which they were particularly famed. The man, a good-looking fellow, wore a smart red shirt, with bands of Indian work, and an embroidered belt. It so happened that every basket of which my mistress asked the price was valued at "one-dollar-half." While waiting for her to make her selection, the young squaw heard a sound we had not noticed in the rear tent, darted in there, and presently reappeared carrying in her arms a rose-bud of a baby.

"Oh! What a beauty!" exclaimed my mistress. "I suppose you will sell him, too, for a dollar and a half."

"Not for all the money in the world!" answered the mother, her stolid face becoming suddenly aglow with feeling, as she hugged her treasure close. It was a pretty little scene.

My mistress bought a square basket with a lid, and a basket without a lid. Everybody does the same at Bar Harbor. When the visitors prepare to go away the agony of packing up these fragile acquisitions is met by the Indians, who put them up in barrels, to be sent to distant points, often across the ocean. And thus it is that in a hundred homes remote from the Maine island arises at midwinter the fragrance of summer walks in the fields beside the sea. Let the wind rave as it lists, the sleet dash on the window-panes, a whiff of sweet grass brings back Mount Desert!

From Bar Harbor Days, *Mrs. Burton Harrison, Harper and Brothers, New York, 1887.*

In 1983 William Ibelle, Mark Emerson and Pamela Wood interviewed Penobscot elders for *Salt, The Journal of New England Culture*:

Violet Francis was born in the early 1900s and spent her life on Indian Island, near Old Town. She recalled, "I was brought up entirely on basketry, the sales from it. Our home was run by it, our food and everything. I used to make baskets after school hours in the winter. My work was sold the same as my mother's was sold. I'd get the money from it and that was for my school clothes and my books and it lasted me all winter.

"I made baskets up until twenty-five years ago–until I learned to work in the shoe factory over across the river. Then that was more money by the week. It was hard making money by basketry because you wouldn't get the money it was worth. We spent an awful long time, night and day, on baskets to make a living.

"When I got work in the shoe factory, I said, 'I'm through with making baskets.' I never made another one again...."

Her husband Clarence also made Indian craft items when he was young. "My father was a good carver and I done it. It was sought in those days. We used to make all kinds of Indian novelties. We go up in the woods to a camping area...take all our equipment with us. I'd make rough stock up there–go as far as we could up there without painting it. Then we'd bring it down–lots–a canoe load. Bows, arrows, tomahawks, everything, war clubs, paddles–get them in rough stock up there, bring them down and finish them up...."

Cottages vs. Hotels

1881

MOUNT DESERT HERALD

There is this difference between the hotels and the cottages. The former are full of life, bustle, activity and moving people after the gas is lit; the latter stand dark and silent behind the shrubbery in the lots and at the head of lawns as smooth and green as new billiard tables. These dwellings of the rich are what they are intended to be—summer retreats far from the "maddening crowd" where they and their families can rest and gain health and strength. While the air of the hotels is heavy with manufactured perfumes and is freighted with the sweet sounds of laughter and music, that of the cottages is laden with ozone and bracing qualities garnered up from the surface of the deep. No lights flash or brass instruments squeak melodiously in these cottages at night. No stranger or vulgar eyes stare in through the windows or boldly scrutinize the forms of its lady occupants. The blinds are drawn, the latticed shutters bowed and the lights turned down, in the front rooms at any rate. At night there is an air of peace, repose and quiet about these aristocratic residences that suggests relief to the minds of tired plodders who are too poor to have such dwellings.

From the Mount Desert Herald, *August 31, 1881.*

The Bar Harbor Swimming Club and view up Bridge Street from the Bar. The Swimming Club (1903 to 1930) was the predecessor of the currently vacant Bar Harbor Club. The large hotel is the St. Sauveur, which stood on Mount Desert Street from 1881 until 1945. (Courtesy of Bar Harbor Historical Society.)

An Evening at the Swimming Club

EARLY 1900S

NAN COLE

The goings-on that were common knowledge among the natives, who never divulged them to the rusticators, weren't by any means limited to the strangers' behavior. The town rocked with laughter when my brother Chet, and four of his friends, decided to sneak a dip at the pool at the Swimming Club—an exploit that called for planning, secrecy, and courage. They met outside the wire fence, scaled it, dived into the pool and swam to the float. Suddenly the night watchman appeared on the roof of one of the bathhouses, fired a shot over their heads and ordered them out. They obeyed hastily, and read in the next issue of "Town Topics" of the unidentified marauders being evicted from the exclusive pool. The item closed with this sentence: "Next day, under pressure, the directors ordered the pool to be drained because of any possible contamination of the water."

Again, the town rocked with laughter, because the boys confided only to natives that, while they were dressing, a group of giggly, illustrious females, fresh from a jubilant party, had arrived to plunge fully clothed into the pool and splash around with mermaid merriment....

From "Personal Glimpses of Bar Harbor's Lush Era," Nan Cole, Down East, *July 1969.*

Bar (Rodick's) Island

Rodick's Island portrayed by David Maitland Armstrong in his painting The Bar, Bar Harbor. *Armstrong painted the original in 1877 and reworked it in 1883. He shows a somewhat idyllic but probably essentially accurate view of the Rodicks' homestead and fishing operations.*

The tide is partially out, exposing most of the large herring weir. The rowboat is typical of those rented to visitors, and it seems likely that Armstrong used it, since the bar is a short row from the harbor. A woman and one or two small children are walking across the bar, and three men or older boys are working with a small dory at the edge of the water. The geese are also out for a stroll.

The schooner in the cove is about to be launched or has taken the ground for repairs, while a small gaff-rigged boat sails or waits at the water's edge just off her stern. Another schooner is moored off the Bluffs, just below Hulls Cove. Both schooners are typical coastal working vessels of the time.

The Rodicks' fish houses, including the smoke house, stand on the far shore. The house occupies a sheltered place at the top of the rise, below the pastures and fields. (Courtesy of Layton Art Collection, Milwaukee Art Museum, Gift of Frederick Layton; photograph, P. Richard Ellis.)

Thanks to politics, Bar Island belongs to the town of Gouldsboro, across the bay, as do all of the Porcupine Islands. It is, however, unarguably linked to Bar Harbor. The island is available to walkers who wish to keep their feet dry for about two hours either side of low tide.

Eugenia Rodick Martin recalled visiting with her aunt and uncles on the island at the turn of the century: "...[W]e could not always wait for the tide and sometimes drove either to or from the island before the tide had ebbed sufficiently to uncover the bar, and many times I remember the water seeping into the bottom of the high carriage and the horse having to swim for a few feet in the low spots. Even more exciting was to gallop across when the tide was rising and we wondered if we could make the other side."

Horses swim better than people or internal combustion engines. In recent years a couple nearly drowned when they tried to swim across the frigid, fast-moving tidal current. Several owners of off-road vehicles have discovered to their sorrow that getting stuck means watching about eight feet of water cover the prized vehicle—and slowly uncover it several hours later.

Except for one private holding, Bar Island belongs to Acadia National Park. The buildings and the herring weir are gone, but clear traces of the busy homestead that occupied the island from the early 1800s until well into this century remain.

A Tour of the Weir

LATE 1860S

BENJAMIN DECOSTA

[Weirs] are huge traps, built on shallows and bars, in which the silly fish are impounded. Selecting some spot on the shore where the tide recedes at low water, a fence of wicker-work is made with strips of deal or spruce saplings, inclosing an area varying from one-half to three or four acres. A good-sized gateway is left for the fish to go in, and when once in they do not have wit enough to attempt to go out, at least in season, but go circling around the sides, shooting past the open gate. When the tide has gone nearly down, the fisherman enters the weir with a skiff, closes the entrance, and, taking a great scoop-net, jumps into the water and soon loads the boat with handsome herring, which are conveyed ashore to be put in pickle or hung up on sticks in the great curing-house whose smoke, in these parts, ascends forever. By the process, the fish, both small and great, are alike destroyed. The small herring, indeed, have no direct commercial value, and should be carefully restored to the water as soon as taken, to perform their part in supplying the future stock; yet these are remorselessly thrown into the barrow and trundled off to manure the ground, which could easily be enriched by the inexhaustible supply of shells and other fertilizing material now lying useless upon the shore. Gentle Islander, I pray you heed the voice of reason and common sense, and, while you slay your lambs at a tenderer age, let the young fish go....

...But while earnestly deploring this waste of wealth, it must be confessed that a visit to the fish-weirs is very instructive and entertaining....

...At Mount Desert they occasionally find a good-sized shark or horse mackerel [tuna], but oftener the porpoise thus comes into the weir. Schools of these continually gambol about the bay for the edification of visitors, or as a prize for the Indians who hunt them for oil. I started once across Frenchman's Bay for their camp on Iron-bound Island, to see them at home, paddling with an old trapper in his bark canoe; but when we got halfway over a hard rain-storm set in, and we thought it best to return at once. Still the trip afforded an opportunity of testing the qualities of the "bark" on the long ocean swell. No boat could have behaved more admirably. But to return.

Sometimes the porpoise show their glittering backs close in by the quay, and seem on the point of landing for the purpose of applying for rooms....

...While visiting the weir at Bar Island, we were not favored by an interview with this creature, yet a numerous assemblage of the finny tribes awaited inspection.

The fisherman in charge was very accommodating, and ferried Amarinta and the rest over the shallow water into the weir, and then waded in with his scoop-net and proceeded to catch the herring, which rushed about the weir exceedingly frightened. When dropped out of the net into the boat, they set up a prodigious drumming. The herring in the water could be distinctly seen, their sides flashing like silver. The rest of the fish did not seem to mind our presence, and swam leisurely around the boat, or lay still while we paddled among them. Besides herring there were menhaden [pogies], silvery hake, dogfish, rockcod, sculpin, flounders, pollock, skates, and goose fish or monkfish. The two latter were extremely tame, and several of the monkfish were five and six feet long. Putting a blade of the oar into its broad mouth, this fish would hold on with its teeth until drawn up to the boat, and when alongside they would swim slowly, so that we could touch their backs with our hands. In the water, their movements are as dignified as those of an empress dragging a long train. On the other hand the skate is rather clumsy, and when I tipped them over on their backs, they had hard work to recover from this position. Such a multitude of fish, for there were thousands of them, all at home in their native element, formed a rare sight, and one for which the naturalist might well afford a journey to Mount Desert.

Cod are not taken in these weirs, but are fished with lines and trawls. This is called boat-fishing. Fishing with lines is very laborious work, as it often occupies the whole night, some fish being taken only at that time. Trawling, however, is more easy. By this method the fisherman fastens a hundred or two baited hooks at regular distances on a small rope, which is sunk to the bottom and left, each end being marked by a buoy to which they are attached. The fisherman leaves it to itself, and only goes at certain hours to rebait the hooks and take off the fish that are caught. This practice is very destructive and should be suppressed by law; that is, unless we wish to banish the cod and haddock to deep water.

Some of the fishermen talk very sensibly on this and other subjects connected with the

The Rodicks' weir in the late 1800s. The weir was taken down sometime in the early 1900s. Smaller weirs remained in Hulls Cove until the late 1970s.

Herring fishermen still trap herring in the coves along the northeastern shore, but set nets when the fish are running. (Courtesy of Bar Harbor Historical Society.)

fisheries. It was quite entertaining to go on board of their vessels as they lay in the harbor, and enter upon conversation. I found two distinct classes of fishermen, that may be called the old school and the new. The former are open to suggestions, and anxious to profit from science, while the latter kept old horse-shoes nailed to the foremast, near the deck, to drive away the witches, and think that there is no danger of exhausting the supply of fish. There were "fish enough" in the sea. "But why don't you catch them?" I inquired. "Well, they didn't know; the people threw so much 'gurry' overboard in the harbors." By this they meant the head and entrails of the fish. They seemed to think that it had something of the effect of pirates hung on the headlands in chains, or the grinning skulls of bold highwaymen, fixed on spikes over London gate. Once, as they had confessed, it was easy to go off in a boat and get fifteen dollars' worth of hake in a few hours, but now they often toiled all the night and took nothing. They did not, however, throw away all the 'gurry.' The liver and sounds, that is, the air vessels attached to the back-bone, are carefully preserved, the livers for oil, and the hake sounds for sizing, and—would you believe it, lads and lasses?—for gum-drops. It is nevertheless so, and when at the confectioner's you roll unhealthy things under your tongue, as a sweet morsel, dreaming away of the Asiatic Acacia bleeding away its rich life in a thick resinous ooze, just remember that your gum may have originated in the fish-tubs of Mount Desert.

From Rambles in Mount Desert: With Sketches of Travel on the New-England Coast from Isles of Shoals to Grand Manan, *B. F. DeCosta, A. D. F. Randolph & Co., New York, 1871.*

Daniel Rodick and Betty Hamor were married in Harpswell in 1764. Five years later they settled in Hulls Cove. Their son David, born in 1768, bought Bar Island from Mme. de Gregoire shortly before her death in 1814. His son David Jr. was born in 1815 on Bar Island and lived his entire life there.

David Rodick Jr. built a large herring weir between Bar Island and the shore. As the summer colony grew, David Jr. and his grown children found ways to fill some of its needs. They kept cows and took the milk to town. They tended and stored racing yachts instead of repairing schooners. The Rodick House and related businesses kept the elder Rodick and at least three of his sons busy. His daughter Flora and her husband Charles Pineo kept the island homestead with hired help. She raised sweet peas for a local florist and overwintered the summer people's tender perennials in her cellar. Charles Pineo was a lawyer and judge, and owned commercial properties and dealt in real estate. In 1909, Pineo sold thirty acres on the west side of the island to Morgan partner E. T. Stotesbury for $100,000. Stotesbury wanted to stop any more talk of bridges to new hotels on the island.

Pineo moved his house to the shore. In later years the family had the buildings torn down instead of allowing weather and vandals to do their work. A couple of cottages stood on the island for a short while. In 1945, John D. Rockefeller Jr. bought the western parcel and gave it to the park. Over the years, the federal government has acquired most of the island.

Exploring the Rodicks' Island

Alas, Eugenia Rodick's Uncle Milt and the boys working at the fish house will no longer hear anyone who stands on the Bar Harbor shore and hollers for a ride in the dory, as she and her brothers used to do.

Today's choices: row, paddle or walk across to Bar Island at low tide. If you go by boat, be sure to pull the boat well up on the shore and tie it off securely above the high tide line so that it does not float away.

On the island shore, only some suspiciously flat spots indicate where the small cottage and fish houses once stood. The harbor shoreline has changed since this photo was taken. The bar's harbor side is protected from wind and seas coming from the northern quarter, but it looks like an oceanfront beach when swells generated by fall hurricanes or winter northeasters break upon it.

Herring caught in the weir were smoked and also sold as fresh bait to passing Banks fishing schooners. The weir crew put up a flag to signal the schooners when the herring were running. The baitfish had to be iced, so the Rodick family cut ice at Eagle Lake and Witch Hole Pond, and stored it in large houses in the harbor. The ice also kept the food and drinks cold in the Rodicks' expanding hotel.

At the turn of the century, Milton Rodick and a small crew ran the fish business. They lived in the small cottage at the foot of the hill. The fish house was two stories high; Eugenia Rodick Martin estimated its dimensions at 80 by 200 feet. A small car ran along a track from the water to one end of the fish house, the floor of which was two and a half feet above the ground-level tracks so the fish could be dumped easily onto the floor. The fresh fish were strung through the gills and mouths on stringers three or four feet long, then fastened to huge racks in the smokehouse. The smokepots were located at one end so that the prevailing winds would carry the smoke through the racks. The crew adjusted vents in the building's walls to keep the smoke circulating.

The Rodick homestead. The date of the photograph is unknown, but it must have been taken after the early 1880s and probably was taken in the late 1880s or early 1890s. (Courtesy of Bar Harbor Historical Society.)

The family gathered at the weir when the fish were running well. At times the weir was so full of herring that it was possible to get out of the boats and "wallow around on the solidly packed fish." In 1891 the *Bar Harbor Record* noted that there were more herring in the Rodick weir that year, but that thousands of bushels were turned loose for want of a market.

The Rodicks also caught other fish in the weir. Mackerel arrived in season, chasing herring or other bait fish. The children hunted flounder with spears whenever the water was still and shallow enough.

The road on the island rises in a gentle curve close to the north shore. The original road followed a different route.

Eugenia Martin described coming up the hill to the house. The road passed a field on the left about halfway to the house, then turned and "ran up to a house which stood very high; four steps from the road, then a sloping walk and four or five more steps." Lilac bushes covered the bank from the house to the road.

Based on the photo above and her description, it looks like the road went directly up the hill from the shore. Sizable trees now completely cover the lower fields and the old road.

Flora Rodick Pineo loved to garden, and her plants give the best clue to the location of the house. The house site is completely overgrown. The lilacs form a nearly impenetrable thicket on the upper side of the road. Hardy survivors of the flower gardens, including lilies of the valley and day lilies, grow in the dappled shade of the now-wooded house site. One small cellar hole is the only remaining remnant of the house.

Eugenia Martin remembered peonies, tiger lilies, sweet william, phlox, lupines, columbines, bleeding hearts, rambler roses, nasturtiums and golden glow growing in her aunt's flower beds between the house and the barn. The lupines, roses and other persistent garden plants still thrive in the same general area and have taken over new territories in the passing decades.

David Rodick picked a sunny spot with a view for his house. The hardwood forest north of the house provided shelter from winter winds and a continuing supply of excellent firewood. Beeches and oaks grow well on this side of the island, where the soil is deep and well-drained. The Rodick children played on swings hung from the oak trees at the edge of the woods overlooking the garden.

Over the years David Rodick Jr. added on to his father's small cape. By the early days of this century, the house had a kitchen and pantry, a dining room with another large pantry, a parlor that was used "only on state occasions," a downstairs bedroom, and a living room with a bay window offering a fine view to the west over the bay. Presumably there were more bedrooms on the second floor. The front door opened to a front hall and had a fanlight and sidelights.

The site of the barn is by far the easiest part of the homestead to locate: a large rectangular shape outlined clearly in the field northeast of the road (especially clear when the grass is short). The barn's ramp now leads into the air.

There was a pasture behind the barn. When Eugenia Martin was a child, the pasture was used for the everyday horses: Nancy, a gray work horse; Fencer, the going-to-town driving horse; Racquet, the children's quarterhorse; and Molly, Charles Pineo's trotting horse. In winter, they used a pung, or a low sledge with a driver's seat, for trips to town. It had wooden runners because steel runners were easily racked up by crossing the stony bar. Wooden ones lasted longer and were easier (and cheaper) to replace.

The Rodicks kept cows and a few pigs. They also raised sheep on the neighboring island, called, sensibly enough, Sheep Porcupine. For many years, the family spun their wool and wove it into cloth. Eugenia Martin remembered her Aunt Flora knitting all the family's stockings and mittens, although the family had long since given up making their own cloth.

The homestead's workers were up at dawn and kept at it until long after dark. The cows had to be milked twice a day, water hauled from the well "in the middle of a big cleared field," and the people and animals fed. Butter was churned twice a week, and chickens or ducks prepared for the pot every Sunday.

A small tool shed and work building stood next to the barn. Sweet pea beds lay just beyond the shed. The flowers were cut every afternoon, stored in the dirt cellar overnight, and taken to the florist's the next day by Royal Young, the hired man.

The family kept a large vegetable garden farther down the road, where they raised beans, peas, potatoes, corn, squash, lettuce, pumpkins, beets, carrots and tomatoes.

A large yellow stable stood on the opposite side of the road. It housed Charles Pineo's collection of fine trotting horses.

The apple orchard lies beyond the barn site. Flora Pineo took particular interest in the trees, and conducted grafting experiments, working alongside the hired men.

A long line of kennels beyond the orchard and vegetable garden housed Charles Pineo's nationally known purebred pointers. He kept about 200 dogs. Eugenia Martin recalled that she was "awed by the dogs, as they jumped up and barked in a most terrifying manner." Ailing dogs, as well as new mothers and their litters, were cared for in the yellow stable. The puppies found favor with the children and appear in several family photos.

The farm road ended at the poultry yards that lay "at the edge of the pine grove" at the foot of "The Mountain," the island's eastern end.

The Rodicks leased a site on the northern shore to the Mount Desert Canoe Club in 1888. By the early 1900s the abandoned club was "a relic," but its porch provided a nice place for a picnic. The family also gathered on the island's western shore to watch the sun set over the bay, a fine way to end the day that can be shared with them by those who visit the island today.

Note: Eugenia Rodick Martin's generation was the last to live on the island and to remember what family life in those times was like. We are grateful to her for sharing those memories. Her 1938 memoir is kept in the collection of the Bar Harbor Historical Society, along with other Rodick family papers.

Bar Harbor from Rodick's Island in the late 1880s. The Rodick House, in the center, is in its glory. The large hotel to the right, above the bar on West Street, is the West End Hotel, which was a close runner-up to the Rodick with rooms for 400 guests. It was built in 1881 and torn down two decades later. The Summit Hotel on top of Green (Cadillac) Mountain is dimly visible through the haze above the West End.

From left to right, the mountains are (old names first): Newport (Champlain), Round Peak or Picket Mountain (Huguenot Head), Dry (Dorr) Mountain and Green. The Gorge is in the middle. (Courtesy of Bar Harbor Historical Society.)

Acadia

Acadia National Park occupies about 40 percent of the town of Bar Harbor.

Nearly all of the land in the park was given by private donors, many of whom were members of the summer colony. A private land trust formed by the summer residents began acquiring land in 1901; fifteen years later the federal government accepted the trust's lands as a national monument after George Dorr did some earnest talking to Congressmen, assuring them that the island was not a desert and not so close to the arctic that no one would ever visit. He convinced them of the island's favorable climate by explaining that he swam in Frenchman Bay every day of the year. Since they did not ask, he did not say that he swam alone during most of the year, especially when it was necessary to break the ice first. The national monument achieved park status in 1919 and grew steadily thereafter through donations from generous individuals.

The Acadia route follows the Park Loop Road from the visitors' center at Hulls Cove to Ocean Drive, Jordan Pond and Cadillac Mountain. The park loop road system is eligible for the National Register of Historic Places and has a fascinating history of its own.

John D. Rockefeller Jr., George Dorr and other early park planners designed the loop road as a system. Road sections were built from 1927 to 1958. Rockefeller's crews built the first section from Jordan Pond to Eagle Lake, and Ocean Drive; park crews took over thereafter, although Rockefeller stayed involved in planning and design. The loop road fits well into the landscape because it was so carefully conceived and built. The Olmstead design firm planned several sections, including Stanley Brook Road (1936) and Paradise Hill to the Kebo Valley Golf Course (1938).

By the second World War the loop itself was essentially complete, except for the connection between Bear Brook and the shore at Schooner Head. Sightseers could drive around a loop by taking a short connector road (still visible just past the Beaver Dam Pool) over to the Schooner Head Road, then returning to the park loop road at Great Head. This final section was a controversial problem; the land between Bear Brook and Schooner Head was all private property. One proposed route that was heavily opposed went down the west side of Champlain and up over the saddle below the Beehive to Sand Beach. It was abandoned in favor of the present route, and the park slowly acquired the properties it needed. The final section along the eastern slope of Champlain Mountain was finished in 1958.

Getting Around

The park loop road is an excellent starting point, but many of the places mentioned in the following stories can be reached only on foot, or by bicycle, skis, horse or small boat. Signs of the past, from the remains of abandoned structures to changes in the landscape, await the curious and careful observer.

Illustration from Souvenir Guide to Bar Harbor and Mount Desert Island, *undated, courtesy of Maine Historic Preservation Commission; loop road information from Jim Vekasi, Chief of Engineering, Acadia National Park.*

1. Visitors

2. The Great Fire: Paradise Hill and Duck Brook

3. The Gorge and Sieur de Monts

4. Robin Hood Park, Jackson Lab and High Seas

5. Schooner Head and Egg Rock

Note: Egg Rock is in the town of Winter Harbor.

6. Great Head, Sand Beach and Ocean Drive

7. Otter Cliffs and Otter Point

8. Jordan Pond

Note: Jordan Pond is in the village of Seal Harbor.

9. Eagle Lake

10. Cadillac (Green) Mountain

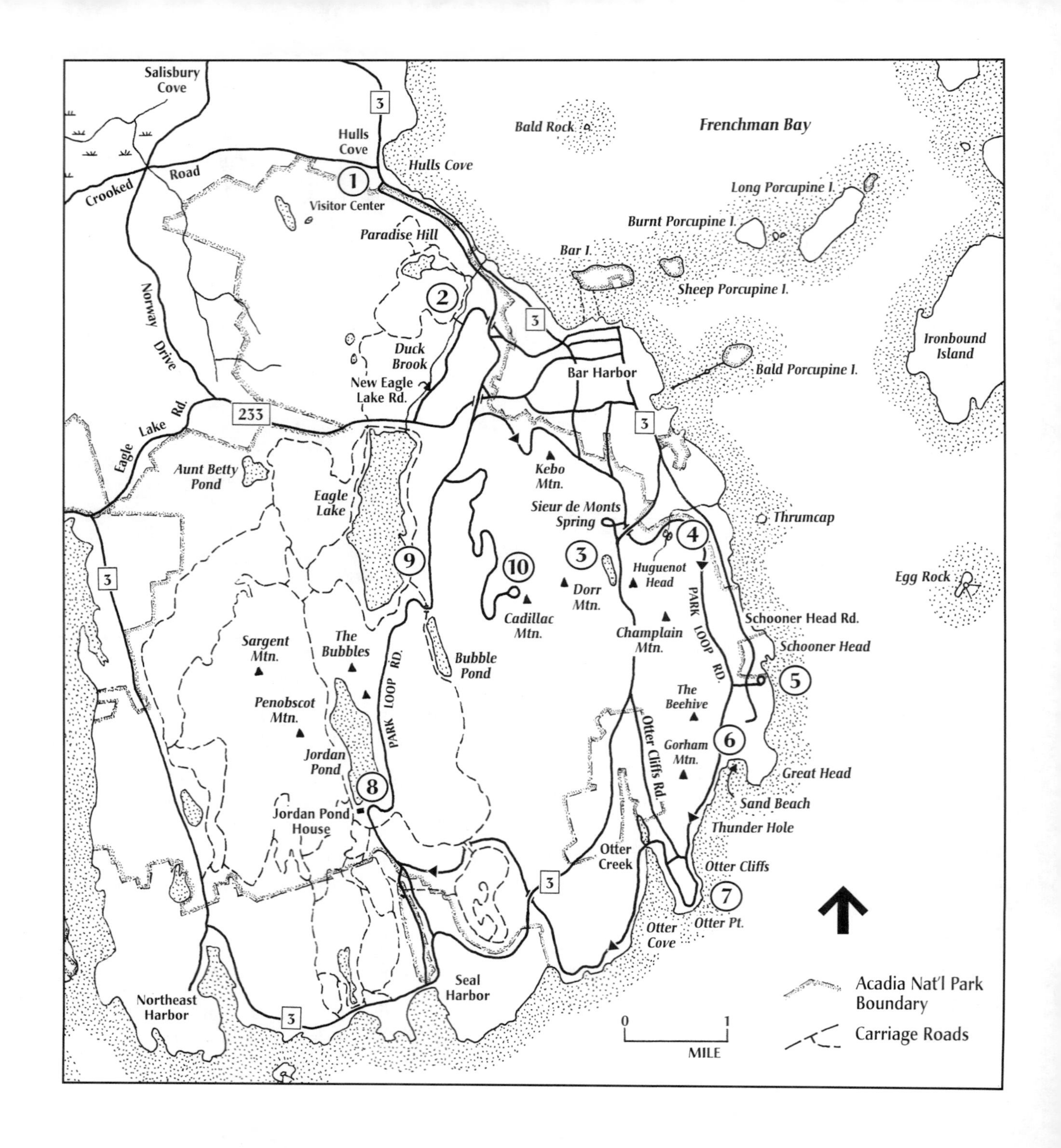

An afternoon picnic on the ledges. (Courtesy of Maine Historic Preservation Commission.)

In the mid-1930s reporter Henry Buxton spoke to former Judge Charles B. Pineo about the creation of Acadia National Park:

"Thirty-five years ago those of us who were really interested in the proper development of Bar Harbor realized something must be done to preserve this natural wonderland for posterity. We did not like the thought that the time was not far distant when these incomparable mountain tops would be disfigured with 'keep off' signs of private owners. We felt that these beautiful acres jewelled with ten fresh water lakes, and bounded to the eastward by the tumbling Atlantic were the natural heritage of the American people, and should be incorporated into a park where they would be available to every beauty-loving citizen. We formed a group of eight with Charles W. Eliot, former president of Harvard, as chairman, but the prime mover was George B. Dorr, now living at the age of eighty. It was due almost entirely to Mr. Dorr's tireless activity that we received authority from the Legislature to buy and hold land in the interests of the public. And now this initial effort has resulted in the establishment of a national park that is second to none in the United States for sheer beauty."

A visitor might do well to share an ocean view, take a child for a hike or go for a quiet ride on the carriage roads in thanks to those who saw what Acadia could be.

My Vacation at Mount Desert

1881

"Shepard"

Mount Desert Herald

Dear Editor.—What shall I send you in exchange for a sweet invigorating breath from Bar Harbor, a breeze from your fragrant mountains, or just one restful feeling coming with sound of rippling brook and dashing wave?

Sitting here at my desk, with only white marble walls between me and intense heat, there comes a longing for another row among the islands in your lovely bay, another tramp along the bed of Duck Brook; a buckboard ride to Spouting Horn, and another to Thunder Cave, the Ovens and the Cliffs; a day's ride to Somesville, a good dinner and home in the evening; a moonlight ride to Salisbury Cove, a row across Jordan's Pond to the foot of the Bubbles, and the lovely ride home through the forest, with grand old Newport [Champlain] and Dry [Dorr] Mountains towering on either side—one 1,200, and the other 1,000 feet above the sea, over a road as perfect as the suburbs of our own beautiful city can boast; or a snug little rocking chair on the Rockaway porch, listening to the whispering, splashing and roar of the ever restless tide, enjoying at the same time one of your spicy *Heralds*, or a pleasant chat with friends—or if it is evening the illuminations from the many yachts in the harbor....

[John James] Audubon visited your lovely island while he was preparing his magnificent "Birds of America." [Harvard geologist Louis] Agassiz also, who has made the pathway of the natural sciences so bright and entertaining, stood with uncovered head in the shadow of your mountains, and laid his hand tenderly upon their rocky brows. How they would start with surprise and admiration could their eyes (long since closed to earthly beauties) gaze upon the wonderful transformation of Mount Desert. Its natural glory is unchanged, but the village of Bar Harbor has since sprung up in all its loveliness, and partakes strongly of the name of the town (Eden). Nestling between mountain and ocean, her streets lined with fine cottages, some of them with elegant pretentions, and her fields covered with the sweet wild rose. Thriftiness also mingles with her beauty in the shape of many fine hotels, and pretty little stores, where almost everything can be purchased, from the dainty skein of silk, to the crawling crocodile; to say nothing of the steam grinding mill built and run by Morrill and Palmer, two enterprising young bachelors from Bangor.

Poets may sing, and artists paint, but one must use one's eyes, ears, lungs and appetite, to fully appreciate Mount Desert, and I am already growing impatient for another summer to come, that its sea-girt shores may again welcome.

Shepard
Washington, D. C.
September 10, 1881

From the Mount Desert Herald, *September 17, 1881.*

Bicycling

Late 1890s

Souvenir Guide to Bar Harbor and Mount Desert Island

There are better roads for bicycling on this island than can be found in any other part of the state. Since the safety pattern of bicycles came into general use, wheeling has become one of the most popular pastimes, and rich and poor, young and old, male and female, enjoy the scenery of the island a-wheel. The hard smooth roads wind about through picturesque glens past bold mountain barriers, skirting the shore of beautiful lakes and ponds, leading to scenes far dearer to the lovers of nature than all the wealth of art. The Bar Harbor Village Improvement Association and several of our prominent summer residents are interested in the plan of building bicycle paths. Already one very charming path has been constructed—It leads from Robin Hood Park on the Gorge Road and intersects the Schooner Head Road near the residence of Mr. Joseph Pulitzer. [It led from the site of Jackson Lab on Route 3 to the Schooner Head Road near the shore at Bear Brook.] The Ocean Drive and Bay Drive [Route 3 from Bar Harbor to Hulls Cove] are very popular with wheelmen, as the roads are comparatively level and in fine condition. There were at least 500 wheels brought into Bar Harbor last season.

From Souvenir Guide to Bar Harbor and Mount Desert Island, Illustrated, *no author, undated; courtesy of Maine Historic Preservation Commission.*

Flora and Geology of Mount Desert

1894

Edward L. Rand and John H. Redfield, With William Morris Davis

Mount Desert and Its Flora

Mount Desert Island, called by the Indians Pemetic ["a range of mountains"] lies about one hundred and ten miles east of Portland, on the coast of Maine, and less than half that distance from Rockland on the western shore of Penobcot Bay. Its coast is washed by the Atlantic Ocean on the south, by Blue Hill Bay and its tributaries on the west, and by Frenchman Bay and its tributaries on the east and north. On the northwest Mt. Desert Narrows, a shallow strait connecting the water of these two bays, is crossed by means of two bridges, connecting Thompson Island with the mainland on the north, and with Mount Desert Island on the south. The area of the island may be estimated at about 100 square miles; its greatest length being about fifteen miles, from Hadley Point in Eden on the north to Bass Harbor Head in Tremont on the south; its greatest breadth, about twelve miles, from Great Head in Eden on the east to the Cape in Tremont on the west. The coast line, especially of the southern and western shores, is extremely irregular. Up the centre of the Island for fully half of its length from north to south, through the mountain range, passed the fiord of Somes Sound (or "The River"), a deep arm of the sea, dividing the island into two almost equal sections. Across the centre from Western Mountain on the west to Newport Mountain on the east stretches the granitic range of mountains that has given Mount Desert its name, rising almost from the sea to heights varying from about three hundred to over fifteen hundred feet. Towards the north the ground slopes to the farming lands of Eden and the great meadow of Northeast Creek, and towards the southwest to the meadows of Marsh Creek, to Great Heath and the boggy wilderness below Hio [in Manset]. Between the peaks of the granitic range lie deep valleys, filled either by an arm of the sea, as Somes Sound, or by a lake or pond of more or less magnitude. These are mountain ponds for the most part, many of them of great depth, with rocky shores broken by stretches of sand or gravel beaches. None of the streams are of much size, and the regularity even of their natural flow has been greatly diminished by the wanton destruction of the woods about their water sheds....

...One of the most marked characteristics of the Island flora is its not only strongly northern, but arctic character. On its coast, enveloped in cold fogs and washed by waters chilled by the arctic current, it's no wonder that arctic plants...should find a congenial home. Moreover, this character of the flora is shown by the fact that, with one exception, *Lycopodium selago* [a clubmoss], the mountain plants descend to sea level. Neither on the one hand is the altitude of the mountain summits sufficient to develop an alpine flora, nor on the other hand is the warmth and general character of the lowlands sufficient to bring many of the plants of the middle temperate region thus far up the coast of Maine. The flora, then, may be said to be essentially Canadian, having close relations with the very similar flora of New Brunswick. It also shows, apart from its maritime character, many points of resemblance to the general flora of the White Mountain region....

With A Note on Field-work From the Geologist

...[T]he reader, if he is not versed in the interpretation of evidence presented in the language of the rocks, is likely to regard the whole subject as something of a mystery.... If the reader will walk patiently over the island, look closely, and think clearly, the whole argument may be apprehended.... Seldom are geological facts more plainly presented....

We have coasted in good company and under good pilotage along the rocky shore, landing for our geological discoveries even as old Champlain may have landed for his geography, and returning to our vessel at night. We have clambered up pathless glens to rugged summits; and if we carried rations for only half a day, we felt nevertheless the spirit of the explorers in unknown lands, and our adventures were recounted around campfires in the evening. Our vacations are shorter now than then, and while recalling them in this writing we must leave to others the pleasures on sea and shore once our own....

From Flora of Mount Desert Island, Maine: A Preliminary Catalogue of the Plants Growing on Mount Desert Island and the Adjacent Islands, *Edward L. Rand and John H. Redfield, University Press, Cambridge, 1894; Thorndike Library, College of the Atlantic.*

Acadia National Park History in Brief

1901: Charles W. Eliot, president of Harvard, calls a meeting of leading men of the summer colony to discuss the creation of a land trust for the island.

1903: The Hancock County Trustees of Public Reservations is chartered by the state of Maine.

1908: The HCTPR receives its first gift of land: a tract containing the Beehive and Bowl on Newport Mountain; George Dorr, with financial support from John S. Kennedy, of New York, acquires the 85-acre old hotel site on the summit of Green (Cadillac) Mountain from Daniel Brewer's heirs.

1908–14: The HCTPR acquires all or part of the following mountains: Dry (Dorr), Newport, Picket (Huguenot Head), Pemetic, Jordan (Penobscot), Sargent, and the Bubbles. George Dorr travels to Washington to seek federal acceptance of the land as a National Monument.

1910–12: With state permission, the HCTPR takes Eagle Lake and Jordan Pond watersheds by condemnation.

1913: A local group tries to get the HCTPR's charter revoked. The effort fails, but Dorr rethinks their options.

1914: John D. Rockefeller Jr. begins building carriage roads on his own land near Seal Harbor and on land owned by the HCTPR. Rockefeller also begins working with Dorr on land acquisition, at Dorr's request.

1916: After two years of legal work and politics, President Woodrow Wilson signs the proclamation creating Sieur de Monts National Monument. The new park includes about 6,000 acres.

1919: After more months of legal work and politics by Dorr, President Woodrow Wilson signs the bill creating Lafayette National Park.

1929: The park accepts a gift of land on the Schoodic peninsula and acquires a new name–Acadia–in deference to the anti-French feelings of the donors.

1935: John D. Rockefeller Jr. informs Secretary of the Interior Harold Ickes of his gifts to date: more than 2,700 acres costing over $250,000; buildings, roads, bridges, forestry and plantings, $500,000; new lands to be given, over $600,000; roads and other improvements on those lands, over $500,000; roads in the park, $2,000,000; total expenditure, $4,000,000. Rockefeller's land gifts would total about 10,000 acres.

1996: Acadia National Park includes 35,000 acres on Mount Desert Island, Schoodic and Isle au Haut. Approximately three million people visit each year.

Getting Around

1930

Acadia National Park

Well-arranged motor bus trips may be taken about the island and through the park during the summer season. The buses run on regular schedules twice a day at 10:30 A.M. and 2:00 P.M. The charge for the morning trip is $1.50 per person; the charge for the afternoon trips is $2.00 per person.

The routes followed are not identical and by taking the combination of the two all points of interest are seen. In addition to the motor-bus trips public cars with competent drivers, or, if desired, cars without drivers, may be hired at reasonable cost for special trips....

Arrangements may be made at the publicity office in Bar Harbor or at the Jordan Pond House at Seal Harbor for buckboard trips or for the hiring of driving and saddle horses, to enjoy the remarkable scenery afforded by the driving road and bridle path system in the park. Buckboard trips leave the Malvern Hotel, Bar Harbor, and the Jordan Pond House, Seal Harbor, daily at two o'clock in the afternoon. The charge is $2.00 per person....

From Circular of General Information Regarding Acadia National Park, Maine, *U. S. Government Printing Office, 1930; courtesy of Patricia Tierney and Heidi Welch.*

I Was Wondering...

Acadia National Park Rangers

1938

- Are you a forester?
- What do you do in the winter?
- How can you tell a virgin tree from the others?
- This is a real rock, isn't it?
- Does the sea cruise include the trip up Cadillac Mountain?
- How does this compare with the Grand Canyon?
- What good are starfish?
- Do the tides come in by daylight or standard time?

At Thunder Hole:

- Is this what they call Cadillac Mountain?
- Is that water salty?
- Is this the whole shore from that point (Otter Point) back to Bar Harbor what they call Thunder Hole?
- I left Bar Harbor for the Municipal Pier. Is this the right road?
- Are there any private beaches around here? (Very few.) Well, we want a place where everyone can go swimming.
- Is this the ocean? (Well, yes.) Well, is it the Atlantic Ocean?
- Is this natural, or did they blast it out?

On Cadillac Mountain:

- How deep is it to the ocean?
- How does this compare with Mount Everest?

From the naturalist notes files; courtesy of NPS, Acadia National Park.

The Great Fire: Paradise Hill and Duck Brook

The Great Fire on October 23, 1947, as it appeared from the Trenton Airport. (Courtesy of Bar Harbor Historical Society; Brown's Studio.)

The trees on Paradise Hill and along Duck Brook are beginning to hide the views. This is progress.

When the 1947 fire passed over Paradise Hill and Duck Brook, it was a gale-driven inferno. The wind drove the fire toward Bar Harbor and over the mountains to the sea. The fire traveled from Hulls Cove to Sand Beach and Great Head, a distance of eight miles, in about five hours. Very little remained in its wake. A few houses were spared or saved. The landscape was a smoking desert; a handful of pines and other fire-resistant species survived, but the dark forests described by 19th-century guidebooks were gone. The fire was especially intense when it raced uphill, burning not only the vegetation but the organic material in the soil.

Mount Desert Island's soils were never especially rich, and regrowth of vegetation after the fire has been slow. Blueberries grew extremely well for many years after the fire, and still provide fine munching on many of the ledgy slopes. Trees are coming back in many places, but the woods are noticeably thin. Birches, popples and other species that colonize sunny openings dominate large areas.

Throughout the park and surrounding territory, changes in the trees show the path of the fire. The fire line is especially clear on Ocean Drive. The fire blew out to sea over Great Head and most of Ocean Drive, but stopped short of Otter Point.

A CHRONOLOGY
OF THE GREAT FIRE – 1947

Essentially no rain fell during the spring and summer of 1947. By mid-October, warm, dry Indian summer winds blew through the colorful, very dry woods.

Friday, October 17: One man with a pump truck is sent to put out a small blaze at Dolliver's dump on the Crooked Road at the edge of Fresh Meadow. The fire spreads rapidly, but reinforcements from town and the park stop the fire on the eastern side of Northeast Creek.

Saturday–Monday, October 18–20: Crews soak the edge of the 100-acre burn and put out hot spots. A few small fires continue to burn underground but do not appear serious. The fire is declared out and the pumps are shut off.

Tuesday, October 21: In the early morning a fire is spotted about 200 feet from the first burn. The cause of this fire will be debated for years to come, but at the moment fire fighters have more important things to worry about. A stiff wind blows the fire southward faster than they can lay hose. The crews make a stand at Norway Drive but are overrun. Fueled by piles of loggers' slash, the fire races toward crews waiting at Eagle Lake and at the New Eagle Lake Road.

Wednesday, October 22: The fire travels past Aunt Betty's Pond, but is held back north of the Bubbles. The northeastern line at New Eagle Lake Road holds.

Thursday, October 23: Hope comes with the quiet dawn. It does not last. The wind picks up, and the fire in the northeast begins to move, pushing past the Breakneck Road to Hulls Cove. Hulls Cove is evacuated, and the fire takes several of the town's oldest buildings.

At 3:00 P.M., the wind shifts to the northwest and increases to a steady gale estimated at 50 mph, with gusts over 70. The fire explodes and races toward Bar Harbor. At 4:00 P.M. the evacuation signal blows in town, and those not fighting the fire gather at the ballfield.

Fire crews make successful stands at the edge of the downtown. Evacuees move to the town pier, but most leave when roads behind the fire are reopened. The fire heads over the mountains, reaching the sea at Great Head four hours after the gale began.

The fire was declared out on November 14, although fires continued to burn underground at Sieur de Monts until spring. In all, 17,128 acres burned.

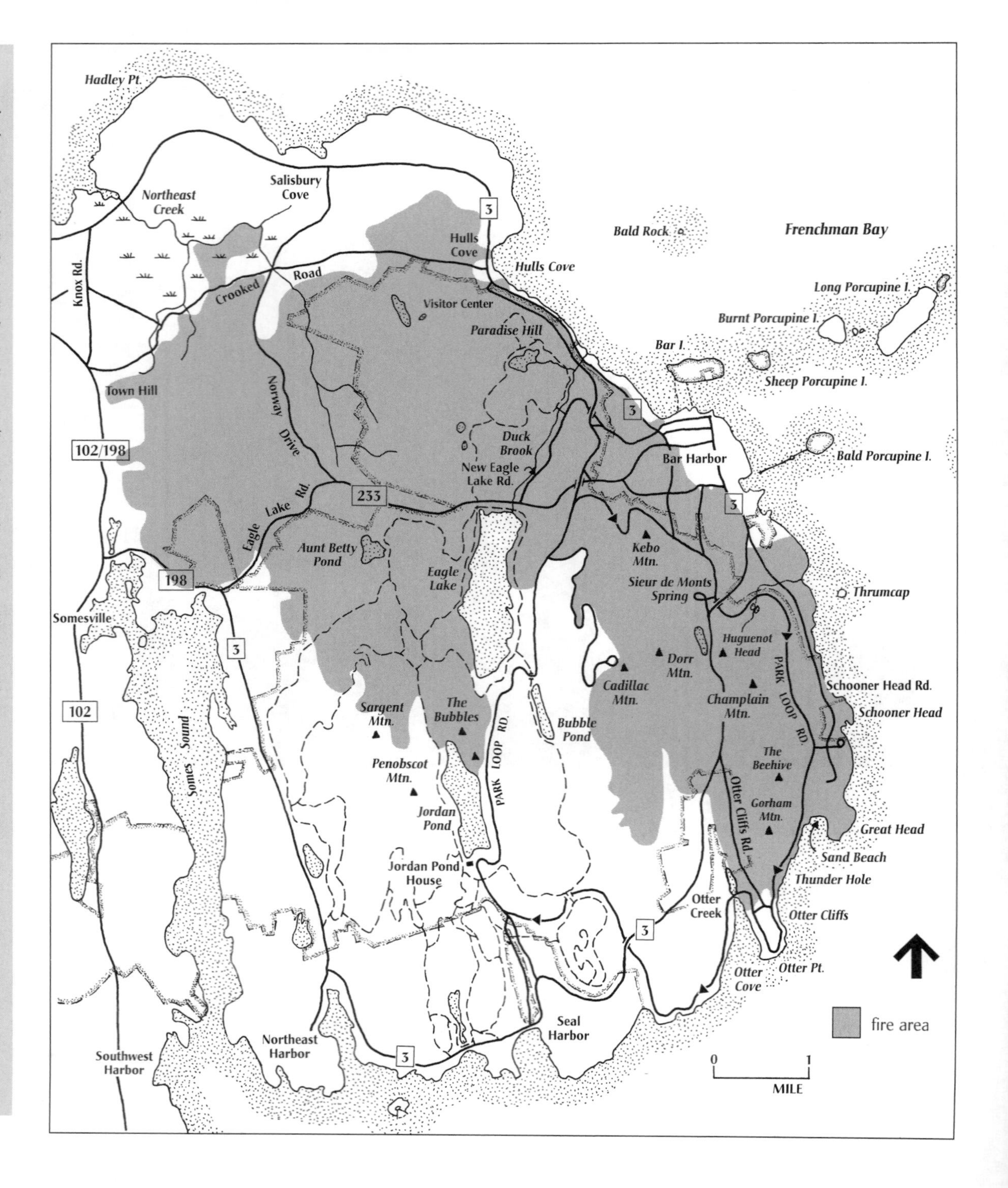

Fighting the Great Fire

1947

PARSON ANSON WILLIAMS

It was mid-October in 1947, and I was sitting in my study in Bar Harbor at the beginning of the day. It was hard to concentrate on anything except the fire situation. The late summer and early fall had been extremely dry in the State of Maine, with very little rain since May. The ground was parched and the grass was burned brown by the heat of the sun, so that conditions were explosive in the fields and woods—the worst, according to the Maine Weather Bureau, in 200 years. In the churches, prayers were made for rain, and notices in the newspapers stated tersely: "no outdoor fires"; "no hunting in the woods."

All that was needed to start a dangerous forest fire anywhere was a bit of flame from a match, or a lighted cigarette tossed aside carelessly. Already there had been disastrous fires [in other Maine communities]. Now we had a fire which had started [near] Dolliver's Dump near [Town Hill]. Fighting the fire were men from the National Guard, Dow Field in Bangor and the University of Maine, as well as householders from Camden, Bucksport, Blue Hill, Ellsworth, Orono, Belfast, and Old Town, (in addition to those from Bar Harbor and MDI). They felt that progress was being made and the fire was being contained.

I leaned over to turn on the radio for the morning's news. The announcer said, "The fire...is burning a swath along a wide front."...I knew that I must volunteer immediately to help. I got on some heavy boots, grabbed a coat and an old hat, and told my wife to keep the radio on; she might have to be evacuated if the fire got too close. When I reached the fire station, I saw volunteers pouring in from all directions, their faces tense and anxious.

I was assigned to the mobile canteen unit to help Mr. Frothingham, the owner and driver. The ladies' groups in the churches and clubs were making hundreds of sandwiches and doughnuts and we were to take these, along with hot coffee, along the line of firefighters.

(Courtesy of Bangor Daily News.*)*

It was gratifying to see how much the food and coffee helped the men. So grimy with smoke and perspiration that they were scarcely recognizable, following their quick snack there'd be a smile and a lifting of the shoulders, as if they could now push back fatigue a little longer. As we fed the firefighters, we got news of the fire itself. In some spots, the men thought it was being contained; in others, it was slowly gaining by moving underground, especially in the woods. We worked on the canteen until about midnight.

The next morning [October 23] I went to the fire station, expecting again to go out with the canteen, but it had left. The man in charge said help was needed in taking several truck loads of hose from the Eagle Lake section to the Duck Brook area, so I was soon aboard a truck and we were on our way.

The air was filled with smoke and bits of cinder ash. The sky was still cloudless and the sun was shining hotly through the smoke, leaving no hope of rain. As we passed houses along the way, the women would come to the door to watch us down the road [Eagle Lake Road]. Each one probably hoped her husband was returning from the fire. Even the small children and dogs seemed to know there was danger, and their romping had given way to a worried unrest. Occasionally, we'd see families wetting down their houses and barns in case sparks might fly over and ignite them.

When we had trucked the mile of hose to where the [New Eagle Lake Road] stopped, we had to drag it into the woods, a strenuous task. The hose was in two units and a "Y" of several hundred feet was put on, the central line going a considerable distance from where I worked with a young airman from Dow Field. We started to wet down the forest bed where the fire was slowly eating its way.

This was on October 23, later called "Terrible Thursday," and no one realized how close we were to sudden danger. At 4:30 my partner had to leave in order to go back to his base with other airmen who had been helping elsewhere on the fire front, and I was left alone. Suddenly, I heard an ominous sound. Except for an occasional slight breeze, it had been very calm until then. I listened closely and soon realized that it was the sound of a mighty wind coming from the northwest.

The fire, which had been confined to the ground, was swept up into the evergreen trees in no time at all. I knew that alone I could do nothing to stop it at any point with the strength of the wind relentlessly pushing it forward. I also knew that in a very short time I could be burned to death.

I dropped the hose and started out of the woods as fast as I could go. Smoke billowed around me, it was dense at times and I could see practically nothing, then it would lift for a moment and I could find the line of hose. My only way out was to follow the hose; otherwise I might find myself going in circles because of the smoke cloud.

I ran at full speed whenever I could see. At one point I was slowed up when a huge pine tree, ahead of the fire and almost in front of me, suddenly burst into flames as if it had been doused with gasoline. The heat around me was intense, and I was relieved to reach the carriage road where three younger men were waiting for a truck to pick them up.

I told them about the inferno that was behind us, and that there could be no waiting for trucks; there was danger of our being overtaken by the fire. I said, "I believe our only means of saving our lives is to get to the Duck Brook Bridge, a mile away." We headed there and didn't stop until we were underneath the bridge, where we'd planned to wait for the fire to sweep over us.

What a relief it was to rest our weary legs! Even though the wind was cool, we were streaming with perspiration and blackened with smoke and soot. We still didn't know whether or not we would escape death by the fire, but for the time being we could get our breath and a bit of strength back. I never knew what was passing through the minds of the other men while we were waiting, but I remember that scarcely a word was spoken. We were too exhausted to talk and also, I think, the mind of each man was engrossed in his thoughts of actual survival.

As the fire approached with a truly frightening roar, I hoped that if we had to go, it would be quick. I'd already suffered from the intense heat of the fire, and I knew from several experiences in my ministry that anyone who is badly burned, but still lives, endures excruciating agony.

We could see the wall of flame and thick smoke approaching. The heat became terrific and our pulses raced, partly with the feeling that in another moment we might become human torches, but with a mighty whoosh, the fire roared over us and we were showered with sparks which we beat out on each other's clothes. What a relief to know that the fire had gone by, and that we were still alive!

We waited there for a while, then went to the Bar Harbor Water Supply Station, which was a few hundred feet from our refuge under the bridge. The building was open and had not been singed by the fire. In it we found an apple, left by the last person there, and four doughnuts, one for each of us. We waited until we thought it was safe to work our way toward Bar Harbor, two-and-a-half miles away.

On every side trees had fallen to the ground. Some were still standing, however, and the bark was burning and the dead limbs were flickering with intermittent flames. We had to walk around trees which had toppled into the road. It was a walk through devastation.

We were fortunate in meeting a truck at McFarland's Corner, and the driver took us from there. We did not know whether we were moving slowly toward our homes or the ruins of homes, and we had to make several detours because of debris in the road. I became more and more anxious. Finally we got to Bar Harbor and, as we approached I could see with great relief that our house on Pleasant Street was still standing, although the fire had come within a few hundred feet of it. I was eager to get home to see if my wife had left me a note, but since no one was allowed to return to his home at that time, the truck driver took us to the police station, where we got extra wraps and had hot coffee and a sandwich.

I walked to the Bar Harbor Pier and tried to find out whether or not the Mission Boat, the *Sunbeam*, had been there. It had, and a load of people had been evacuated earlier in the evening. That eased my mind somewhat; I was sure my wife had been on the boat.

Back again to the police station. Around one A.M. I was allowed to go home. I found a note from Margaret saying she had gone to Seal Harbor, as all women and children had been evacuated from Bar Harbor. I couldn't get in touch with her because all phone connections were out.

First I attended to the bruises and scratches I had acquired while running through the woods, and a warm, relaxing bath which I'd been thinking of for hours was now a reality. Rest seemed delightful.

From "The Big Fire," by Anson R. and Margaret Williams, as told to Mary Wilkes Haley, Down East*, October 1962.*

Note: Margaret Williams tells her story of the fire beginning on page 68.

The Gorge and Sieur de Monts

Thomas Cole painted this romantic scene about 1845, after he spent part of the late summer of 1844 exploring and sketching throughout the eastern side of Mount Desert Island. Cole's view of the natural and bucolic paradise he found on Mount Desert Island entranced his audience in New York.

The painting is a condensed, dramatized view of the gorge between Huguenot Head and Champlain on the left and Dorr Mountain on the right. It is impossible to be certain exactly where Cole's vantage point was, but it looks like he was near Great Meadow. The log cabin is reasonably typical of the first settlers' simplest dwellings. It appears abandoned. The clearing was fenced, but Cole shows the fence in disrepair and a pair of deer hidden in the shadow to the left of the house. According to George Dorr, Great Meadow and nearby Harden Farm were among the oldest cultivated lands in Bar Harbor. (Courtesy of Fogg Art Museum, Harvard University Art Museums, transfer from Harvard University, bequest of Edward Charles Pickering, 1919.)

Until the park loop road was finished in the late 1950s, the Gorge and Sieur de Monts was the beginning of Acadia's natural wonderland for most visitors. It was Bar Harbor's backyard, a pleasant walk or carriage ride from any house or hotel.

There were functional and scenic paths in existence when the rusticators started climbing the mountains, but pathmaking became an avocation for a devoted group of summer colonists. The island village improvement societies had active path committees dedicated to creating wonderful walks through all the beautiful places. The Bar Harbor Village Improvement Association published two trail maps in 1896 and had to issue revisions five years later.

The pathmakers did not simply clear and mark trails, they *built* trails with stone steps and iron rungs to aid the cautious and less agile. On occasion, they rearranged the landscape for dramatic effect, setting immense boulders in apparently threatening positions, for example. The Beachcroft Trail (1915) up Huguenot Head and Waldron Bates's Ladder Trail (1891) up Dorr Mountain, each with over 1,000 stone steps, are fine thigh-strengthening examples of their handiwork.

The 1947 fire tore through the Gorge and over the mountains. On the way, it burned Great Meadow and Strawberry Hill, which were recovering nicely from a heavy burn in the late 1880s.

A Choice of Excursions

1888

M. F. Sweetser

The Climb Up Newport Mountain

Newport [Champlain] Mountain is a long ridge, parallel with Green [Cadillac] Mountain, and between it and the sea. It is 1,060 feet high, and nearly two miles long. An entire day should be devoted to the trip hither, so as to avoid breathless haste, which is attended with some peril along the slippery ledges. It is about two miles south of Bar Harbor, and the path branches to the right from the Great-Head road, a little way beyond the divergence of the Otter-Creek road. It is at first a lonely little forest-lane, which changes into a rapidly rising footpath; and after emerging upon the ledges is marked by a pile of stones. Leaving Round Peak [Huguenot Head] to one side, the trail mounts straight to the summit, where there is a tall pole, and also a cairn of rocks.

The charm of this vast pile of granite is its nearness to the sea, which fringes its base with an embroidery of white surf. Nowhere else on our American Atlantic coast is there such a wonderful sea-view. As an experienced traveller has remarked, the prospect from Green Mountain is for the delight of the geographer, while Newport's view is for the artist.

The west is impressively filled with the huge reddish-brown mass of Green Mountain, against which lies the contiguous Dry [Dorr] Mountain. Above the long northward slope of the latter appear bright reaches of Mount-Desert Narrows, the white houses of Lamoine, and far-away mountains on the mainland. Farther to the right is the long point of Hull's Cove, with the lake-like Raccoon Cove above it, on the main. The hotels and villas of Bar Harbor next appear, with the gate-like opening of the Skillings River above them, at the head of the bay. The Goldsborough mountains and the bold islands of the bay make a noble appearance on the vast blue expanse. Directly over the left flank of Schoodic Mountain, and much more remote, are the nameless blue peaks of the eastern counties. The waves are seen whitening among the ledges of Egg Island; and here and there steamboats or yachts noiselessly move up and down the bay, over their snowy paths, and seeming so near that one might throw pebbles upon their decks. Farther around rise the bold headlands about Otter Cove, the Cranberry Isles, and the Placentia group, Isle au Haut, and the great archipelago of Penobscot Bay.

An inspiring (but arduous) walk leads along the ridge to the south peak, whence a still finer view of Otter Cove and its cliffs is given. This route is marked by little cairns; and gives noble views down into Echo Notch, and over the open sea. Beyond and far below the south peak is Loch Anna (so named by Church, the painter) a beautiful mountain-

Hikers on Huguenot Head above the Gorge in the early 1900s. (Courtesy of Bar Harbor Historical Society.)

pond on the contiguous spur, 475 feet above the sea, which is but half a mile distant. This sequestered tarn (called *The Bowl* by the islanders) was in past years well-stocked with trout. A path leads from its eastern side to a wood-road which soon enters the Schooner-Head road. Close to Loch Anna, and quite conspicuous from the Schooner-Head road, is the foot-hill called The Beehive, 540 feet high; and about a mile S. S. W. is the Peak of Otter [Gorham Mountain], 506 feet high.

The ascent of Newport is made by many ladies, during bright summer days. It is best to ride to the base, and so avoid perplexity about the entrance of the path. In dry seasons, climbers should carry up something wherewith to appease thirst, for it is a very dry mountain, and the violent exercise of climbing produces an amazing thirst.

The Road
Through the Gorge, or Echo Notch

The road to Otter Cliff is one of the most interesting in this wonderful region, since it combines in an unusual degree the noble and notable features of mountain scenery and sea-coast. The distance down there is five miles, by the road running south from Bar Harbor, and swinging off to the right from the Great-Head road, something over a mile from the village. For a long distance it drives directly towards the tremendous cliffs of Dry Mountain, which seem to overhang the glen from an Alpine attitude. Then the road swings around and makes a dash toward the lofty and ledge-environed northwest peak of Newport Mountain, and so ascends into the magnificent Echo Notch. On one side, across a narrow morass [now The Tarn, thanks to George Dorr's dam], the Cyclopean masonry of Dry Mountain rises for over a thousand feet; and on the other, over the débris of ancient slides, the rocky walls of Newport Mountain reach far into the sky. It is one of the noblest mountain-passes in New England, for although its walls lack the great height of the Crawford and Franconia Notches, they are more wild and stern in their rocky strength, and are not masked by miles of arching woodlands, or draped with softening forests. Here we see huge overhanging masses of splintered red granite, towering high above the rich forest of spruce and hemlock; and the long heaps of ancient avalanches; and on one side a lush meadow, overgrown with rank deep-green grasses. From all appearances, the scene might be amid the fastnesses of the Catskills or the Adirondacks; yet the great eastern wall of the gorge is hammered down along its whole length by the heaviest waves of the ocean; and the little brook singing its way down the intervale will be swallowed by the sea in a short league. Thomas Cole truly said, here, that "One might easily fancy himself in the forests of the Alleghanies, but for the dull [faint] roar of the ocean breaking on the stillness."

When Longfellow made his great collection of "Poems of Places," he found room in it for an anonymous poem to Echo Notch, containing this word-picture:

> Adown thy steep and rugged flanks,
> The black fir glooms and the pale aspens quiver,
> And o'er thy glistening, windswept cliffs,
> The mossy, perfumed streamlets leap forever.

From Chisholm's Mount Desert Guide-Book, *M. F. Sweetser, Chisholm Brothers, Portland, 1888.*

Visitors take a close look at Sieur de Monts Spring. The 1947 fire spared Dorr's springhouse. (Courtesy of Maine Historic Preservation Commission.)

Dorr's Spring

1909

George B. Dorr

Springs, from boyhood on, have always held a singular interest for me, an interest heightened by years of travel abroad where, from the earliest historic period on, they have been objects of mystery and worship. And this spring was wonderfully placed, with the mountains rising steeply up beside it, contrasting with the Great and Little Meadow lands on either side. Hidden as it was by the concealing woods, I had not realized its existence till Strout and Prescott's work [to develop it as a commercial spring] began, but now that it had come to a halt, I set myself to see for what price it could be obtained and added to our Reservations. But the price was high, five thousand dollars, and there was no other purchaser in sight, so I let the matter lie, entering only into an agreement with Ora Strout not to sell to another without first giving me opportunity to buy. And there the matter rested; there seemed no need for haste.

The[n] one fair spring morning in 1909, when I was out, here and there, looking after work I had in hand, Mr. Harry Lynam, knowing my interest in the tract, drove up hastily, out searching for me, and said:

"Mr. Dorr, a bunch of them up town have got together and raised the money to take over the option on the spring, which they believe to be essential to your plans. Ora Strout gives you until noon to take it, but will sell to them upon the stroke of twelve unless you close with him first. [T]hey are waiting by the clock upon the Village Green till noon shall come to make the purchase. What will you do?"

This was in the old, slow horse-driving days. Mr. Lynam had spent some time in search for me and when he found me there was but a scant fifteen minutes left in which to reach the Village Green, a mile or more away. There was no time to spare. I made up my mind on the spot to take the option, and Mr. Lynam drove back as rapidly as the team which had brought him down could carry him, to so tell Mr. Strout. He found him waiting on the Village Green, where were also gathered the group that sought to take the option from me, waiting, cash in hand, for the hour to strike. When Mr. Lynam drove up, with but two or three minutes to spare, and told Mr. Strout that I would take it, they could not conceal their anger and hot words ensued between them and Strout. But the spring was mine, and became, as it proved, one of the foundation stones on which the future park was built.

Robert Abbe Museum researchers excavate a shell midden in 1928.

Physician Robert Abbe developed a keen interest in prehistory and began collecting artifacts. Abbe died in March 1928, five months before his Museum of Stone Age Antiquities opened at Sieur de Monts.

The Abbe Museum sponsors educational programs involving the descendants of prehistoric peoples—Maine's Native Americans—in addition to continuing exhibits and fieldwork. The museum is open from June through October. (Courtesy of Cameron Bradley; Robert Abbe Museum.)

Freeing it from a concealing cover of sphagnum moss and fallen leaves, which hid the full abundance of the flow, I shaped the sloping ground about it into a shell-like, concave basin, deeply draining it around to carry off all surface water from the mountainside above. I then built over it the octagonal, tiled-roof cover house, of old Florentine design, which is there today [1942], with the arched openings upon the sides protected to a man's height and over with plates of purest glass, so that all who wished might look in and see the water gushing out in a generous rush, to be led away by pipe to where the public might drink of it freely, if they would.

To the spring I gave the name of the founder of Acadia: The Sieur de Monts. And in memory of two spring-fountains I once had visited, on opposite shores of the Bosphorus, built by the Greeks in classic times and named by them respectively, The Sweet Waters of Europe and The Sweet Waters of Asia, I called these waters, flowing out at the mountain base in such purity and abundance, The Sweet Waters of Acadia, carving this upon a granite rock I placed beside the spring.

From Acadia National Park: Its Origin and Background, *George B. Dorr, 1942.*

A Wild-life Sanctuary

1930

ACADIA NATIONAL PARK

One important aspect of our natural parks and monuments is that they—unlike the [national] forests, devised to follow economic lines—are absolute sanctuaries, islands of shelter for the native life in all but noxious forms. Like the monasteries of the Middle Ages that sheltered—all too fragmentarily—the literature and learning of the classic period, they are a means of incalculable value for the preserving in this destructive time the wealth of forms and species we have inherited from the past and have a duty to hand on undiminished to the future, so far as that be possible.

In this aspect of a wild-life sanctuary, plant and animal, Acadia National Park is remarkable. Land and sea, woodland, lake and mountain are all represented in it in wonderful concentration. In it, too, the northern and temperate zone floras meet and overlap, and land climate meets sea climate, each tempering the other. It lies directly in the coast migration route of birds and exhibits the fullest of the Acadian forest which at the land of De Monts stretched without a break from the St. Lawrence to the Gulf [of Maine] and is the oldest, by the record of the rocks, and richest in existing species of any mingled hardwood and coniferous forest in the Temperate Zone. And it possesses, also, a rich biologic field in the neighboring ocean, the parent habitat of life. Deeper waters apart, the sea beach and tidal pools alone form an infinite source of interest and study, while the ocean climate, like the land one, is profoundly different from that to the southward, off the Cape Cod shore.

To take advantage of this opportunity an association has been formed, incorporated under the name Wild Gardens of Acadia, to cooperate with the Government in the development of the educational and scientific features of the park and environment. By means of it a marine biological laboratory has been established on the shore [in Salisbury Cove], material has been gathered for a book on wild flowers of the park and wild gardens for their exhibition started, and entomological collections, and studies of bird life and geology of the region have been made. The park itself is a living natural history museum, a geological and historical area lending itself remarkably to the nature guide and lecture service which is rapidly becoming a valuable feature in our national parks.

Botanically Acadia National Park forms an exceedingly interesting area. Champlain's term "deserts" in description of the mountains meant "wild and solitary"; not "devoid of vegetation." [The exposed summits probably were bald and sparsely vegetated to some extent.] Vegetation, on the contrary, grows upon the island with exceptional vigor, and in wide range of form. The native forest—before it was invaded by the axe—must have been superb, and superb it will become under the Government's protection. Wild flowers are abundant in their season, among them a number of species of conspicuous beauty, because of their loveliness in danger of extinction until the national park was formed and its lands became a sanctuary. The rocks, frost split and lichen-clad, with granite sands between, are of a character that makes the mountain tops, with their bearberries, and blueberries and broad ocean outlook, wild rock gardens of inspiring beauty, while both mountain tops and woods are made accessible by over a hundred miles of trails built by successive generations of nature-loving summer visitors.

In addition to ocean, rocks, and mountain heights, to woods and wild flowers, and to trails trodden by feet of generations, Acadia National Park has a rich possession in an inexhaustible spring source of pure, delicious water rising—cool and constant—from beneath the mountain at the entrance from Bar Harbor, and made, with its free gift of water to the passing public, a memorial to Sieur de Monts, the founder of Acadia.

From Circular of General Information Regarding Acadia National Park, Maine*, U. S. Government Printing Office, 1930; courtesy of Patricia Tierney and Heidi Welch. (Note: no author is named for this piece, but the writing appears to be George Dorr's.)*

George Dorr built the first "wild gardens" on family land near the Beaver Dam Pool in the late 1800s. His mother enjoyed planning and taking care of the gardens for many years. In the 1890s, Dorr built a narrow bicycle path loop through the gardens. The path was wide enough for Mary Dorr's small carriage, allowing her to visit the gardens in her declining years.

In 1961, the national park and Bar Harbor Garden Club established the Wild Gardens of Acadia at Sieur de Monts.

Friday Hikes for Girls

1933
BAR HARBOR TIMES

Each Friday at 11 o'clock in the morning girls leave the Y. W. for a hike of some sort or another. For the last two weeks they have been taking some of the hikes offered by Mr. Arthur Stupka, the Ranger-Naturalist of the National Park. Last Friday the girls took a hike to Huguenot Head in spite of the fog and mist. Any girls in town are invited to attend these hikes, whether they are "town girls" or girls visiting Bar Harbor for the summer. It is a good way to get acquainted if they are strangers to each other. There has been no fee thus far, since no transportation has had to be provided; the only requirement being to bring a lunch. Next Friday, the group is planning a hike to the Bowl and Beehive Mountain, returning for a dip at Sand Beach. Any offers for transportation to the Bowl would be greatly appreciated. For further inquiry, contact the Y. W. office.

From the Bar Harbor Times, *July 5, 1933.*

Christmas Bird Count

1933
ARTHUR STUPKA

Under a clear sky with the temperature at eight degrees above zero a little party, consisting of Dr. A. E. Brower of Bar Harbor, Mr. Vernon Lunt of Indian Point, and myself, began our census of Christmas birds. Our plans, like the plans of so many other groups of bird enthusiasts who were compiling similar records for *Bird Lore Magazine's* 1933 census, were to spend the daylight hours in the field and, keeping within a prescribed area, list the species and numbers of birds observed. The area in which we worked lies within the eastern half of Mount Desert Island and includes various sections of Acadia National Park.

Snow covered the ground to an average depth of ten inches and a light wind was blowing from the northwest. The highest temperature reading for the day was twenty degrees.

Twenty-four species numbering 446 individuals were observed. Most outstanding of these, and the ones which gave us the greatest thrill, were American Crossbills and a lone female Arctic Three-toed Woodpecker. The former were seen with the more common White-winged Crossbills feeding in the spired cone-laden crowns of the tall-growing red spruces which stand on the grounds of the Jackson Memorial Laboratory. The Arctic Three-toed Woodpecker, working low on a large dead balsam fir, permitted me to approach within five feet before moving up the trunk. While all three of us were watching the bird, a Ruffed Grouse alighted upon a nearby tree in the snowy woods, but upon catching sight of us hurried away, sending the snow which lined the branches flying.

The birds seen in the course of the day were as follows:

Holboell's Grebe 3
Red-legged Black Duck 71
American Golden-eye 8
Old Squaw 28
White-winged Scoter 2
Bald Eagle 1
Canada Ruffed Grouse 1
Herring Gull 164
Northern Downy Woodpecker 10
Arctic Three-toed Woodpecker 1
American Crow 13
Black-capped Chickadee 18
Red-breasted Nuthatch 17
Brown Creeper 4
Eastern Robin 3
Eastern Golden-crowned Kinglet 16
Starling 10
English Sparrow 2
Pine Grosbeak 10
American Crossbill 21
White-winged Crossbill 27
Slate-colored Junco 4
Eastern Tree Sparrow 10
Eastern Song Sparrow 2

From Nature Notes, *Arthur Stupka, Ranger-Naturalist, November and December, 1933; courtesy of Acadia National Park.*

Robin Hood Park, Jackson Lab and High Seas

ABOVE: Surrey (or cutunder) parade at the horse show at Robin Hood Park.

LEFT: Jackson Laboratory founder Dr. Clarence Cook Little with genetically mutant mouse "adba."

The laboratory complex can be glimpsed over the Beaver Dam Pool from the Park Loop Road; the main entrance is on Route 3 north of Sieur de Monts. The lab offers regular tours in the summer.

(Courtesy of Bar Harbor Historical Society; The Jackson Laboratory.)

From 1900 to 1912, extravagant horse shows were held at Robin Hood Park, on the plateau northwest of the Beaver Dam Pool. The land belonged to Colonel Edward Morrell of Philadelphia, an enthusiastic show sponsor and competitor.

University of Maine zoologist Dr. Clarence Cook Little brought a group of students to Bar Harbor in 1924 for a summer field course. They camped near the shore south of Bar Harbor.

Dr. Little was convinced that a lab that worked with mice could make great strides in mammalian genetic research. Over the next few years, he attracted committed supporters, including Edsel Ford and Roscoe B. Jackson, founder of the Hudson Motor car company. George Dorr gave thirteen acres near the old Robin Hood Park for the project. Dr. Little's lab opened in 1929, named in memory of Jackson.

The lab lost nearly everything in the 1947 fire, including 60,000 specially bred mice. Dr. Little and his staff were determined to rebuild. Donations of all kinds, including breeding pairs of mice, came from scientists and supporters throughout the country.

The present lab employs 735 people and maintains more than 1,700 different strains of mice, many of which are mutants essential to research throughout the world. Lab researchers are at the forefront of genetic research in many areas, including work on cancer.

The brick mansion High Seas is the only survivor of the 1947 fire along this stretch of coast. It was built in 1912 by Princeton professor Rudolph Brunnow, a widower with several children, for his new bride-to-be, who sailed on the *Titanic*. She never saw the house. A dedicated pathmaker, Professor Brunnow spent years building the "trail" up the Precipice.

Mrs. Eva Van Cortland Hawkes, of New York, bought the house in 1924 for $25,000. She seldom entertained but nevertheless employed a large staff: a butler, two footmen, a downstairs maid, a cook, a kitchen maid, a laundress, an upstairs maid, a personal maid, a cleaning woman, a chauffeur and a gardener. Her tea roses regularly took first place at the flower show. Her twenty-four Sealyham terriers had their own brick house.

During World War II, Mrs. Hawkes tried to hide the estate from enemy bombers by having the roof painted green, a tactic presumably more effective before the nearby trees burned in the fire. She held parties for American and English sailors stationed in Bar Harbor, serving plenty of champagne and lobster newburg.

The 1947 fire destroyed several of the estate's outbuildings, but the gardener saved the main house by keeping the hoses on it. Mrs. Hawkes was ill in New York at the time and died without learning of the fire.

In 1951, Mrs. Hawkes's heirs gave High Seas to Jackson Lab. Student interns working in lab progams stay in the house. The two white additions were recently built by the lab.

"High Seas"

LATE 1940S

PREVIEWS INCORPORATED

This spacious estate has approximately 1,500 feet of ocean frontage and magnificent views overlooking Frenchman's Bay. The stately brick house was carefully located to provide a setting of mountain and ocean scenery, with absolute privacy and seclusion. From the open terrace and covered veranda one overlooks the ocean, dotted with spruce-covered islands in the foreground.

Aside from estate purposes, this property lends itself for use as an exclusive inn, sanatorium, or school. Uses for other than estate may be permitted by appeal to the zoning appeal board. Swimming, boating, and mountain climbing are all within access. The picturesque Ocean Drive with its famed Thunder Hole begins two miles south of the estate.

TABLE OF FACTS:

LOCATION: Bar Harbor, Maine. Shopping center, two miles; Seal Harbor, eight miles. R.R. station at Ellsworth, twenty-three miles, with direct train service to New York and Boston.

GROUNDS: *About fifteen acres*, mostly wooded. About 1,500 feet shore frontage on Frenchman's Bay. Grounds about the house pleasingly landscaped. Small rose terrace facing the water. Meadow brook crosses property to sea.

RESIDENCE: *Twenty-two rooms*, (nine master bedrooms, six baths, lavoratory; four servants' bedrooms, bath lavoratory; five third floor rooms, bath). Brick Georgian Colonial on brick foundation, with canvas asbestos roof. Hardwood floors, brass plumbing; copper leaders, gutters and screens. UTILITIES: Coal-fired steam heating system for spring and fall use; separate coal unit for domestic hot water. PS electricity; tank gas; telephone; town water. Included in the sale price: Gas range, coal range, built-in refrigerator, and Bendix washer.

FIRST FLOOR: Large Entrance Hall with Coat Room and Lavatory; *Recreation Room* with fireplace; Living Room (30' x 50') with fireplace, museum-piece carved mantel, French doors opening to covered brick Porch; paneled *Library* with built-in bookcases and fireplace; *Dining Room* with fireplace; glassed-in *Breakfast Room*; butler's pantry; large *Kitchen* with Magic Chef gas range; Servants' Dining Room; pantries; Lavatory. *Elevator* to second floor.

SECOND FLOOR: Six double *Master Bedrooms*, three single *Master Bedrooms* (six with fireplaces). Six Master Baths. *Four Servants' Bedrooms* and Bath.

THIRD FLOOR: *Play Room* (40' x 60'). Three large and two small *Bedrooms*. Bath. Storage Rooms.

BASEMENT: Laundry, Servants' Lavatory; furnace room.

GARDENER'S COTTAGE: Brick construction, six Rooms and Bath.

GARAGE: Detached. Brick building with space for *Four Cars*.

PRICE: $55,000 Unfurnished

From a sales brochure, Previews Incorporated, New York, undated; courtesy of Bar Harbor Historical Society.

Note: High Seas is not open to the public.

Schooner Head Shore and Egg Rock

The view toward Schooner Head, about 1895. Mr. and Mrs. L. F. Brigham's cottage stands in the open. When Frederic Church sketched the Lynam farm house in 1850, the headland was nearly treeless, open ground. The small creek that flows into the cove (just out of view to the left) powered a small seasonal mill. The summer cottagers got their water through an aqueduct from the Bowl, a small lake located next to the Beehive.

The 1947 fire was traveling at maximum speed and intensity when it passed through here. It burned everything in its path, including the cottages on the head and nearby (except High Seas). The present homes on the headland are on private land, and were built during the last fifteen years.

Thomas Cole included a bald eagle eating its catch on the rocks in his 1845 painting of lower Frenchman Bay. Although it may not be common to see an eagle dining upon the rocks at Schooner Head, the area is still part of an active bald eagle territory and the birds periodically hunt fish and ducks along the shore. (Courtesy of Bar Harbor Historical Society.)

Winter may well be the best time to visit the lower Frenchman Bay shore below Schooner Head. It is certainly the most dramatic. The park overlook is a fine spot for watching storms and contemplating the force of breaking seas, which is on the order of three tons per square foot.

In 1890, the *Bar Harbor Record* observed: "Though the stormy days are far from conducive to the comfort of the visitor, he may employ them to great advantage in visiting some of our beautiful shore scenery...It is when the fierce surges of the old Ocean are breaking in foam upon our rockbound coast that these places should be visited. Then the Spouting Horn and Thunder Cave are at their grandest; and he is but a shallow lover of Dame Nature who would not risk a slight wetting and damp feet to behold them at such a time...."

In the summer of 1844, Thomas Cole walked to Schooner Head from Somesville to stay at the Lynams' farm house and draw. The following year, Cole painted an imaginative but identifiable grand view of Schooner Head and a tumultuous lower bay after a squall. He apparently reversed the squall's direction and enhanced the shoreline rocks, but the effect was magnificent, and it made a favorable impression on the folks back home in New York, including Cole's student, Frederic Church, who came to Mount Desert most every summer in the 1850s and early 1860s.

Sightseeing at Schooner Head

1888

M. F. Sweetser

The road to Schooner Head leads south from Bar Harbor for three miles through the woods, usually out of sight of the sea, but with frequent glimpses of great Newport [Champlain] Mountain. In the vicinity of Schooner Head are the pleasant estates of George S. Hale, George H. Homans, and Charles Francis and Henry Sayles, all of Boston. Schooner Head is a bold headland on the coast, with high rocky cliffs, breasting the surf. In one of these is a long, tunnel-like opening, from whose inner end a cleft opens away into the top of the Head. During rough water the waves rush madly into this passage, and dash out at the top, throwing showers of white spray many feet into the air. This is the famous Spouting Horn, which, on the pleasant days usually chosen for this excursion, forbears to spout. Venturesome persons have climbed up through the Horn, at low tide, but it is a perilous and uncomfortable journey.

An early rusticator studies the Spouting Horn. (Courtesy of Maine Historic Preservation Commission.)

There are various wild legends connected with the white stain on the seaward face of the Head, which bears a singular resemblance to the lower sails of a schooner. One of these tells of a pirate-schooner, one of Capt. Kidd's, running in to make a harbor and land treasure at Otter Cove, and disabled off this shore by a broadside from a British corvette, after which she was dashed to pieces on the Head. Hence the mariners along the coast, a century or more ago, often fancied they saw, off this point, the ghost of a schooner, with a shadowy helmsman, flitting past in the white moonlight. There is also a tradition that one of His Majesty's cruisers ran in here, during the War of 1812, and opened up brisk fire upon the cliff, under the impression that its white face, dimly descried through the fog, was the mainsail of a flying Yankee schooner.

Anemone Cave is a picturesque grotto, forty feet deep, across the cove south of Schooner Head, full of interesting sea-mosses, sea-lettuce, pale-green sponge, kelp, barnacles, green echini [sea urchins], red-backed crabs, star-fishes, and other wonders of the shore...The exquisite sea anemones, once so abundant in its rocky pools, have well-nigh vanished at the hands of visitors; and the owners of the Head now strenuously forbid the removal of the treasures of this loveliest of aquaria. [This has not changed; the present owner, Acadia National Park, strongly discourages visitors from entering the cave.] A favorite name for Anemone Cave, among the old islanders, was The Devil's Oven; and the roaring and rushing of the waves in its dark depths, during a stormy high tide, certainly suggests demoniac activities....

Something less than a mile beyond Schooner Head, the road reaches a lonely farm-house, whence the path leads up through woods, for a long half-mile, to the seaward front of Great Head. Sturdy climbers sometimes follow the shore between the two Heads, and enjoy the wild rock-scenery, with its caverns and bowlders and birch-groves....

From Chisholm's Mount-Desert Guide-Book, *M. F. Sweetser, Chisholm Brothers, Portland, 1888.*

It takes a good sea to make the famous Spouting Horn function. As one of the late 19th-century guidebooks noted: "The Spouting Horn does not spout unless after an easterly gale and at half flood tide, when the scene along the cliffs is magnificent." With over ninety feet of water right in front of the head, swells travel essentially unimpeded until they hit the cliff face.

About ten years ago, a group of local folks, including the author, were out for a traditional trip to see the sights along the shore after an excellent winter storm. Immense southeasterly swells were assaulting Schooner Head, along with lesser seas. On this particular winter afternoon, the big swells, traveling in sets of three or four, produced jets that sent spray up over the chimney of the recently built summer cottage at the top of the cliff.

Notable Events at Egg Rock Light

1874 TO 1908

EGG ROCK LIGHT KEEPERS

1874: An appropriation of $15,000 was made by an act approved June 23, 1874, for a light-house and fog signal at or in vicinity of Egg Rock. Plans are now being prepared and steps have been taken to secure a site. The work will then be taken in hand without delay.

1875: ...After considerable delay in obtaining title to the site, and cession of jurisdiction, measures were taken for the erection of the buildings. The situation of the rock is very similar to that of Avery's Rock, and the difficulty experienced in landing material much the same. The work was commenced in June. The iron-work is now completed and ready to be set into place. Nearly all the material has been landed, the foundation is laid, and the brick-work nearly finished. The station will probably be ready for lighting November 1. A fog-bell, similar to that placed at Avery's Rock, will be placed at this station.

1876: The buildings at this station which at date of last annual report were in process of construction...were completed and the light exhibited for the first time on the night of the 1st of November, 1875. During a gale on the 21st of March, 1876, the sea washed over the rock, carrying away the fuel shed and moving the bell-tower some thirty feet. The windows of the dwelling were broken in on the seaside, and the dwelling flooded to such an extent that the oil-butts were moved from their benches.

Egg Rock Light at the turn of the century. Built in 1875, the light was manned for a century. Today's automated light flashes red at five-second intervals; a sensor triggers the fog signal. (Courtesy of Bar Harbor Historical Society.)

Jan. 11, 1877: Gale of wind, S. E., bell-tower washed down and sea striking heavy against dwelling.

1882: A boat slip, 145 feet in length, was built, and the exterior walls of the dwelling were repainted.

1884: A boat-house was built, the roof of the dwelling was covered with canvas laid in paint, and a bell-tower built.

1888: The damage to the bell-house by the storm of December 28, 1887, was repaired and the house converted to a skeleton tower bolted to the ledge. A 1,000-pound bell, with striking machine, was mounted and placed in position.

1890: A foot bridge was built across the chasm in the rocks to enable the keepers to reach the oil-house and store-house from the dwelling. A fuel-house was built and the fog-bell machinery was overhauled and repaired.

1895: The boat slip was extended seaward thirty-five feet and was provided with a hard-wood capping. Various repairs were made.

1899: The tower is of brick, twelve feet square, and stands in the center of the dwelling, so dispersing the rooms that they can not be kept warm during the long and severe winters of this locality. It is estimated that at a cost not exceeding $1,700 a suffi-

Although Egg Rock poses an obvious hazard to navigation, it did not get a lighthouse until 1875. The motivation for the light was the desire to keep the passenger steamers from running into the island. On a clear day, this seems a foolish concern, but a look at the records for Egg Rock gives an idea why a fog signal was as important as a light. During the early years, Egg Rock had a whistle and a back-up bell.

July was (and is) usually the foggiest month, but the 1889 to 1910 records note remarkable fog signal runs for January, February, April, May, June, August and September. The noisiest month was July 1897 when the signal sounded for 360¾ hours. The longest continuous run was 105 hours during June 21 to 25, 1895.

In 1903, the warship *Massachusetts* ran aground at Egg Rock in the fog. The keeper vehemently assured the top brass that the signal was operating at the time. The following year, the Coast Guard installed a loud horn driven by compressed air. This drove Joseph Pulitzer wild, since the same southeasterly wind that brought the fog carried the horn's repetitive moan straight to his estate, Chatwold, which was located at the outlet of Bear Brook, opposite the Thrumcap. Pulitzer tried to get the foghorn shut off, but succeeded only in getting it turned to face the open ocean.

In 1881, a *Mount Desert Herald* correspondent asked Captain Robinson of the steamer *Mount Desert* why he did not hit anything coming up the fogged-in bay. The captain retorted, "I couldn't see anything to run into."

cient number of rooms for one family, arranged so that they can be easily heated, could be provided by adding a second story to part of the dwelling. It is therefore recommended that an appropriation of this amount be made therefor.

January 21, 1899: Gale of wind, E. to S. E., washing completely over rock, washed away walks and box of bell tower that weights run down into....

December 24, 1899: Fishing pinky *Julia Ann* came ashore during the night, complete wreck, kindling wood by morning, nearly calm, hazy, two men, all on board, drowned, mysterious. Probably (?) asleep.

March 2, 1900: Gale of wind, S. S. E., heavy sea breaking completely over rock, boat house washed away, government boat and boat belonging to a man hired by the keeper, completely ruined; keeper's boat badly smashed. Heavy storm shutters on seaward side of dwelling closed, sea coming around dwelling but doing no damage. The worst gale for twenty-four years as the records at this station show.

1900: The boathouse which was carried away by the storms of March, 1900, was rebuilt, twenty feet of new boat slip made, and the tower deck repointed.

1901: The interior of the dwelling was improved, a cellar built under it, and the old striking machine replaced by one rebuilt in the light-house machine shop in Boston.

1902: The intensity of the light was increased by changing the lens from fifth to fourth order and the characteristic from fixed red to flashing white every five seconds. The fog-bell striking machinery was repaired.

February 22, 1902: E. S. E. gale, heavy sea coming around dwelling, water driving in around storm shutters, washing away heavy deal walk and building 20 by 80 [30?] feet, all movable articles and other small damage.

August 14, 1903: Battleship *Massachusetts* while putting to sea from Bar Harbor in a dense fog run ashore and was badly damaged.

1904: A fog-signal operated by compressed air was established.

1905: The axis of the trumpet was changed to approximately magnetic south. Various repairs were made.

1907: The first-class Daboll trumpet, in duplicate, was in operation some 1,813 hours during the year and consumed about 762 gallons of oil.

February 1, 1908: Strong gale, S. E., snow, rain, very heavy sea breaking and washing completely over rock, breaking in shutters and windows of the whistle house and flooding same, all small articles being afloat, ripped shingles off bell tower and roof off whistle house, tore railing away from rock, etc. In fact, everything movable being washed away, rocks weighing from two to thirty tons were moved and the sea running between dwelling and whistle tower was seven feet deep, a solid body of water.

From the Egg Rock Light annual reports, courtesy of United States Coast Guard, Southwest Harbor Group; and the Bar Harbor Times, *February 1, 1911.*

Note: Egg Rock is owned by the town of Winter Harbor; the light is maintained by the Coast Guard.

Great Head, Sand Beach and Ocean Drive

At Newport (Sand) Beach. (Courtesy of Maine Historic Preservation Commission.)

The track from Bar Harbor to Ocean Drive is well-traveled. A trip on the O. D. has been one of the required activities on the island for more than a century.

At first there were two drives to the southern shore. One followed the path now taken by Route 3 through "The Gorge" between Newport (Champlain) and Dry (Dorr) Mountains, then turned onto the Otter Cliff Road. The other followed the Schooner Head Road, ending at the farmhouse just south of the head. A road connecting the two was built in 1888 by the Village Improvement Association. It was improved for autos and extended by John D. Rockefeller Jr.'s crews in the early 1930s. The Park Loop Road from Sieur de Monts was finished in 1958.

Sightseeing by buckboard was the way to go until automobiles took over. Buckboards were very popular, though many customers reached home happy but sore. Passengers frequently got out to walk alongside in the rougher sections, sparing the horses and, no doubt, themselves.

In 1881, the editor of the Salem (Massachusetts) *Gazette* spoke of Bar Harbor's buckboards thusly: "They bend under their burdens in a manner to awaken suspicion; but the accommodating drivers are always comforting in the assurance that, while they have sometimes been known to break, they always give warning by cracking first."

Seaside Rambles: Great Head

1871

BENJAMIN DECOSTA

Our next ramble is to Great Head, the finest headland on the island, and the highest, it has been said, between Cape Cod and New Brunswick. It lies a short mile beyond Schooner Head and is reached by the same road. Approaching the Head, we have a fine view of Newport's southern end descending to plunge into the sea. High up on the ledges are the nibbling sheep, foraging among the closely cropped grass. Reaching the farmhouse, most persons here leave their carriages; though the road extends some distance farther into the woods. The way is perfectly plain. The left-hand track leads by a gradual ascent directly to the Head. The woods are here and there largely sprinkled with fine old birches. Arriving at its highest point, a view is had far and wide of the grand old ocean, while landward rise the mountains.

This whole peninsula recently became the property of a Philadelphia family that has a taste for landed trifles. Among their effects, it is said, is an islet in Lake Superior, and a snow-peak in the Swiss Alps. But Great Head need not feel ashamed of itself in any company.

In one place there is a rough and steep descent nearly to the water, while in another a sheer wall leans forward, threateningly, over the sea. By descending the former a fine view of the face of the cliff is had; while a little way west, just below the gulch sprinkled with white rocks, is a cyclopean den called Stag Cave, from the resemblance to a stag which the imagination may easily conjure up when looking steadily upon some intrusions of milky quartz in the side of the wall.

Visitors are fond of coming to Great Head again and again to spend the whole day in sauntering from point to point, catching each new expression of the cliffs; or book in hand, bestowing themselves under some convenient rock, to keep one eye on the stereotyped page and the other on the changeful deep.

From Rambles in Mount Desert: With Sketches of Travel on the New-England Coast from Isles of Shoals to Grand Manan, *B. F. DeCosta, A. D. F. Randolph & Co., New York, 1871.*

In 1910, J. P. Morgan gave his daughter Louisa Satterlee a very large present: Great Head and Sand Beach. Louisa and her husband, Herbert, built several cottages near the beach, and a caretaker's house and barn near Schooner Head. The western side of the beach was open to the public.

The Satterlees built a stone tea house at the brink of the headland. It was a simple column eighteen feet high by fifteen feet wide, with a few small windows, a front door and a ladder to the rooftop observation deck. The famed donkey Melba carried thirty-odd tons of material up to the head and retired with honors.

The 1947 fire destroyed the Satterlees' cottages and damaged the tower. Their daughter Eleanor gave the family property to the park two years later.

Driving Out to See the Scenery

1892

SHERMAN'S GUIDE TO BAR HARBOR

Driving is a favorite pastime in Bar Harbor and everyone indulges in it, from the millionaire cottager who rides out in state in his costly equipage, to the hotel guest who is contented with the more modest and distinctly local production, the buckboard. Everything is favorable for driving here. The roads are in capital order, and an intricate network of them overspreads the island taking in every place of interest and introducing the tourist to some of the grandest and most beautiful scenery on the coast of America.

The buckboard deserves particular mention, as being the vehicle best suited to the roads of the island. The first buckboard was rudely fashioned out of two pairs of wheels with a couple of planks stretched between them and seats nailed or tied on the planks. But it has developed wonderfully, and some of the buckboards of the present day are marvels of the builder's and painter's arts. Many of them are now shipped to all parts of the country for persons who have first seen the vehicle here. The gentle swaying motion of the board while traveling at full speed over the hilly roads is simply delightful; and no person who has ever ridden in one, wishes to use any other kind of vehicle during his stay. They are now built to carry any number of passengers from two to twelve, and the largest ones are drawn by four horses.

The stables in the village contain many

ABOVE: Driving past the Beehive.

LEFT: Buckboard party ready for a day's adventures.

(Both courtesy of Maine Historic Preservation Commission.)

fine specimens of horse flesh, and there is no danger of the traveler being furnished with a poor "rig" if he is at all careful. The livery men employ skillful drivers who are well acquainted with all the points of interest on the island and can impart all manner of interesting information to the passengers.

The town authorities issue a list of the drives with all the fares for one or more passengers annexed, and this list is carefully revised each year. All drivers and liverymen are licensed, and any guilty of overcharging will be fined or lose their license.... It would be well for those starting out on a long drive to provide themselves with plenty of wraps, including waterproofs, as showers may come up very suddenly at times and the evenings are generally pleasantly cool....

The Ocean Drive is one of the grandest shore roads on the island. Here the visitor has a remarkable ocean view. The road leads southward from the village, entering the woods at Schooner Head Road, coming out again at Schooner Head...then on past Great Head and Thunder Cave to join the Otter Cliffs Road near the summer residence of Mr. Aulick Palmer. On one side of the road tower the Peak of Otter [Gorham Mountain] and Newport Mountain, the sides overgrown with noble forests of pine and spruce; while on the other is a grand battlement of cliffs. In some places the road runs down close to the water's edge; in others it winds along the edge of a precipice, at the base of which, hundreds [scores] of feet below, the ocean is beating and throbbing continually. Nothing but sea meets the eye to the eastward; but what a sea! Nowhere in the world can the ocean present a more pleasing prospect under the rays of the summer sun, or a grander one when tempest-tossed.

The places of interest which may be visited on this drive besides those above stated are Newport Beach on the western side of Great Head; Stag Cave so called from the fancied resemblance to that animal on its white quartz cliff; and a tall, battlemented cliff known as Castle Head. Otter Cliffs are well worth visiting, especially after a storm when the surf breaks grandly against them....

From Sherman's Guide to Bar Harbor, *W. H. Sherman, 1892; courtesy of Maine Historic Preservation Commission.*

Schooner Wrecked

1911
BAR HARBOR TIMES

In the great storm of wind and rain which was almost terrifying in the heart of town last Friday night, and has proven to have been most fearful at sea, the two-masted schooner *Tay*, Capt. I. W. Scott, of St. John, N. B., bound from St. John to Boston with lumber, went ashore on the Sand Beach at Great Head, about three-and-a-half miles from Bar Harbor, at 12:15 o'clock Friday night and was a total loss. One man was lost, J. B. Whelpley, the cook, of St. John, N. B., who is survived by a wife and three children. The schooner was owned by Peter McIntyre of St. John.

The lumber was owned by Stetson, Cutler Co., of Bangor.

The captain's son, Erving Scott, was a passenger and the crew numbered six besides the captain.

The *Tay* was doing well, according to Captain Scott and was bowling along in the face of a heavy southeast gale, when the schooner sprung a leak. At this time he was keeping her off shore and when the leak was discovered he squared away and intended to make the harbor here.

The mainsheet parted and then he lost his main boom. Capt. Scott attempted to stand off shore under head sails, but he was too far in and was swept inside the breakers. The *Tay* struck hard and was dismasted fore and aft at the first shock and began to go to pieces rapidly. The deck load of shingles was carried away but her cargo of plank below deck is safe on the beach.

The wreckage of the schooner Tay *and her cargo of shingles and lumber on Sand Beach. Lumber schooners like the* Tay *typically carried deckloads piled as high as possible, leaving just enough room for the booms to swing over. It was not unusual for the helmsman to have a hard time seeing forward. Since the entire cargo was buoyant, lumber carriers could, and did, load until the decks were awash.*

The remains of the Tay *lie under Sand Beach, far up on the shore near the stairs. Severe winter storms remove sand from the upper beach and periodically expose her timbers. Summer seas bring the sand back, gently burying her again. (Courtesy of Bar Harbor Historical Society.)*

The Sand Beach is the property bought by J. P. Morgan for his daughter, Mrs. Satterlee.

That more deaths did not result from the accident is almost miraculous. The captain and crew attempted to save themselves by swimming or scrambling to the shore. Although the task was a very difficult one all reached the beach in safety after a desperate struggle with the exception of the cook.

All day Saturday and Sunday, great crowds drove or cycled or walked to Great Head to view the wreckage strewn all over the Sand Beach. It was an impressive spectacle and a very sad one, and helped many who had little comprehension before of the might of the sea to realize what it was when aroused by the wind....

From the Bar Harbor Times, *August 2, 1911.*

Otter Cliffs and Otter Point

Early rock climbers at Otter Cliffs, ostensibly hunting and fishing. (Courtesy of Maine Historic Preservation Commission.)

Those who come to Otter Point to see the otters are destined to be disappointed. Sea otters do not inhabit the Atlantic. River otters occasionally visit salt water, but they prefer fresh. And the species that is a likely candidate for the name of the place has been extinct for well over a century.

Sea minks were largish minks that lived along rocky coastlines and on offshore islands, including Great Duck Island, eight miles southwest of Otter Point. Early records called them otters.

The last sea mink was converted to fur sometime in the mid-19th century. By the time naturalists got around to identifying the species several decades later, they were forced to work from a few specimens dwelling in museums. Park naturalist Arthur Stupka considered himself fortunate to see a dilapidated stuffed sea mink in the 1930s.

Visitors to Otter Point will find the same fascinating rock formations, crashing waves and grand view that have drawn sightseers and "rocking parties" for generations. On early summer mornings or winter afternoons when it is possible to mentally remove the roads, Otter Point returns to the days when people were few and sea minks might surface nearby. The developments of the last two centuries—fishing camps, farmhouses, summer cottages and a Navy radio station—are gone now, leaving scant traces behind.

The Journey to Otter Point

1888

M. F. Sweetser

After [passing through the Gorge], the road turns up along the Peak of Otter; runs high along the ridgy east wall of Otter Cove, with charming views of the cove and its settlement of farms; and finally stops at a little house. A fee is paid at the farmhouse at the end of the road; and leaving the carriage, the holiday rambler walks along a pleasant path, through a short stretch of evergreen woodland, and emerges on the vast cliffs, at whose foot, [nearly] a hundred feet below, the sea roars and whitens ceaselessly. The trend of the shoreline is visible as far as the yellow Newport Sands [Sand Beach] and the high promontory of Great Head. Otter-Creek Point is over a mile long, between the sea and Otter Cove, and rises to a height of 188 feet, covered with woods, and fronted on either side by noble cliffs. A little way off-shore is a lonely spindle; and farther out swings a bell-buoy, with its perpetual melancholy music of warning. A mile inland rises the Peak of Otter, a wild foot-hill of Newport [Champlain] Mountain. This region received its name from the otters that once abounded here, but have long since passed away. When the tide favors, people can cross from Great Head to Otter Cliff by way of Newport Beach and the rugged hills above. (In 1887–1888 a road nearly two miles long was built along these rocky cliffs, from Sand Beach to Otter Cliff, giving remarkable views of marine scenery.)

Beyond Otter's Nest, the summer-residence of Lieut. Aulick Palmer, of Washington, a road runs on to the end of Otter-Creek Point. Unless it is nominated in the bond, the buckboard drivers oftentimes decline to drive out over this noble road. On the western side of the point is a notable cavern, near which the natives have dug a deep pit, in the search for Capt. Kidd's buried treasures.

Otter Cove makes in for half a mile, between high wooded shores; and has on one side a quarry of fine (but hard) red granite. In ancient times the head of the cove was occupied with beaver-dams (beaver-skins were shipped from Eastern Maine to Boston as late as the year 1822). Here Champlain first made the acquaintance of the Mount-Desert Indians, according to his narrative: "The next day we sailed two leagues, and perceived a smoke in a cove at the foot of the mountains. We saw two canoes rowed by savages, which came within musket-shot to observe us. I sent our two savages in a boat to assure them of our friendship. Their fear of us made them turn back. On the morning of the next day, they came alongside of our barque, and talked with our savages. I ordered some biscuit, tobacco and other trifles to be given them. These savages had come beaver-hunting and to catch fish, some of which they gave to us." The friendly savages piloted the French ship through Penobscot Bay, and up to the present site of Bangor.

Conspicuous across the bay rises Schoodic, which is thus described in the *North-Atlantic Pilot*: "This prominent peninsula, one of the great landmarks on the coast of New England, is a range of high, barren, rocky hills, terminating to the southward in a low, bare, rocky point called Schoodic Point. They are composed of bare yellowish rock, with their slopes cut into very peculiar-looking steps, and a few low trees dotting at wide intervals their eastern sides. The general appearance is barren and desolate in the extreme. These hills are usually made by vessels from Europe coming upon our coast, bound to either the northward or southward." Farther to the eastward rises Petit Menan, a group of low rocky islets, destitute of vegetation, and surrounded by dangerous shoals...On the southern islet is a granite tower 107 feet high, with a fixed white light varied by flashes, 125 feet above the sea, and visible for seventeen miles. There is also a steam fog-whistle, and two or three dwelling-houses.

Fifteen years ago a well-known author predicted that in a short time the Otter-Creek village would surpass Bar Harbor, with a road up the south-eastern side of Green [Cadillac] Mountain, and easy rambles to the neighboring Great Head and Schooner Head. This consummation lies far in the future. A little way west of Otter Cove, Cornelius Wellington has built a costly road a mile and a half long, to a far-viewing plateau on the ridge between Green Mountain and Pemetic, north of the old Boyd camp. It is in contemplation to extend this road by the west shore of Turtle Lake [Bubble Pond], and the east shore of Eagle Lake, to the Eagle-Lake Road, thus making a beautiful round drive of about fifteen miles from Bar Harbor, encircling Green Mountain.

From Chisholm's Mount Desert Guide-Book, *M. F. Sweetser, Chisholm Brothers, Portland, 1888.*

Alessandro Fabbri was too old to enlist in World War I. He decided to offer his expertise as an amateur radio enthusiast, and his wealth in the form of a new radio station. Secretary of the Navy Daniels, an adamant Democrat, was not interested in any gift from a blue-blooded Republican with ties to the Morgans. Fabbri's friend, Assistant Secretary of the Navy Franklin Roosevelt, Maine's Senator Hale and supporting naval officers forced the Secretary to accept the plan, but Fabbri did not enjoy the process: "The earnest conversation continued for sometime until my now guilty conscience could no longer stand the strain, and I slipped out of the private door into the outer hall, undoubtably an object of suspicion to all passers-by."

Fabbri's battles were not over, but his radio station, Radio NBD, was commissioned August 29, 1917. Within a year, it was relied upon for all trans-Atlantic communications, since it functioned phenomenally well under all conditions. By mid-1918 the 200-man crew was handling more than 20,000 messages daily from France, serving as Washington's contact with General Pershing and the American Expeditionary Force. Many messages were in cipher; the operators had one chance to get it right. Radio NBD was the only station to hear the German "Surrender" broadcast on October 6, 1918.

Fabbri received the Navy Cross in 1920. He died of pneumonia two years later. In 1935, the station was dismantled and operations shifted to Schoodic as required by John D. Rockefeller Jr. in his agreement to extend the Ocean Drive auto road.

Very Loud and Clear

1918

Ensign Alessandro Fabbri

My dear Mr. Cooper,

I have read your kind letter of Monday night with the greatest interest.... Evans and Castner beamed all over when I read them those extracts from your letter that were intended for them and they seem to be fired with new enthusiasm.

Today, signals from all foreign stations have been received with phenomenal loudness. This may be due to the fine atmospheric conditions, in part, and partly due to the new counterpoise and the lengthening by 1,000 feet of the trans-Creek aerial, which has given an increase in the fundamental from 1,960 to 3,850 meters. With Dr. Austin's amplifier on IDO [Italy] and POZ [Nauen, Germany] this afternoon, both Castner and Evans said they had never heard such tremendously loud signals. The sound was so loud as to be unendurable for more than an instant, with the receivers close to your ears. I am quite certain that you could have heard it over the long distance telephone in Washington. I happened to have to call up Mr. Proctor, Chief Engineer of the Wireless Specialty Apparatus Company, in Boston and as a joke I asked if he wanted to hear POZ. As I was talking from an extension telephone on that floor, I placed one of the Baldwin ear pieces over the mouth piece of the telephone and, although he could not believe his ears at first or my assertion that it was POZ, both he and Mr. Picard, who was in his office, could read the signals at eight feet from the telephone in Boston. As

Lieutenant Fabbri and the Radio NBD crew. (Courtesy of Bar Harbor Historical Society.)

both Mr. Proctor and Mr. Picard have shown the greatest interest in the construction of the apparatus and the erection of the Station, I was glad to be able to give them this experience, which I imagine is a unique one. If you have time some day, let's try it all the way to Washington. Mr. Picard said that the energy of the signals received in Boston was easily sufficient for them to go in all the way to San Francisco by land wire, with the usual system of relays. When you think that the origin of this energy is thousands of miles away, being transmitted by etheric vibrations, it is truly wonderful....

From a January 23, 1918, letter to Lieutenant J. C. Cooper, Office of the Director of Naval Communications, in Alessandro Fabbri's personal files, reprinted in the Winter Harbor Naval Radio Station newsletter The Acadian *by T. F. Hahn, August 11, 1967; courtesy of Bar Harbor Historical Society.*

In the early summer of 1692, Cadillac stopped by a small ledgy island at the mouth of Frenchman Bay, and later reported that he found "six hundred dozen" eggs there.

Egg Rock was one of many seabird nesting islands along the Maine coast. The most common species were herring gulls, greater black-backed gulls and common eider ducks. There were also colonies of alcids: guillemots, puffins, murres, razorbills and the now-extinct great auk.

Before automated chickens, people looked forward to fresh seabird eggs in spring. They also collected down from the eider nests. Eiders and alcids were shot for food and many were packed in barrels, like the eggs, and shipped to city markets.

Settlers moved onto the habitable islands, bringing predators: rats, cats and dogs. By the turn of the century, there were just a few pairs of nesting common eiders and the alcids left on the coast of Maine.

There were also very few gulls, which is why they so rarely appear in coastal photos of the time. During the late 1800s, fashionable ladies wore hats decorated with feathers or bird parts, including white gull feathers. To protect the endangered gulls, the National Audubon Society pressured the ladies to give up their feathers and hired lighthouse keepers to keep gunners off the nesting islands.

Eiders from farther north recolonized Maine, and the nesting population has recovered. The gulls have proliferated to the point that they threaten vulnerable nesting neighbors such as terns. Once again, eiders and gulls nest on Egg Rock.

Observations of Seabirds

1934 TO 1935

ARTHUR STUPKA, RANGER-NATURALIST

A NOTE ON THE HERRING GULL

Captain Rodney Sadler of Bar Harbor, well known as an observant and capable mariner in these waters, tells me that some thirty-five or forty years ago a group of about two dozen Passamaquoddy Indians would leave their homes above Eastport, Maine, and journey by canoe to Heron Island, ten or eleven miles southwest of Mount Desert Island, where they would spend the entire summer shooting gulls. In those years there were no laws protecting these common birds of the ocean front, and the feather trade heaped great sums of money at the feet of an army of bird-butchers. The white-feathered breast of each mature gull, skinned and tanned, would be cut up into three pieces which, on the market, sold at four dollars per dozen pieces—hence one dollar per gull. After the skinning of the breast portion, the Indians discarded all that remained. At one time the Captain saw a pile of these discarded carcasses which he and his companion estimated as being "as big as five cords of wood."

A MEMORABLE SIGHTING OF THE AMERICAN EIDER

On February 10, 1935 in the immediate vicinity of the bell buoy which rings, rising and falling on the sea just off Otter Cliffs, it was the good fortune of Mr. Vernon Lunt and I to see a great flock of American [Common] Eiders. These birds, among the largest of the northern sea-fowl which winter off the Maine coast, described a great living arc on the surface of the deep blue water. Looking them over with a telescope I estimated that there must be approximately 5,000 birds in the flock. The clean white upper parts and black under-plumage of the male birds contrasted with the plain brown of the females presented a gala spectacle, for few birds are more handsome than these big male eiders. Here, off Otter Cliffs, I have seen them time and again in winter, but never in such numbers. In all probability they come to the ledges here and elsewhere to feed on mussels—a food which these birds appear to hold in great favor.

From Nature Notes, *Arthur Stupka, Acadia National Park, 1934, 1935; courtesy of NPS, Acadia National Park.*

One theory holds that the ledge just off Otter Point is the one that Samuel de Champlain ran into when he passed by in 1604. He reported a minor hole that was easily fixed after grounding the boat in a nearby cove (Otter Cove?).

The ledge would be easy to hit; it is barely awash at low tide. When a ground swell passes over, it can look like a large being rising up in the water–like a whale, in fact. On occasion Minke whales do come in between the headlands, but the one that stays right next to the green buoy is a ledge, despite what everyone else says.

Jordan Pond

The Jordan Pond House near the turn of the century.

In the 1890s, the Pond House advertised thusly:

> This house is situated on a picturesque spot at the southern end of Jordan's Pond, and from it can be had magnificent views of the mountains, the ocean and the many islands which separate Frenchman's Bay from the Atlantic.
>
> A new dining room has been built and dinner parties will receive special attention. Orders for party dinners should be sent in advance.
>
> Lunches at all hours.
>
> Ginger ale on ice, Confectionery and Cigars.
>
> A good fleet of boats will be kept in readiness for rowing and trout fishing. The fishing is better than ever this year.
>
> The signal at the head of the pond for boats for parties via Eagle Lake, will be attended as in years past. Fishing parties can also be accommodated overnight, for early or late fishing. Telephone connection with all parts of the island.

(Courtesy of Bar Harbor Historical Society.)

Blissfully, some things change very little. It is still possible to indulge in a program more than a century old: a quiet morning row followed by luncheon upon the lawn at the (second) Jordan Pond House. (The original building burned in 1979.)

In 1881, M. H. Sweetser recommended "an interesting route from Bar Harbor to Jordan's Pond [that] is entered by traversing Eagle Lake in boats, and then walking across a forest-path of a mile or two, under the round peaks of the Bubbles, and so emerging at the head of Jordan's. Upon signals being made here, the little local navy starts up the lake, and conveys the adventurous travellers to the outlet.... The lonely and weather-beaten little farmhouse of Mr. Tibbets stands at the foot of the lake, and here one (or a score) can get a good rural lunch for a small rural price, or a pitcher of rich milk, or various and refreshing beverages of the State-of-Maine unintoxicating variety, or loyal American cigars, or confectionery for the children...."

In 1871 Benjamin DeCosta observed that "Only the more persistent climber penetrates into the recesses of Mount Desert...." By 1888, a land development company had laid out plots for scores of little cottage lots on 3,500 acres from the slopes of Cadillac to Seal Harbor. This venture failed. Most of the land was protected in the early 1900s and became one of the first areas included in the national park.

In 1887, speculators set up shop on Mount Desert Island. The *Bar Harbor Record* reflected upon the boom a decade later:

"...The wonderful advance of Bar Harbor at that time started the fire of speculation till it glowed wildly in the breast of every man or woman who was possessed of or could buy a piece of property...."

Men mortgaged whatever they could to buy more land "in the enchanted regions." Land companies "sprung up in the night."

Some men profited greatly; pieces of land that had been bought for $200 sold for $20,000. Land in Bar Harbor was going for $11,000 an acre, at a time when a decent day's pay was a couple of dollars. According to the *Record*, "Fabulous stories of the real estate transactions are told, and most of them are true. Many lucky individuals who held a small piece of land retired after its sale recently with comfortable fortunes...Land [value] is increasing steadily and it is said that land in Bar Harbor is worth more than at any summer resort in the world."

The valuation of the town of Bar Harbor increased from $622,901 in 1880 to $5,034,958 in 1890.

Following the normal pattern, the Bar Harbor land boom burst suddenly, and "the wreckage fell upon mostly the native residents." The ruins of the Mount Desert and Eastern Shore Land Company filled over a column of very tiny type in the December 4, 1890, issue of the *Record*—under the heading "Sheriff's Sale."

Description of Mount Desert Island and the Magnificent Property of this Company

1888

MOUNT DESERT AND EASTERN SHORE LAND COMPANY

The following report from our resident superintendent at Bar Harbor will present only a brief and limited idea of the value and extent of the property of the Mount Desert and Eastern Shore Land Company.

The near future will develop new, valuable, and interesting features. A large number of charming sites on mountain, lake-side, and seashore, suitable for the erection thereon of cottages, villas, and chalets, have been opened up by the completion of four miles of road, and construction has begun on the road recommended by our superintendent which will make a grand and popular drive, without parallel on Mount Desert Island. The scenery is most beautiful, grand, and varied, the air pure and bracing, and hay fever unknown. A demand has already been created for the lots, and we shall offer for sale at once at our offices 500 choice lots, to be selected from the plan, varying in size from 10,000 to 40,000 square feet [under an acre], and prices from $150 to $600 per lot. This is a rare opportunity to invest in Bar Harbor property at a very low figure, with assurance of an early advance in price.

Charles H. Lewis, President Mt. D. and E. S. L. Co., Boston, Mass., Oct. 11, 1888.

Bar Harbor, Me., Oct. 4, 1888
Col. C. H. Lewis,
President Mt. D. and E. S. L. Co.

DEAR SIR,—In obedience to your instruction I have examined the property of the Mount Desert and Eastern Shore Land Company, with the following result: The new carriage road to the summit of Green [Cadillac] Mountain passes for its entire distance, about two miles, through your mountain lands, a gradual ascent, opening up at different levels on both sides of the road a large amount of elevated and sightly property with grand and extended views. Although this road was not open for travel until about the middle of July, between that time and the middle of September over 3,000 visitors drove over it to the summit, an evidence of its attractions and popularity as well as proof that cottagers, residents, tourists, and visitors of Bar Harbor will gladly welcome and avail themselves of any opportunity to enjoy new and beautiful drives. The proper development of this property will produce an astonishing result in this line, to be attained by opening up and building a road down the shore of Eagle Lake, thence through grand forests with picturesque streams and brooks, mountains looming up on either side, overhanging crags and cliff, until we reach the head of Jordan's Lake, nestling in the mountains. Eagle Lake is over two miles in length and three quarters of a mile wide. By reference to the accompanying map you can better understand my description. The proposed road then follows at the foot of Pemetic Mountain, along the eastern shore of Lake Jordan to its southern end, and thence to Seal Harbor at the ocean.

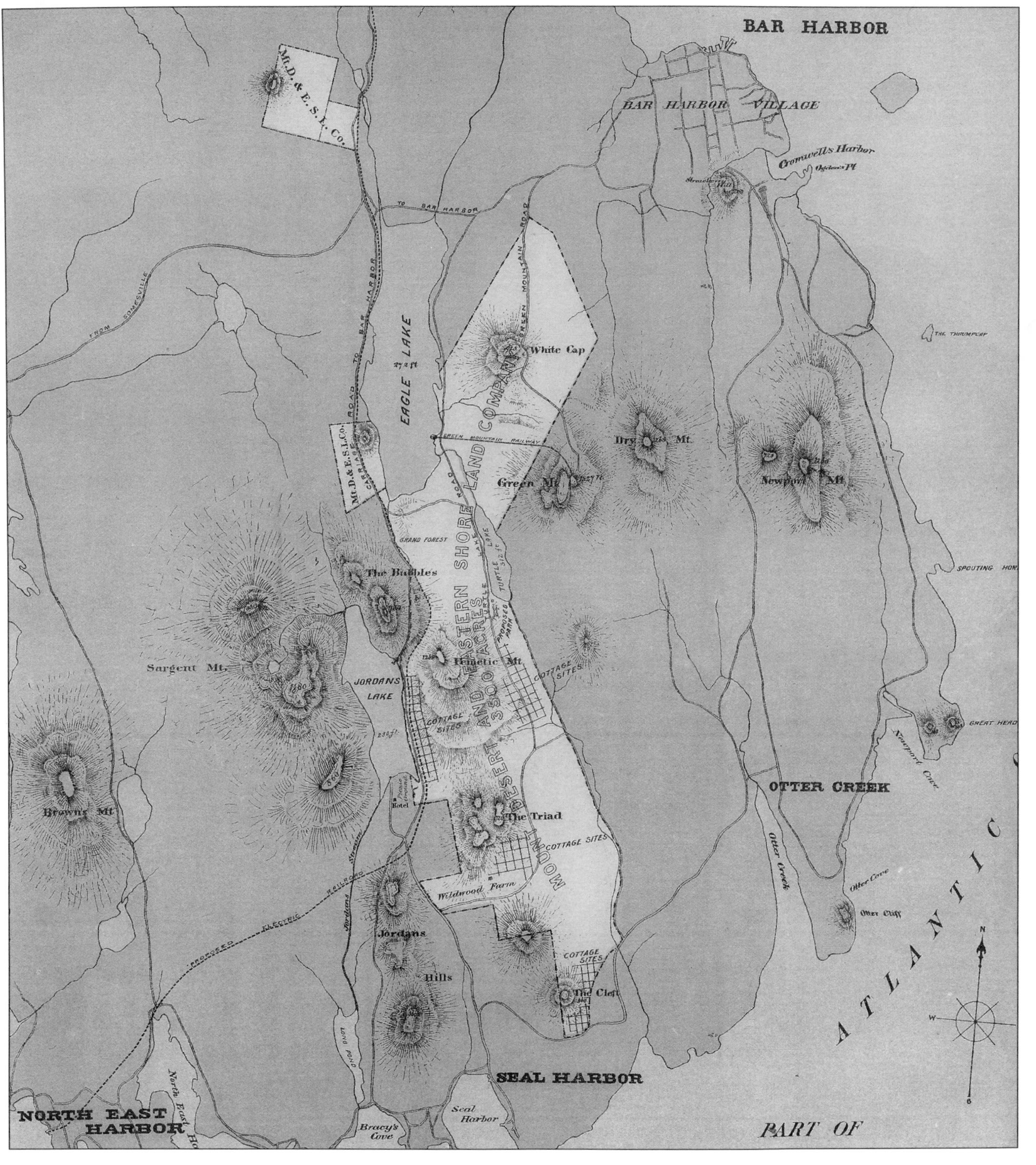

The land company partially completed a rough track from Jordan Pond to Eagle Lake, passing by Bubble Pond. Most of the land company's other plans never developed, including the electric railway, a controversial idea that was proposed at intervals over the years, and appears to have always found more vehement objectors than defenders.

Thirty years later, John D. Rockefeller Jr.'s crews built carriage roads over much of the land company's route. Rockefeller's crew, with the support of George Dorr and many others, also built an auto road from Jordan Pond to Eagle Lake in 1923, despite loud objections from summer colonists who felt the park's special places would be opened up to hordes of trash-dropping, unappreciative tourists driving loud and smelly automobiles. (Courtesy of Maine Historic Preservation Commission.)

A large area of this land is available for the erection of mountain cottages, villas, and chalets with charming, picturesque, and sublime views of the ocean, lake, and mountains. I can conceive of no part of this country where such a combination can be found, all within an area of five or six miles in diameter, available to the large and wealthy summer population of Bar Harbor. At the south end of this lake is a small old farm-house which has been for the past five years used as a place of entertainment for man and beast; last year 5,000 guests registered there and many failed to do so. Of course the accommodations were very limited, and the attraction was the beautiful scenery. Most of this large number drove from Bar Harbor. On the livery cards this drive is called twenty-two miles the round trip, several miles of which is over a road with no special interest or beauty therein. The proposed road will decrease the distance seven miles, while the entire drive will arouse the wonder and admiration of all. On the west side of Jordan's Lake, near the north end, a perpendicular precipice of dark granite rises to the height of 900 feet, while towering above the proposed road is Pemetic Mountain, 1,200 feet in height. This lake is one and a half miles long by one half mile wide, of great depth, from 100 to 140 feet in several places, and abounds in trout.

The probabilities of establishing a successful and popular resort near this lake can easily be understood. There is a complete and invigorating change from sea to mountain breezes, from salt ocean to clear, cool mountain lake, 230 feet above sea level, while some of our roads will wind around the mountainsides at double that elevation. Leaving Jordan's Lake we follow the road for about a mile bordering your property; thence turning in, is a road about three miles in length which we have just completed, opening up a large amount of desirable land with an ocean and lake view; following this road we pass up between Pemetic and Green Mountains through a lovely valley about a half a mile in width, along the west side of Turtle Lake [Bubble Pond]. This is indeed a most desirable and available part of your property. Turtle Lake is truly the gem of the mountains. I have said so much about Jordan's Lake, that any repetition is unnecessary. Turtle Lake is about one mile long and a quarter mile wide, with high mountains nearly all around it. It is 100 feet higher than the other lakes, the water is clear and cold, evidently pure spring water; a rare and healthy spot. What more can be desired? All the requisites of the White Mountains, Adirondacks, and the Berkshire Hills can be found here within six miles of the shore at Bar Harbor....

...To sum it up, you have about 3,000 acres of land upon which you will be able to take one continuous drive of fifteen miles, replete with surprising changes of wilderness, mountains, lake and ocean views, traversing hitherto almost inaccessible lakes, the scenery combining lovely, picturesque, sublime and sylvan features. Hunting and fishing are fine. Deer and smaller game are frequently seen. In Eagle Lake, land-locked salmon and trout abound, and brook trout in two other lakes. This property, well managed and well developed, will produce one of the grandest parks and mountain resorts in this or any other country, and transform Bar Harbor into a fall as well as summer resort. The transient and permanent residents are deeply interested in this enterprise and its success.

Yours very truly,
John J. Pratt
Resident Superintendent

From the Maine Historic Preservation Commission collection.

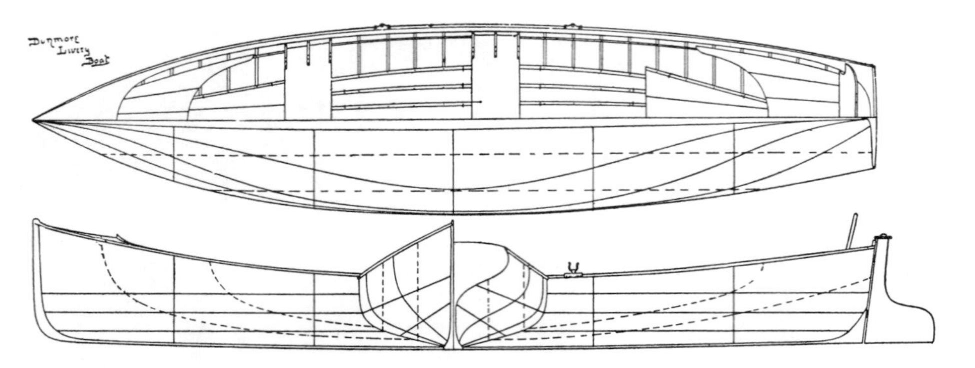

A typical livery boat, from the 1893 catalog of the St. Lawrence River Skiff, Canoe and Steam Launch Company. Her essential dimensions: Length, fifteen feet; beam, forty inches; depth amidships, fourteen inches. She was advertised to be "a safe, staunch craft, and perfectly safe even in inexperienced hands." She cost $60, varnished, with a copper-fastened cedar hull; oak keel, stem, ribs and gunwales; butternut or cherry deck; pine seats; and two pairs of ash or spruce oars. (Courtesy of David Gordon.)

Eagle Lake

Rowboats could be rented on the lake for most of the late 1800s and early 1900s, from the proprietor of Eagle Lake House and other entrepreneurs. Despite the difficult winds and rough chop common on many summer afternoons, people rowed across the lake and explored along the shore.

The small sternwheel steamer Wauwinnet *carried visitors across the lake from the north shore to the Green Mountain cog railway from 1883 to 1890. To reach her new route, the boat steamed to Bar Harbor from Newport, Rhode Island, then was hauled and winched the two-and-a-half miles to Eagle Lake under the direction of Elihu Hamor and Daniel Brewer. The trip took a month. Reports of the* Wauwinnet's *fate after the railroad failed differ, but it is clear that no one was interested in winching her back to the sea. Some say that she was left untended during the winter and was wrecked by ice; others say that she was stripped and sunk in the lake, either in deep water or in the cove. It seems likely that she suffered untended during the winter, then was stripped and sunk in fairly deep water.*

The framework and gears on the left were part of a conveyor system used by the Brewers to bring harvested ice onto shore to their two ice storage houses. They also maintained two ice houses in town on Brewer Avenue. The ice business operated from 1875 to 1951; parts of the conveyor are still visible on the bottom of the cove. (Courtesy of Bar Harbor Historical Society.)

Eagle Lake is one of the most popular destinations in Acadia National Park, but relatively few people come to spend time on the water. The carriage roads are the main attraction, offering miles of beautiful auto-free roads for walking, running, biking and skiing.

In 1910, John D. Rockefeller Jr. and his wife, Abby, bought a cottage in Seal Harbor after renting in Bar Harbor for a couple of seasons. He enjoyed horses and carriage rides–and designing roads–so he began building quiet woodland carriage roads on his increasingly large property.

Five years after the Rockefellers settled in peaceful Seal Harbor, automobiles arrived to stay on Mount Desert Island. At about this time, George Dorr asked Rockefeller to help with the work of protecting land. With the approval of most, Rockefeller expanded the carriage road system to the newly acquired protected lands.

Most of the work on the carriage roads was done between the park's founding in 1919 and the 1930s. The work progressed steadily, with general public support punctuated by occasional heartfelt objections from some of the summer people, including Harold Peabody.

When Rockefeller and his crews finished, they left a legacy of fifty-seven miles of thoughtfully designed and carefully built carriage roads throughout the eastern portion of Acadia.

Winter Sports at Eagle Lake

1890–1891

BAR HARBOR RECORD

JANUARY 2.—There has been rare sport at the Witch Hole Pond during the week and crowds have taken advantage of the excellent skating there. Ice boats are also numerous and the pond has presented a very gay appearance. A large number of these crafts are now being constructed and as soon as Eagle Lake freezes over a fleet of nearly forty boats will furnish pleasure for our people.

JANUARY 16.—There was rare sport on Eagle Lake, Tuesday. The ice was clear and smooth as crystal and a fleet of about twenty-five ice boats flew over its shining surface. Skaters by the hundred were there and the lake was alive with people of all ages. The snow of yesterday put an end to the sport for the present but the owners of the ice boats are hoping they will be able to clear the snow from the ice and renew their favorite sport.

JANUARY 23.—[Eagle Lake measures one and three quarters miles, but] judging from the time it takes an ice boat to go across it when there is a good breeze, one might think it not over half a mile in length.

MARCH 20.—Ice boating and skating on Eagle Lake have attracted crowds of people to that place during the week and even though Bar Harbor is noted for having the largest number of churches of any village in Maine, it must be confessed that Sunday found many of our people enjoying these popular sports. The wind was very strong that day and the ice boats made some wonderfully fast time. By actual measurement, Eagle Lake is one and three-fourths mile long from the steamboat wharf [at the north end] to the road leading to Jordan's pond and, although it hardly seems possible, Mr. Chas. Conners's boat covered the distance in one minute and forty-five seconds, or at the rate of about sixty-two miles per hour.

January 1.—A novel sight was witnessed at Eagle Lake one day last week. Mr. Isaac Moore, who is an enthusiastic bicyclist, wound the tires of his cycle with heavy emery paper, and started out to beat the skaters. The ice was smooth but on a straightaway course he could hold the skaters good play. It required about an acre of space to turn in but Isaac could do it.

From the Bar Harbor Record, *1890 and 1891.*

The fleet of ice boats on Eagle Lake. (Courtesy of Bar Harbor Historical Society.)

At Eagle Lake House

1881

Mount Desert Herald

[O]ur party secured the services of a buckboard seating nine comfortably, besides the driver. We were careful to make a trade with the owner of the team before starting, as the sharp Yankees of Mount Desert will overcharge when they get a chance, as some of our party found out. But satisfactory rates were agreed upon and we started off for Eagle Lake, which we reached after a hilly ride of about an hour.

"Eagle Lake in the moonlight."
(Courtesy of Bar Harbor Historical Society.)

We know of no reason why the lake should be called Eagle, unless it was named after a stuffed specimen of the national bird which spreads its wings benignly over a lunch table in the Lake House, kept by a bald-headed Hungarian. After taking in the wide expanse of the lake, something over a mile in length, and tasting the delicious ice cream and Hungarian chips served for us, and witnessing the intelligent tricks of a huge Newfoundland dog, for which the proprietor had refused offers of "t'ree hun'ded dollars," and listening to the pathetic story of how the animal saved the life of his boy from drowning, we could realize that it would take more than money to buy him.

We had seen Eagle Lake and after securing about a ten acre lot to turn our lengthy vehicle in, we rode back at a lively rate, it being down hill this time, arriving at the hotel in time to do justice to a good dinner.

—*Eastport Sentinel.*

From the Mount Desert Herald, *September 3, 1881.*

The Hungarian and his Newfoundland offered more than chips and ice cream. One correspondent reported that the establishment was "a sort of saloon and beer-garden. Around the house, in a grove, are tables with rustic seats, where visitors sit and sip their ale while enjoying the breeze from the lake." Eventually the forces of justice caught up with the Hungarian, whose disregard for the "Maine Law" cost him $200. (Maine passed its first prohibition law–the unloved and much ignored "Maine Law"–in 1851.)

By the late 1880s, "four-horse barges" left town several times daily for a fancier Eagle Lake House. It featured "billiards, bowling and refreshments."

A Lament for Past Times

1894

F. Marion Crawford

The principal characteristic of the place was an air of youth—it did not seem as if any one could ever be more than twenty-five years old. Parties of half a dozen girls were often under the nominal care of one chaperon, generally chosen because she was good-natured and not too strict, but as a matter of fact the young people protected themselves and one another. Large picnic parties frequently went off for the day in buckboards, and there is a lonely sheet of water among the hills, called Eagle Lake, which used to be a favorite goal for afternoon expeditions. There were canoes and row-boats to be had, and in the evening supper was obtainable, and better than in the Bar Harbor hotels, at a little tavern where the prohibition laws of the state were defied. The usual result followed, and very bad things to drink were sold at very high prices, after paying which the party came home, making the woods-roads ring with laughter and singing.

That is all changed now. The tavern is burnt down, and a great wooden box in the lake marks the sluice which takes the village water supply, people only cross [the lake] on the way to Jordan's Pond, and on moon-light nights it hears but the occasional splash of a fish, or now and then the wild laughter of the loon.

From Bar Harbor, *Francis Marion Crawford, Charles Scribner's Sons, New York, 1894.*

From 1914 to 1941, landscape designer Beatrix Jones Farrand created dozens of gardens on Mount Desert Island, including the sunken Oriental sculpture garden at Mr. and Mrs. John D. Rockefeller Jr.'s Seal Harbor estate, The Eyrie. Rockefeller also asked her to work with him on landscaping along the new carriage roads.

The final landscaping work involved far more than cleaning up construction debris and planting a few pines. Rockefeller and Farrand planned a carefully contrived "natural" landscape, built with a wide variety of mostly native species propagated by the thousands in the Rockefeller nurseries under the supervision of head nurseryman Charles Miller. The landscape was designed to please the eye with its natural beauty, while also satisfying the human need for order.

Beatrix Farrand conversed about ideas, plans and progress with Rockefeller through a series of Road Notes. The following selection of notes covers carriage road sections from Aunt Betty's Pond on the west side of Eagle Lake southwest to Bubble Pond. The area around Aunt Betty's Pond burned in the 1947 fire, but the southern and eastern shores of Eagle Lake, and all of Bubble Pond escaped.

Road Notes: Eagle Lake Area

1929 TO 1932

BEATRIX JONES FARRAND

On the edge of the road between Aunt Betty's Pond and the road lines it was suggested that a low screen of shrubs of native types be used. The varieties mentioned were cassandra [leatherleaf], wild rose, *Ilex verticullata* [winterberry] and clematis. (1931)

A note was made to ask Mr. Miller whether or not he thought *Lobelia cardinalis* [Cardinal flower] would thrive and would be appropriate to plant on the edges of Aunt Betty's Pond. (1931)

Mr. Rockefeller felt that he would like to leave a dead branch on many of the trees, at any rate experimentally, for the next season and felt that this experiment might be tried on the new Aunt Betty's Pond road and others in this vicinity. Mr. Rockefeller and Mrs. Farrand both agreed that the dead trees, where the whole plant was dead, should be cut out. (1931)

Mrs. Farrand again greatly enjoyed the beauty of the road leading southward from Aunt Betty's Pond. The coloring of the hardwood trees was magnificent and the glimpses from the road winding up the brook were admirable. (1931)

A note was taken to thicken heavily the plantation between the Y, the Sargent Mountain road, the west Eagle Lake road and the new bridle path, as these roads are now unpleasantly open to each other. (1931)

Additional planting is also needed when possible on the banks south of Eagle Lake. Birches might be well added to the ledges, especially in the places where recent cuts have been made. This planting suggestion applies to the road line parallel to the south shore of Eagle Lake. (1931)

Yellow birches would be attractive if planted above the road (southwest) on the banks in the birch wood southwest of Eagle Lake on the slope of the Bubble. (1931)

Bubble Pond bridge: Pockets were thought desirable to have made by Mr. Ralston on both the north and southwest sides of the Bubble Pond bridge. These would not be difficult to build, as a shelf on the south side of the bridge would permit a good-sized pocket, and there seemed also to be space on the road level which would allow the placing of several big rocks and possibly a cubic yard of soil. Mrs. Farrand thought that it was altogether desirable, if possible, to add bush honeysuckle (*Diervilla* [*lonicera*]) and wild roses to the planting of the banks near the Bubble Pond bridge. Mr. Miller felt that there might not be soil enough but he was urged to try and find a few pockets as even a few groups of roses, etc. would break up the somewhat bleak appearance of these road shoulders in the neighborhood.... (1929)

Mr. Miller promised that he would fill the spaces around the Bubble Pond bridge as thickly as the ledge permitted, even perhaps stretching a point and putting in a larger tree here and there. (1931)

From Beatrix Farrand, Road Notes, Home Series, Record Group Two, Office of the Messrs. Rockefeller (OMR), Rockefeller Family Archives, Rockefeller Archive Center, North Tarrytown, New York.

Cadillac (Green) Mountain

The first accommodations on Green Mountain were basic, but served. Patrons usually walked, although some hired a wagon. The road ran up the mountain's north ridge and featured boggy mud, rough, rocky ground and open ledges with a little earth thrown upon them to offer some footing for the horses. Those who chose the horse-drawn option often found themselves walking beside the wagon on the more interesting parts of the road. (Courtesy of Maine Historic Preservation Commission.)

The urge to climb Cadillac (Green) Mountain is irresistible. Its first ascent went unrecorded, but George Dorr recalled his first trip: "I remember driving up the old road to the summit in an old wagon drawn by two stout horses among the first things we did—my father, mother, my older brother and myself—when we visited Bar Harbor in the summer of 1868.... I remember well the old house of entertainment there, a simple structure which was admirably placed looking broadly out to the southward across the ocean...."

The Brewer family bought the mountain from the Bingham Heirs, who had acquired it for its speculative timber value. The land was part of the vast holdings sold by Madame deGregoire in the early 1800s. The Brewers logged the mountain's slopes and ran a mill at the outlet of Eagle Lake. They eventually developed the mountain for summer visitors, building the first Summit Hotel in 1883. In the years following, a cog railway and toll carriage road competed for visitors. By the late 1880s, weary persons could leave Boston in the morning on the luxurious Bar Harbor Express train and be on the summit by the next noon.

George Dorr bought the mountain summit from the Brewers in 1908. He promoted an auto road, and by the 1930s, autos were passing hikers on the slopes of the mountain renamed Cadillac.

A Night on Green Mountain

LATE 1860S

BENJAMIN DECOSTA

Green [Cadillac] Mountain elevates itself above all the rest, both in pictorial interest and in commanding height.

In crossing the island to Bar Harbor, our friend Oldstyle, and others averse to climbing, were left behind, while new friends and acquaintances entered the circle. Here the mountain tramp is never a solitary excursion. At a signal, troops of pedestrians issue forth to explore the neighboring regions, and two or three in nearly every circle were always ready to climb the highest peak and the most difficult pass.

But happily Green Mountain presents few obstacles in the way of visitors. For a number of years the officers of the Coast Survey had an Observatory on its summit, and when work was suspended a tolerable road was left, which has since been improved to such an extent that carriages can, if necessary, ascend to the top; though it is the custom for most persons to perform the last two miles on foot. The whole distance, four miles to the village, is a pleasant excursion for a pedestrian in full strength.

As we ascend, Eagle Lake comes in view on the right, lying along the flank of the mountain in a trough-like depression, while beyond the ranges rise in regular order. The view towards Newport and the sea is shut in by the woody ridge of Green Mountain, along the back-bone of which the road runs, though at several points about half way up may be had charming glimpses of Goldsborough Mountains and Frenchman's Bay. Finally, on reaching the top, a glowing prospect greets the eye, land and sea mingling in the most captivating forms. On a clear day the view is extensive. Katahdin shows a clearly defined peak many miles distant, while Mount Washington at times will even vouchsafe to unveil its head.

On the ocean, Mount Desert Rock may be distinguished with the aid of a glass about fifteen miles distant, while a maze of islands rise up along the shores.

The top of Green Mountain is grooved out by two little valleys which run nearly north-west and south-east. The western valley, which descends towards the sea, is filled with small trees and shrubs. Crossing near its head and descending in a westerly direction, we reach the brow, where may be had a fine view of the wild region lying between Green Mountain and Sargent. Pemetic is close at hand, lifting up its sharp barren ridge; the Bubble Mountains next appear, rejoicing modestly in their green crowns of lesser height; beyond is the dark but splendid range of Sargent, shutting in the sky; while Eagle Lake stretches northward at our feet. Only the more persistent climber penetrates into the recesses of Mount Desert, where he may any day come face to face with the fierce-looking but inoffensive wild-cat, or the harmless deer. One never tires of looking down upon the dark, tangled woods, the jagged peaks, and dusky glens, where the light and shade hold perpetual play, bringing out the strongest and most beautiful effects.

Other very fine views may be had, to see which we must scramble around the entire summit. But only one of these can be mentioned here, though in some respects it is the grandest to be had on the whole island. It is seen from the north-east brow, where the visitor looks down into the Otter Creek Valley, lying between Green Mountain and its spur known as Dry [Dorr] Mountain. The prospect is marked both by variety and magnitude. Immediately before us is the valley, a thousand feet deep, clothed in the dark green forests, well-watered in the centre by a cool, invisible brook, and terminating in the blue fiord of Otter Creek; beyond is the ridge of Dry Mountain and the peak of Newport, rising in bold relief against the sea; while to the left, far down upon the shore, is the village of Bar Harbor, fronting the isles and waters of Frenchman's Bay. Language cannot fitly convey an adequate impression of the beauty of this scene, which when once viewed will linger forever in the memory.

It was a beautiful July morning when we made our first excursion to the summit, in company with a merry party. Occasionally we saw the glacial marks on the rocks, that Agassiz views as records of the Ice-period in Maine; but we were chiefly interested in the prospect, which unfolded some fresh charm at every step. On reaching the summit, we were denied a view of the more distant objects, such as Katahdin and Mount Washington, which are seen only in remarkably clear weather, but objects far out at sea were distinctly visible. We enjoyed a beautiful sunset, yet as night came the fog rolled in from the sea, shutting out the view of the numerous beacon lights that twinkle on the coast. Only the light on Bear Island appeared at intervals.

The world below being wrapped in darkness, we were obliged to confine ourselves to the little house erected here for the entertainment of visitors. It is a rough-built structure, thrown together on the umbrella principle, with all the framework showing on the inside, being braced up without by light timbers of spruce planted in the rock to enable it to withstand the heavy gales. The little parlor in the centre is flanked by the dining-room, and a couple of dormitories, while overhead, in the loft, a double tier of berths is arranged, steamboat fashion, for the further accommodation of disciples of Morpheus. During those cold, stormy nights which occur on the mountain even in the middle of July, the well-filled stove is no unwelcome companion, but tends to promote jollity in the circle of wayfarers gathered around it. Here, when supper is over, the adventures of the day are recited, the song is sung, and the story told, while the walls at times will crack with peals of laughter.

At an early hour the weary pedestrian usually retires, with a firm resolution to be up betimes and receive the first greetings of Old Sol as he rises from his ocean bed. Our company followed the custom of the place, though not before some young sons of Yale had executed a grand bear dance on the rough board floor in the loft which had been assigned to their use. Mine host looked slightly aghast when he heard the timbers groaning about his ears, but on being assured that the party was no less sage than noisy and "all right" he took a candle and sought out his downy couch, simply enjoining us to put out the lights when we got ready.

The tired Collegians, however, had hardly ended their performance on the light fantastic toe, when a fearful thunder-storm arose, which set the sky all ablaze and made the mountains reel. When morning came no glorious sunrise greeted our eye, but the heavens were still pealing, while the lightening seemed fairly to rain down upon every part of the country below. It was one of those storms such as the inhabitants of Mount Desert experience but once in a lifetime, being tropical in its characteristics and disastrous effects.

When breakfast was over the storm abated, and we went forth to view as much of the prospect as could be discerned through the mist. The rain had fallen in floods, and cascades were tearing over the rocks and shooting down the steep ledges, while the fog veiling Otter Creek Valley only occasionally opened and gave a glimpse of the half-drowned woods below.

Soon the most of the party grew weary of watching the fog, and all but two departed for Bar Harbor. By four o'clock in the afternoon my own patience was exhausted, and in the midst of a driving gale and blinding fog, Amarinta and I left the house, started down the deluged road, and pushed on without pausing, until at the end of an hour and a half we entered the hotel at Bar Harbor. Thus, for the time, ended our dreams of Green Mountain.

From Rambles in Mount Desert: With Sketches of Travel on the New-England Coast from Isles of Shoals to Grand Manan, *B. F. DeCosta, A. D. F. Randolph & Co., New York, 1871.*

A Visitor's Guide to Green Mountain

1888

M. F. SWEETSER

Green Mountain, the chief elevation on the island, is nearly five miles long, from Duck Brook to Otter Creek, with Echo Notch in the east, and the deep bowls of Eagle Lake and Turtle Lake [Bubble Pond] on the west. Among its subordinate peaks are Dry Mountain, on the east; and the White Cap and Great Hill, on the north. The highest point of the ridge is 1,527 feet above the sea, being the most considerable elevation on the Atlantic Coast of North America.... The United States Coast-Survey officers, who occupied the peak for some time, named it Adam's Grave (because it was just outside Eden), but this singular title fortunately failed to stick.

The old carriage road up Green Mountain has long been discontinued, and is impassible for wheels. It is still used as a foot-path, by climbers,—entering the woods on the left of the highway, at the top of the long hill before descending toward Eagle Lake, about half a mile beyond the race-course [now the Kebo golf course], and more than two miles from the summit of the mountain. The mountain-road at its junction with the highway looks much like the bed of a stony brook. It ascends a mile through the woods and comes out on the rocky northern ridge, with views of Eagle Lake and a vast expanse of country. Beyond the shaggy slopes of Great Hill, the steep road climbs the White Cap, whose peak (925 feet high) is left on the right. It is a long mile from this point to the summit, during which a rise

In the early 1880s, the summer tourist population swelled to thousands, offering glorious prospects for making money. The satisfying vision of throngs taking a cog-railway ride up Green Mountain's western slopes came to a group of forward-thinkers. Passengers would travel to the railroad by ferry across Eagle Lake, after a buckboard ride from town.

Crews started work on the railroad in February 1883, putting in twelve-hour days for $1.50 per day. They used oxen to haul timbers for the trestles from the nearby woods. Going up to work was a chore, but heading home was a breeze–or, rather, a gale, since the ride down on a slide board took a little over a minute. The railroad was ready for business by July.

The locomotive was brought up from Portland on a schooner and hauled overland by fourteen horses. The crew hauled it and the rest of the machinery over the lake ice in late March and early April. They were forced to extend supporting timbers out from shore, since the ice on the edges was getting a little soft.

The locomotive burned wood. The first year's supply came from along the tracks, but the railroad bought its fuel thereafter: 175 cords at $2.50 per cord, delivered.

The railroad did very well for a few years, but competitors built a new carriage road in 1887. To stop them, the railroad men put up gates and finally applied explosives in the dead of night, to no avail. The railroad went bankrupt in 1890. Its equipment was salvaged or scrapped. The locomotive went to Mount Washington in 1895, where she served until 1927.

of over 500 feet must be made. In 1882, a famous highway robbery occurred on this road, when the Howe brothers, summer visitors ascending the mountain, were halted by a modern Claude Duval, and compelled to surrender all their valuables.

The Green Mountain Railway was chartered in 1882 and built in 1883, having been begun in April and finished in June. It is 6,300 feet long, the route being nearly a straight line; and the sleepers and supports are bolted to the ledges, without trestles. For 500 feet the grade is one foot in three. This is the second cog-road in the United States, the other being on Mount Washington. Europe has two, one on the Rhigi [near Luzern, Switzerland], and one on Mount Vesuvius. The road is four feet, seven and a half inches in gauge, with T and cog rails; and the fat humpbacked little locomotive weighs ten tons. The ascent takes half an hour. The ride upward is most notable for the mechanism of the railway, the queerly tilted cars, and the pudgy little locomotive, sticking its toes in the rounds of the middle iron cog-rail. From time to time, the passengers alight and pick berries or flowers, as the engine puffs its slow way upward. Meanwhile, Eagle Lake sinks away in the downward distance, and wider horizons open magnificently on the west and north. The view is clear and unobstructed, owing to the great breadth of the cutting through the forest. At length the little train stops amid wind-swept gray ledges on the summit.

The top of the mountain is a long and narrow plateau cut off from similar adjacent ridges by shallow and woody ravines. One can walk for a half-mile or more along this lofty promenade without much descent, so that sojourners at the mountain-inn need not want for exercise. The ridge is mainly composed of bare ledges, in whose hollows grow mountain-cranberries, blue-berries, bunch-berries, and delicate highland flowers, in great richness and profusion.

Green Mountain House in 1888. The hotel was torn down in 1896. (Courtesy of Maine Historic Preservation Commission.)

The view from near the summit, looking down the Green Mountain cog rails.

Mae D. McFarland, whose father worked on the railroad, recalled one of the crew's favorite stories in a reminiscence published in the 1938 Bar Harbor Times*: "[A] very stout and fashionable lady, when the train was laboring up the steep mountain grade, almost at the mountain top, asked nervously, 'Conductor, if these cogs break, where would we go to?'" The conductor glanced back at Eagle Lake, far below, and replied, 'Well, madam, that depends on the kind of life we've been living before we got on this train.'" (Courtesy of Bar Harbor Historical Society.)*

The hotel is of modern construction, high-studded and airy, with twenty commodious rooms, broad encircling piazzas, an observatory tower, and a dining-hall where good meals are served at a low figure. It is several hundred feet from the railway. Invalids are sometimes brought here as to a sanatorium, the clear sweet air of the mountain-top working favorably for their recovery; and worn-out men find in the quietude of the place, and its novelties of view and air, much that tends to revive and strengthen them. The old hotel on the summit stood some way to the southward, and was burned in 1884, the present handsome Gothic building dating from the year 1885.

The best view-point is the cupola on the hotel, where there is a telescope, with which the remoter objects are clearly identified. At the foot of the mountain the winding roads and red roofs and great hotels of Bar Harbor cover the point, with a fleet of yachts and steamboats offshore. Beyond are the Porcupine Islands, Bar Island over the left of Bar Harbor, with Sheep Porcupine next, and then Burnt Porcupine, and then Round [Bald] Porcupine and Long Porcupine nearly over each other, and above the villas on Ogden's Point....

From Chisholm's Mount Desert Guide-Book, *M. F. Sweetser, Chisholm Brothers, Portland, 1888.*

Sky-Watching on Cadillac Mountain

1932

Arthur Stupka, Ranger-Naturalist

Shortly after midnight, on August 12, we left Bar Harbor and made for the Cadillac Mountain road. The moon had set and the sky overhead was bright with stars. All indications were that this was to be an ideal night during which to observe the annual spectacular shower of meteors which streak across the northeastern sky in the general direction of the constellation Perseus....

Halfway to the summit we encountered fog banks and these only became more dense as we continued upward. On the very top the fog was quite heavy and we therefore decided to make our observations from a lower point on this highest point on the island. About two-thirds of the way down, we stopped and made ready for our count of shooting stars. It was now 1:45, and the sky was exceptionally clear.

We sat back to back, each intent on counting as many meteors in one-half of the sky as could be observed. From this point on our story may as well be in periodic form:

1:45–2:15: Together we saw twenty-eight of the Perseid meteors in this first fifteen-minute period. A cool steady wind kept rustling the nearby low birches creating the only night sound....

2:00–2:15: A total of twenty-six streakers across the sky.

2:15–2:30: At least thirty-eight visible shooting stars, several of which were spectacular streamers. At 2:20 we were entertained by the wild lonely laughter of a loon on the lake below us and at 2:25 the northern horizon was illuminated by short rays coming from a low dim bow of the Northern Lights.

2:30–2:45: Our greatest number of meteors was counted in this period: fifty-four in all. Many of these were bright and sometimes three or four followed one another in rapid succession. The Northern Lights growing dim.

On the afternoon of August 31, at least 3,000 people armed with fogged film negatives and colored glasses assembled upon the summit of Cadillac Mountain to witness the sun's eclipse.... The afternoon was fairly clear with very little wind.

Shortly after 2:15 the first exclamation, "It's starting on the right," was heard and by 2:30 the nick in the sun was prominent. At least fifty percent of the sun was obscured by the moon's shadow at 3:00.

An air of tenseness was felt throughout the group at 3:25 when the sun was almost obliterated by the moon. The eclipse was now at a maximum (ninety-eight percent total) for this region. The air had become cool and the distant islands were enveloped in a noticeably grayish light. Overhead the sky was blue. The sun now appeared as a very narrow crescent. Little clouds of gnats suddenly became noticeable on the mountain top.

But the climax was soon at an end. Slowly the sun's bright crescent began to increase and the crowds on the summit began to disperse. The grand celestial performance was now on the wane.

From Nature Notes, *Arthur Stupka, Acadia National Park, 1932; courtesy of NPS, Acadia National Park.*

Dear Mr. Dorr,

1936

Rubey A. Butterfield

I have just returned home from a most delightful vacation spent in Acadia National Park.... The courtesy and efficiency of your Park Naturalist Mr. Sullivan and his assistant, Mr. Favour, does so much to familiarize strangers with various plant life, rock formations, bird and animal habits that are so often overlooked by the casual observer.

Indeed I have never spent a more varied week in one area. If I were asked which I enjoyed most—your naturalist walks, mountain climbing, bathing, fishing, motoring, sea cruising or watching sunset and sunrise from Mount Cadillac, I could not answer. The combination of all is so perfect.

I wish to personally thank you for the privilege of a campfire enjoyed the night I spent on Cadillac. The party numbering approximately forty-six or forty-seven found a real pleasure in it.

What a hospitable center for our camp songs. At least ten states were represented in our gathering and many spoke gratefully of your gracious permission for the first campfire kindled there.

My thanks to you and your assistants for the most enjoyable of vacations.

Gratefully yours,
Rubey A. Butterfield
Houlton, Maine

From George Dorr's papers; courtesy of NPS, Acadia National Park.

Further Reading

Local Histories

An Island in Time: Three Thousand Years of Cultural Exchange on Mount Desert Island, essays by David Sanger and Harald E. L. Prins (Robert Abbe Museum, Bar Harbor, Maine, 1989, revised 1994) and *The Indian Shell Heap: Archaeology of the Ruth Moore Site*, by Dr. Stephen Cox and Gary Lawless (Robert Abbe Museum, Bar Harbor, Maine, 1994). Reports describing recent Abbe Museum archaeological research at two local sites: Fernald Point and Gotts Island, background information on prehistoric people in Maine.

A Souvenir of Bar Harbor and Mount Desert Island (W. H. Sherman, Bar Harbor, 1893, reprinted by the Bar Harbor Historical Society, 1995). A tourist's picture book of Bar Harbor's fine homes, hotels and other memorable sights.

Lost Bar Harbor, by G. W. Helfrich and Gladys O'Neil (Down East Books, Camden, Maine, 1982). An exceedingly useful collection of photographs and short descriptions of cottages and other important buildings of Bar Harbor's summer colony years that are now gone; from the collection of the Bar Harbor Historical Society.

Mr. Rockefeller's Roads: The Untold Story of Acadia's Carriage Roads and Their Creator, by Ann Rockefeller Roberts (Down East Books, Camden, Maine, 1990). A fascinating and essential history of John D. Rockefeller Jr.'s carriage roads along with his other contributions to Acadia National Park.

Mount Desert and Acadia National Park: An Informal History, by Sargent F. Collier, revised and edited by G. W. Helfrich (Down East Books, Camden, Maine, 1972). A distillation of Sargent Collier's three histories: *Mount Desert: The Most Beautiful Island in the World* (1952), *Green Grows Bar Harbor* (1964) and *Acadia National Park: George B. Dorr's Triumph* (1965).

The Artist's Mount Desert: American Painters on the Maine Coast, by John Wilmerding (Princeton University Press, Princeton, New Jersey, 1994). A well-illustrated study of works depicting the island from the early 19th century to the early 20th century.

The Story of Acadia National Park, by George Dorr (Acadia Publishing Company, Bar Harbor, Maine, combined edition 1985). This volume includes both of George Dorr's memoirs of the founding of the park: *Acadia National Park: Its Origins and Background* and *Acadia National Park: Its Growth and Development*. Dorr's separate volumes are available in local libraries.

To Be Young Was Very Heaven, by Marian Lawrence Peabody (Houghton Mifflin, Boston, 1967). Marian Lawrence Peabody, a member of the Boston aristocracy, was born in 1875 and kept a journal for most of her life. In this book, she shares her memories of the Bar Harbor summer colony in the late 1800s and early 1900s, as well as other important events of her youth. Available in local libraries.

Trails of History: The Story of Mount Desert Island's Paths from Norumbega to Acadia, by Tom St. Germain and Jay Saunders (Parkman Publications, Bar Harbor, 1993). Fascinating facts and fables about the island's footpaths.

The following are the three classic histories of Mount Desert Island and Bar Harbor. Each was written by a summer colonist who visited the island for many years during Bar Harbor's "golden years."

The Story of Bar Harbor, by Richard W. Hale, Jr. (Ives Washburn, Inc., 1949). Available in local libraries.

The Story of Mount Desert Island, Maine, by Samuel Eliot Morrison (Little, Brown and Company, Boston, 1960).

Mount Desert: A History, by George E. Street, edited by Samuel A. Eliot (Houghton Mifflin Company, Boston, 1905, revised 1926). Available in local libraries.

General Maine and New England Histories

Coastal Maine: A Maritime History, by Roger F. Duncan (W. W. Norton, New York, 1992). Coastal history from the viewpoint of an accomplished sailor.

Lobstering and the Maine Coast, by Kenneth R. Martin and Nathan R. Lipfert (Maine Maritime Museum, Bath, Maine 1985). The history of lobstering from the 1600s to the present.

Maine: The Pine Tree State from Prehistory to the Present, edited by Richard W. Judd, Edwin A. Churchill and Joel W. Eastman (University of Maine Press, Orono, Maine, 1995). The best comprehensive history of Maine.

Our Own Snug Fireside: Images of the New England Home, 1760–1860, by Jane C. Nylander (Alfred A. Knopf, New York, 1993). An exploration of the intersection between reality and reminiscence of daily life in New England. Although the book focuses on the more settled parts of New England, it is nevertheless helpful in understanding life on Mount Desert Island through the period.

Wake of the Coasters, by John F. Leavitt (Wesleyan University Press, Middletown, Connecticut, for Marine Historical Association, Mystic, Connecticut, 1970). The story of Maine's coasting schooners from a man who worked on them.

Index

Boldface
indicates a photograph or illustration

More good reading from Down East Books

If you enjoyed *Discovering Old Bar Harbor*, you'll want to know about these other Down East titles:

Lost Bar Harbor, by G. W. Helfrich and Gladys O'Neil. A tribute to the days before the Great Fire of 1947, when many of America's and Europe's wealthiest families summered in Bar Harbor. Includes photographs of 86 of these vanished summer palaces, selected from the collection of the Bar Harbor Historical Society. 0-89272-142-1

Mt. Desert Island and Acadia National Park: An Informal History, photographs and text by Sargent F. Collier. The best from three classic books about Bar Harbor, Mount Desert Island, and Acadia National Park. Edited by G. W. Helfrich. Illustrated with Collier's photos of the contemporary scene and earlier prints. 0-89272-044-1

Mr. Rockefeller's Roads: The Untold Story of Acadia's Carriage Roads & Their Creator, by Ann Rockefeller Roberts. Acadia's 51 miles of carriage roads are the results of decades of personal effort by philanthropist John D. Rockefeller, Jr., whose granddaughter recounts the fascinating story behind their creation. 0-89272-296-7

Acadia National Park: Maine's Intimate Parkland, photos and text by Alan Nyiri. From its impressive vistas to its tiniest treasures, Acadia is an island parkland of haunting beauty. This magnificent collection of 68 color photographs captures that beauty. 0-89272-219-3

The Mt. Desert Island Pocket Guide Series

A Pocket Guide to Biking on Mt. Desert Island, by Audrey Shelton Minutolo. Eighteen selected loop routes, ranging from all-day circuits to shorter routes designed for families with small children. 0-89727-367-X

A Pocket Guide to Paddling the Waters of Mt. Desert Island, by Earl Brechlin. Eighteen different canoe and kayak routes are described in sections covering creeks, wetlands, ponds, and salt water. 0-89272-357-2

A Pocket Guide to Hiking on Mt. Desert Island, by Earl Brechlin. Thirty-one of the best hikes and walks, from easy to strenuous, covering all parts of the island, along with tips for preparing for outings. 0-89727-356-4

A Pocket Guide to the Carriage Roads of Acadia National Park, 2nd Edition, by Diana F. Abrell. An updated guide to Acadia's 51-mile carriage road network for hikers, skiers, bicyclists, and horseback riders. 0-89272-349-1

CHECK YOUR LOCAL BOOKSTORE, OR ORDER FROM DOWN EAST BOOKS AT 800-766-1670

Visa and MasterCard accepted